# Rural Design

This book is the first step along the path for rural design to emerge as an important new design discipline.

Rural areas worldwide are undergoing profound change, creating considerable challenges and stress for their residents and on the ecosystems upon which they depend. Rural design brings design thinking and the problem-solving process of design to rural issues, recognizing that human and natural systems are inextricably coupled and engaged in continuous cycles of mutual influence and response.

This book establishes the theoretical base for rural design and the importance of looking at connecting issues to create synergy and optimal solutions from a global, national, state, region, and local perspective. These directions and others will help enable rural design to:

- help rural communities make land use, architectural, and aesthetic decisions that enhance their quality of life and the environment;
- connect social, artistic, cultural, technological, and environmental issues that create rural place;
- promote sustainable economic development for rural communities and improve human, livestock, crop, and ecosystem health;
- integrate research and practice across the many disciplines involved in rural issues to meet rural needs, provide new data, and provoke new research questions.

This book promotes participation by all involved in a shared process of discovery, learning and problem solving. Including a range of case studies and written by a world leading expert in rural design, this book is an essential resource for students, academics, and design professionals involved with rural design at any level.

**Dewey Thorbeck** is Adjunct Professor of Architecture, and Founder and Director of the Center for Rural Design at the University of Minnesota. A graduate of Yale University, Thorbeck won a Rome Prize Fellowship to the American Academy in Rome. An award-winning architect, he is involved in regional and national projects and has published internationally.

# Rural Design

## A new design discipline

*Dewey Thorbeck*

Routledge
Taylor & Francis Group

LONDON AND NEW YORK

First published 2012
by Routledge
2 Park Square, Milton Park, Abingdon, Oxon OX14 4RN

Simultaneously published in the USA and Canada
by Routledge
711 Third Avenue, New York, NY 10017

*Routledge is an imprint of the Taylor & Francis Group, an informa business*

*British Library Cataloguing in Publication Data*
A catalogue record for this book is available from the British Library

*Library of Congress Cataloging-in-Publication Data*
Thorbeck, Dewey.
Rural design : a new design discipline / Dewey Thorbeck.
p. cm.
Includes bibliographical references and index.
1. Rural development–Research. 2. Community development–Research.
I. Title. II. Title: New design discipline.
HN980.T487 2012
307.1'412–dc23
2011020297

ISBN: 978-0-415-59319-9 (hbk)
ISBN: 978-0-415-59320-5 (pbk)
ISBN: 978-0-203-16254-5 (ebk)

Typeset in Charter and FS Albert
by Keystroke, Station Road, Codsall, Wolverhampton


Printed and bound in India by Replika Press Pvt. Ltd.

# Contents

*List of figures*                                                                         ix
*Acknowledgments*                                                                   xv
*Foreword: rural design arising*                                               xix

1  **Introduction**                                                                      1
   Rural change   3
   Rural design: a new way of design thinking   3
   The Center for Rural Design   8
   Global issues and impacts   10

2  **Rural heritage**                                                                   13
   Ancient roots and European origins   13
   English landscapes and influence on America   18
   Immigrants' dream   21
   Farmsteads   26
   Buildings for agriculture   34
   Indigenous people and the land   40

3  **Rural character**                                                                 43
   Geological forces   43
   Cultural forces   44
   Immigration to America   45
   Landscape patterns   49
   Rural character defined   50
   Rural policy   54
   Forces changing rural landscapes   56
   Managing forces of change through rural design   57
   Aesthetic issues   58

Contemporary working buildings in rural landscapes   63
Form follows function, climate, and place   79

4   **Regional vision**                                      **81**
Thinking regionally   83
A regional vision   86
Regional landscapes   89
Regional thinking worldwide   91
Regional thinking in Minnesota   105
Looking ahead   108

5   **Research foundation**                                  **111**
Research issues   112
Definitions   114
Sustainability challenge   117
A new approach to rural issues   120
Evidence-based rural design   122
Research opportunities   123
Social capital   126

6   **Rural design strategies**                              **129**
Strategies   129
Building codes   130
Rural outreach   134
Case studies of the Center for Rural Design   135

7   **Interdisciplinary connections**                        **190**
Rural design and design thinking   191
Urban/rural synergy   196
Land use and urban/rural edge   198
Problems with animal agriculture   199
Multifunctional agriculture and land use   202
Designing for food supply, food security, and health   205
Design economy   206

8   **Rural futures**                                        **208**
Connecting the dots   211
New design technologies   214
Rural design education   215
Rural Design Certificate program   216
Rural sustainability   218
The International Organization for Rural Design   219
Global challenges   220

**9 Epilogue**     **223**

Process of discovery  224
Integrating buildings and landscapes  227
Drawing and rural design  229
Shaping rural futures  235

*References*     237
*Illustration credits*     241
*Index*     243

# Figures

**1.1** A bank in the rural town of Owatonna, Minnesota designed by
Louis Sullivan    4

**1.2** Tall grain elevators in rural towns throughout the Midwest are as
common as church steeples    5

**1.3** Vineyard shelter in Napa Valley, California    6

**1.4** The diagram used by the CRD to explain the foundation for
evidence-based rural design    10

**2.1** A Roman mosaic from the second-century Liberii farm villa in
Tunisia    14

**2.2** Exterior view of the Coxwell Barn in England    16

**2.3** Interior of the Coxwell Barn    16

**2.4** Contemporary Swedish farm with a cluster of swine buildings    17

**2.5** An integrated dairy farm in the Netherlands    18

**2.6** A farmstead near Zell am See, Austria    18

**2.7** Typical English landscape    19

**2.8** A sketch of the Village Green in Camden, Maine    20

**2.9** A map illustrating the three ecosystems that converge in Minnesota    22

**2.10** Slierping Farmstead in western Minnesota    24

**2.11** Schiltgen Farmstead in the historic village of Lake Elmo, Minnesota    25

**2.12** A handsome stone barn in northern Iowa    25

**2.13** Stone and wood barn in northern Illinois    26

**2.14** Aerial view of a typical farmstead in northern Minnesota    27

**2.15** A large gable-roof bank barn in eastern Pennsylvania    28

**2.16** Farmstead in Lancaster County, Pennsylvania    28

**2.17** An historic vineyard farm in Napa Valley, California    29

**2.18** A large wood horse barn in Nashville, Tennessee    29

**2.19** Large wood horse barn constructed at a State Hospital in western
Minnesota    30

**2.20** Round barn in southwestern Minnesota    31

| | | |
|---|---|---|
| 2.21 | An arched-roof barn in Door County, Wisconsin | 31 |
| 2.22 | A string of tall, free-standing grain elevators along the railroad tracks on the Minnesota prairie | 32 |
| 2.23 | A small connected grain elevator and feed mill | 33 |
| 2.24 | An enormous grain elevator complex in Ada, northwestern Minnesota | 33 |
| 2.25 | Fertilizer storage tanks along a rural highway | 34 |
| 2.26 | The Two Rivers church in northwestern Minnesota | 34 |
| 2.27 | A stately brick country church in northern Iowa | 35 |
| 2.28 | A handsome masonry corn crib | 36 |
| 2.29 | Interior view of a typical metal-skinned, chemically treated wood post-frame confinement-type dairy barn | 36 |
| 2.30 | A typical metal-skinned confinement-type swine barn | 37 |
| 2.31 | A dairy barn with Harvester silos | 37 |
| 2.32 | Simple, small swine barn with adjacent silo | 38 |
| 2.33 | A contemporary ethanol plant in southwestern Minnesota | 38 |
| 2.34 | A lone wind turbine in a field with horses, beside the highway | 39 |
| 2.35 | An array of photovoltaic solar collectors adjacent to agricultural fields at Saint John's University, Collegeville, Minnesota | 39 |
| 2.36 | Exterior sketch of the Tonto Cave Dwelling east of Phoenix, Arizona | 41 |
| 2.37 | Interior sketch of the Tonto Cave Dwelling | 41 |
| 3.1 | The Fosston Map of 1896 | 46 |
| 3.2 | My Norwegian maternal grandfather's steamboat 'Lilly' | 47 |
| 3.3 | A map of Minnesota from 1895 | 48 |
| 3.4 | Rolling farmland and fields in southern Minnesota, illustrating a landscape *regional* unit | 53 |
| 3.5 | Farmland and farmsteads, illustrating a landscape *setting* unit | 53 |
| 3.6 | A dairy farm, illustrating a landscape *character* unit | 53 |
| 3.7 | A GIS map illustrating generalized land cover | 54 |
| 3.8 | A GIS map illustrating topography | 55 |
| 3.9 | Cows in a field – an icon that typifies the rural Midwest landscape | 59 |
| 3.10 | New low-density housing development in rural areas near a major metropolitan region | 60 |
| 3.11 | A CRD diagram of a land-use scenario, illustrating different zoning for rural areas | 61 |
| 3.12 | A CRD diagram of a land-use scenario, illustrating an overlay land-use concept | 61 |
| 3.13 | Typical post-frame construction system | 62 |
| 3.14 | Bodega Salentein in the Uco Valley near Mendoza, Argentina | 64 |
| 3.15 | Chapel at Bodega Salentein | 64 |
| 3.16 | Sketch of Kilka Museum | 65 |
| 3.17 | Sketch of the chapel and site layout of Bodega Salentein | 66 |
| 3.18 | Purina Farms Visitor Center | 67 |
| 3.19 | Purina Farms courtyard and amphitheater | 67 |

3.20  A small holiday house on the Isle of Skye, Scotland                    68
3.21  The holiday house, gently sitting on posts, floats above the
      ground                                                                 69
3.22  Agricultural Management Center, University of Minnesota,
      Crookston                                                              70
3.23  Interior view of riding arena, Agricultural Management Center          71
3.24  Winter view of a proposal for reconstructing a sheep farm in
      southern Minnesota                                                     72
3.25  Close-up view of the sheep farm proposal                              72
3.26  Site plan of proposed Animal Education Center at the Milton
      Hershey School, Pennsylvania                                          73
3.27  Elevation of the Animal Education Center                              74
3.28  The Mitchell-David house entry tunnel                                 75
3.29  The Mitchell-David house courtyard                                    75
3.30  Exterior of the Straitsview barn                                      76
3.31  Interior view of the Straitsview barn                                 77
3.32  Somis hay barn on a foggy day                                         78
3.33  Interior view of stable in Somis hay barn                             78
4.1   Drawing created for a CRD meeting with a regional planning
      commission                                                            83
4.2   A cluster of wind turbines in southwestern Minnesota                  87
4.3   A CRD illustrative diagram showing four different scenarios for
      development                                                           88
4.4   Map of Beijing, showing existing agricultural and natural
      landscape zones                                                       92
4.5   Map of Beijing, showing existing food-growing areas                  93
4.6   Map of Beijing, showing proposed rings around the city               93
4.7   Northern Europe map of cross-border twin-city collaborations         95
4.8   Street in the central area of Tornio, Finland                        96
4.9   The historic City Hall and modern hotel in Haparanda, Sweden         96
4.10  The city of Kirkenes, Norway in the summer                           97
4.11  QwaQwa Township village in Free State, South Africa                  103
4.12  Newly constructed round house in QwaQwa                              103
4.13  A CRD diagram prepared for a meeting in Detroit Lakes, Minnesota     107
4.14  A map of Minnesota, illustrating potential cooperation regions       108
4.15  A vision map, prepared by the CRD, of Minnesota in 2058              109
5.1   A drawing from one of the sessions at the First International
      Symposium for Rural Design in 2010                                   112
5.2   A diagram used by the CRD to illustrate the design process           117
5.3   Diagram illustrating interrelated performance metrics for
      environmental and human health                                       118
5.4   A CRD community workshop in Scott County, Minnesota                  127
5.5   A research field with professors, graduate students, and visiting
      farmers                                                              128

6.1   Aerial view of Riverview Dairy farm in northwestern Minnesota   131
6.2   Interior view of animal stall and feeding lane in the larger
      Riverview barn   131
6.3   Rotary milking parlor in the larger Riverview barn   132
6.4   Map showing the relationship of Wyoming Township to the Twin
      Cities metropolitan area   135
6.5   The planning process ground rules agreed to by the Citizen's
      Advisory Committee   137
6.6   Alternative Scenario A prepared for the Wyoming Township
      workshop   141
6.7   Alternative Scenario B prepared for the Wyoming Township
      workshop   141
6.8   Alternative Scenario C prepared for the Wyoming Township
      workshop   142
6.9   The final revised Comprehensive Plan for Wyoming Township   143
6.10  Aerial view of the flood of June 2002 in Roseau, Minnesota   146
6.11  The Conceptual Vision Plan for Roseau   149
6.12  New Roseau Community Center building   152
6.13  Entrance to the new Roseau Community Center   152
6.14  Strategic Master Plan proposed for the Jennissen Dairy Farm in
      Stearns County   154
6.15  Image from the Offset study, illustrating the spatial relationship
      between animal agriculture and residential dwellings   156
6.16  Offset diagram assessing impacts on urban areas and residential
      dwellings   157
6.17  Methodology diagram illustrating protection zones   161
6.18  Diagram of the Environmental Quality Assurance Pri- for a single
      dairy farm   163
6.19  Location map of Isanti County in relationship to the Twin Cities
      metropolitan area   165
6.20  The process diagram that illustrated how the project was going to
      flow and interconnect with community workshops   167
6.21  The recommended vision plan for the Isanti County Parks and bike
      paths   169
6.22  Location map of Scott County, one of the seven in the Twin Cities
      metropolitan area   170
6.23  Guiding principles prepared by the CRD as criteria for the four
      township planning study   172
6.24  Integrated rural character map for the four township planning area   173
6.25  Aerial map of the City of Morris   176
6.26  The historic elementary school, constructed in 1914   177
6.27  The Vision and Reuse Plan for the elementary school site   179
6.28  An example of the imagery expected to be an outcome of the
      Digital Town project   182

**6.29** Map illustrating Vermillion Highlands and its regional context — 183

**6.30** The concept master plan drawing for Vermillion Highlands — 184

**6.31** Zones plan for Vermillion Highlands — 185

**6.32** Research zones for Vermillion Highlands — 186

**6.33** Recreation zones for multiple use in Vermillion Highlands — 186

**6.34** Hunting and Trapping definitions for the Vermillion Highlands wildlife management areas — 187

**6.35** Map to delineate different levels and intensity of land use related to zones — 187

**6.36** Management zones for land-use management among the multi-party partnership — 188

**7.1** Entrance road to the Brooklyn Park Historic Farm — 196

**7.2** Entrance road to a specialized swine farm in southwestern Minnesota — 197

**7.3** The pole-barn construction system transformed into architecture for a beef and sheep barn — 197

**7.4** A 2,500-cow dairy barn with fabric roof and walls — 201

**7.5** Entrance road to a farmstead in southern Minnesota illustrating change over time — 203

**8.1** A CRD image to illustrate one of the various land-use scenarios for abandoned mines — 210

**8.2** A CRD diagram to illustrate the synergistic impact of connecting the dots to create solutions that cross boundaries — 212

**9.1** Drawing of Casa Di Diana, an apartment building in Ostia Antica, the ancient seaport of Rome — 225

**9.2** A sketch from two books about first-century Roman villas in Germania — 227

**9.3** The Minnesota Zoological Garden, overlooking the central lake — 228

**9.4** Interior of the Tropical Exhibit at the Minnesota Zoological Garden — 229

**9.5** Orvieto, a typical Italian hill town — 230

**9.6** A working harbor in Henningsvær, in the Lofoten Islands, Norway — 231

**9.7** A fish house and home on the Lofoten Islands — 231

**9.8** Large stone and wood barn and granary on Minister's Island, St Andrews, New Brunswick, Canada — 232

**9.9** Machu Picchu in Peru — 233

**9.10** Aerial photograph of Machu Picchu from the top of the mountain — 234

**9.11** Sacsayhuaman, the fortress guarding Cusco, the capital of the Inca empire in Peru — 235

# Acknowledgments

Through the years of working on this book I have met many rural people who have inspired me, and I greatly appreciate their character, friendship, ideas, and insights. The passion they have for the rural landscape, agriculture, and the rural places within which they live and work greatly influenced my thinking.

The book started with a grant from the Graham Foundation for Advanced Studies in the Fine Arts, to write about the architecture of agriculture and how contemporary working buildings in the rural landscape can and should be more place- and climate-oriented. The focus of the book changed, however, as – in both my professional and academic careers – I experienced (and grew to understand) the enormous changes taking place in rural America and around the world.

Since design schools and the design professions had fundamentally ignored rural regions, the book is now an introduction to rural design as a new design discipline and what it can accomplish as a problem-solving process in shaping rural environments for the future. If urban design is one side of a coin, then rural design is the other. Urban design is a well-understood arm of the design professions, but rural design does not exist in any academic unit, and I hope the book helps to resolve that omission

Family, colleagues, and friends also contributed to the ideas expressed. I am indebted and thank them all, but the following deserve special mention: my immigrant grandparents, who came from Norway and Germany and settled on small diversified farms in rural Minnesota where I first experienced farming and working with animals; my parents, who guided my life in a small town in northern Minnesota and instilled in me the importance of higher education; and Burton Fosse, the college professor who introduced me to the world of architecture.

Teachers who inspired me to think and act holistically and systemically were: architects Ralph Rapson, James Stageberg, John Rauma, and Leonard Parker at the University of Minnesota; Paul Rudolph, James Stirling, and Ulrich Franzen at Yale University; and Christian Norberg-Schulz from Norway. Others were residents at the American Academy in Rome, including: architectural historian William MacDonald; classical historian Frank Brown; and architects Louis Kahn and Edward Larabee Barnes.

Partners in professional practice who greatly influenced my thinking include: landscape architect Roger Martin, a fellow at the American Academy in Rome and faculty member at the University of Minnesota, who helped me understand connections between landscape and buildings; systems analyst and computer specialist Stephen Kahne who showed me how systems thinking and the computer are powerful design tools; and graphic designer Peter Seitz, who I first met at Yale University. It was he that opened up the world of design and visual communications.

I appreciate very much the encouragement and assistance of administrators who supported the founding and work of the Center for Rural Design at the University of Minnesota, and wrote the Foreword to the book. They are Tom Fisher, dean of the College of Design; Al Levine, dean of the College of Food, Agriculture, and Natural Resource Sciences; and Mike Martin, former dean of the College of Food, Agriculture, and Natural Resource Sciences and now chancellor of Louisiana State University.

I wish to thank my colleagues at the Center for Rural Design who have been most instrumental in shaping the vision and mission of the Center and in accomplishing the cases studies in the book: Steve Roos, Senior Research Fellow and landscape architect and his special skills in computer visualization and geographic information systems; Tracey Kinney, Research Fellow, planner, and landscape architect and her excellent skills in community organization and community-based planning; Stephen Streng, landscape architect and former Research Fellow, whose communication skills provided early guidance in writing and editing the book; and architecture graduate student Eddie Krakhmalnikov, who assisted in assembling the images for the case studies in Chapter 6.

I greatly appreciate the support, creative advice, and assistance of Francesca Ford, Commissioning Editor; Laura Williamson, Editorial Assistant; and the entire Routledge team who patiently nurtured a first-time author and made this book happen. And, Professor David Witty, former dean of the Faculty of Architecture, University of Manitoba and now Vice-President Academic and Provost, Vancouver Island University, who reviewed the manuscript and offered excellent insight and advice as to how I could improve it from the perspective of students and professionals. I also want to thank the diverse group of architects Bormida & Yanzow, Burr and MacCallum, Loom Architects, StudioKAP, Thompson & Rose Architects, and Studio Palia Fekete Architects who supplied images of their beautiful rural buildings in Chapter 3; and research academics Aileen Espiritu, Judith Read Guernsey, Claudia Parliament, and Fengrong Zhang who provided the information regarding their important research work in rural regions around the world in Chapter 4.

Especially, I want to thank Sharon. She is my wife, best friend, and business colleague, who organizes and manages our life and travels. Without her love, patience, and encouragement this book would not have been written. The book is dedicated to her and our seven beautiful granddaughters – Callie, Julia, Bailey, Riley, Remy, Addison, and Siena – who like to draw and create wonderful things. They remind me daily why visioning a better future is so important.

# Foreword: rural design arising

We often think of cities as designed and the countryside as not, as if the highways, high-rises, and housing developments in urban areas and the roads, fields, and farmsteads in rural areas represent fundamentally different environments. This book, the first ever written about the emerging field of rural design, puts that illusion to rest. It shows how much design has shaped the country as well as the city, and how much design thinking can offer us a way of dealing with the most intractable problems of rural areas.

Most new fields emerge from the vision of outliers, as the author Malcolm Gladwell has argued, and the author of this book, Dewey Thorbeck, is no exception. Trained and licensed as an architect, Thorbeck has long lived and worked in the Minneapolis/St Paul metropolitan area. And yet, born a country boy, he remains passionate about his rural roots and committed to doing all that he can to enhance the economy and quality of life of the countryside. This has led Thorbeck to dedicate much of his career to creating a new field and to go where few architects ever have before: applying the creative problem-solving process of design to situations rarely thought of as designed at all.

Rural design goes far beyond what many might assume would interest Thorbeck as an architect – the design of rural buildings. This new field encompasses the design of everything from our food systems and factory farms to the land uses and landscapes that help support them. And never have these systems needed the careful analysis and creative ideas of architects more than now.

Take the question of how we will manage to feed the world's population, now 6.5 billion and estimated to be at 9 billion by 2050. That may not seem like a daunting task when you consider that the United Nations' Food and Agriculture Organization estimates that the planet can support 33 billion people, if every person ate the minimum needed to live and if we had every available piece of land in high-intensity food production.

Such austerity and efficiency will likely never occur, at least willingly. However, given the thousands of calories required to produce each calorie we eat in the USA, designing a more sustainable food system that doesn't destroy ecosystems, pollute the air and water, or degrade our quality of life in the process represents an enormous – and urgent – challenge.

Or consider the fact that some of the most intense concentrations of poverty occur in rural areas because of a lack of economic opportunity and a shortage of human services in many remote rural locations. A more thoughtful approach to rural design can help us confront these challenges and potentially come up with innovative new solutions.

Rural design has much to offer situations like this. By applying a design process that involves the development, assessment, and refinement of possible future scenarios, rural design can help us imagine what a more ecologically friendly and less environmentally damaging form of cultivation might be like, one that allows farmers to make a decent living while still feeding the world. These scenarios will need to build on the work of scientists and social scientists, who help us understand and expand the limits of our knowledge about the world as it is. But based on that knowledge of what *is*, design asks: What *could be*? How might we, in this case, manage to feed ourselves without destroying the very ecosystems upon which agriculture depends?

Nor does rural design deal only with the primary industry of rural areas – our food system. It also addresses the human issues of rural areas, such as the quality of life of people working in agricultural industries or living in places dependent upon those industries. An example of this involves the ironic and tragic situation of the obesity epidemic in North America. We have so successfully industrialized agriculture that we produce calories at such a low cost that it far exceeds people's daily needs, a dilemma that includes the very people who grow our food. Obesity rates have risen the farthest in predominantly rural states, and such increases have paralleled poverty rates, which plague rural areas as much as urban neighborhoods. Envisioning a healthier rural existence as well as a rural economy remains one of the key activities of rural design. Altering food subsidies to make vegetables and fruits more affordable would most likely decrease the body mass index and improve the general health of the population.

That has considerable support from rural politicians. The Center for Rural Design began, not just with the vision of Dewey Thorbeck, but also with the active lobbying of the then dean of agriculture at the University of Minnesota, Michael Martin, now the Chancellor at Louisiana State University. Martin secured a 'state special' from the Minnesota legislature dedicated to the Center of Rural Design, giving it a sound financial base and creating a resource for rural communities and a model for other universities and agencies to join in the search for solutions. He also helped legislators recognize the value of rural design extending the reach of traditional agriculture beyond farms and fields to the main streets and mainstream communities where most rural residents live and work and where many of the major problems of such places arise. As with any industry, the food industry's success depends upon its ability to attract and keep the best employees, and so the quality of the rural economy has everything to do with the quality of rural life.

From those modest origins in Minnesota, rural design has grown into a field of widespread interest and international importance. An indication of that became clear in the First International Symposium on Rural Design, organized by the Center for Rural Design and held in St Paul, Minnesota, in 2010. Attendees from the United States and Canada assembled to share their experiences of working in rural communities and seeking innovative solutions to the intertwined problems that face such places: rising pollution and declining population, growing social dysfunction and shrinking economies. Most strikingly, the symposium revealed the urgency that people feel in tackling such problems and the diversity of disciplines (seventeen in all) and range of institutions (twenty in total) eager to address the challenges of rural communities.

Such disciplinary diversity defines the Center for Rural Design. Comprised of staff members from architecture, landscape architecture, and regional planning, the Center also has faculty fellows from agronomy, forest resources, veterinary medicine, and housing studies. That intellectual variety reflects the institutional structure of the Center, located in the University of Minnesota's College of Agriculture, Food, and Natural Resource Sciences and yet overseen in partnership with the College of Design. It reflects, as well, the nature of the challenges that rural communities face and the structure that universities will increasingly need to adopt in order to successfully address the complex problems of rural areas. We cannot address the needs of agriculture without also dealing with the health, housing, education, and economic needs of those who work there.

The nine chapters of this book explore the meaning and potential of rural design, drawing from case studies of projects of the Center for Rural Design. The book covers both the history and future of the rural design movement, the diverse issues and disciplines that rural design encompasses, and the regional sensibility, research opportunities, and design strategies that underlie it. As such, this book represents the founding text of a phenomenon that promises to offer a fundamental change in how we approach the challenges of rural communities.

The vast majority of those challenges arose out of conscious decisions about how we use our land and its resources, and if we have designed our way into problems, we can also design our way out of them. Design doesn't have to be expensive or difficult to achieve. Even simple changes, such as trees along the roadside of farms, can stop whiteout conditions because of blowing snow and improve road safety in rural areas. Clearly, design is needed in the country as well as the city, and no book makes a better case for that than this one.

Thomas Fisher
*Dean, College of Design, University of Minnesota*

Allen Levine
*Dean, College of Food, Agriculture, and Natural Resource Sciences,*
*University of Minnesota*

Michael Martin
*Chancellor, Louisiana State University*

# Chapter 1

# Introduction

*No man is an island, entire of itself; every man is a piece of the continent, a part of the main. If a clod be washed away by the sea, Europe is the less, as well as if a promontory were, as well as if a manor of thy friend's or of thine own were; any man's death diminishes me, because I am involved in mankind; and therefore never send to know for whom the bells tolls; it tolls for thee.*

*(John Donne, 1624)*

Design is a powerful tool for integrating knowledge across disciplines. Rural design is a new discipline that currently does not exist in any academic program in the United States or around the world. It is a methodology to bring design as a problem-solving process to rural regions to nurture human ingenuity, entrepreneurship, creativity, and innovation. It provides an opportunity to reflect upon and integrate human and natural systems into a viable, sustainable design process to improve quality of life. Never has the time been more opportune for such an approach, nor is it more needed.

On June 8, 2002, fourteen inches of rain fell on the rural City of Roseau in northwestern Minnesota near the Canadian border. The damage from the deluge was enormous, resulting in destruction of downtown businesses and private residences. Ninety percent of the 150 commercial buildings and most of the public buildings and public utilities suffered major damage. More than fifty homes needed to be demolished and replaced – many owned by low-income families.

The city was overwhelmed by the reconstruction process because there was no plan or consensus about how to proceed. Working with the University of Minnesota's Center for Rural Design, the city's leadership and concerned citizens developed a community-based reconstruction vision plan for rebuilding the community that holistically looked at land issues, demographics, economics, recreation, and the qualities of life desired by the residents. According to Todd Peterson, Roseau's Community Development Director, 'The City of Roseau could not have achieved the success in reconstructing the community as it did after the flood without having public buy-in of the reconstruction vision plan.' As evidenced in Roseau, rural design offers a new approach to meeting the needs and challenges rural communities face as they manage change or respond to needs in a time of crisis.

Rural design is an emerging design discipline that was started at the University of Minnesota in 1997 when I founded the Center for Rural Design (CRD). Since that time the CRD has been involved with a number of projects that impact quality of life in rural areas, primarily in the State of Minnesota. Yet we have learned that the principles of rural design can be applied anywhere. The intent of this book is to inform readers about rural design as a new design discipline – what it is and what it can do for rural communities worldwide.

I am a designer who was trained as an architect, taught architectural design, and has practiced the profession as a registered architect for a number of years. It has been an experiential journey of discovery and everything in this book reflects what I have learned about rural people, rural issues, rural landscapes, rural planning, and rural architecture. There are other design and research disciplines with different points of view from a cultural, social, economic, and environmental perspective, however most respond from an urban point of view. Landscape architecture may have the strongest connection to rural design because it is so closely linked with cultural and natural landscapes and their ecosystems.

The book is intended to be an introduction to rural design and an outline of multidisciplinary and evidence-based research that responds to the variety of rural issues that need to be resolved. Design can integrate knowledge across disciplines, and while not directly engaged in research, designers can translate and apply research knowledge to the design process – helping bridge the gap between science and society.

This issue of applied research through design is not well understood by many funding organizations that support scientific research regarding agriculture and rural environments. To them, research is discipline-oriented and focused on subjects that end up in scientific journals to inform other researchers. This book is not a traditional research-oriented textbook. Rather it is about design thinking as a means to utilize research knowledge and translate that evidence through the rural design process to benefit rural society. With the world changing so rapidly, design thinking and rural design, as a community-based problem-solving process, is becoming more and more important as a means to manage and shape rural futures.

Rural design brings the methodology of design to rural issues. Through that process, other academic disciplines involved with agricultural, cultural, and natural landscapes have embraced the concept. Rural design can assist academia in making connections holistically and systemically, and through its practice contribute to rural economic development, environmental protection, and improved quality of life.

## Rural change

Over the past fifty years, rural regions in North America and worldwide have undergone enormous changes impacting quality of rural life and their economic, social, and environmental sustainability. Critical global issues, such as population increase, climate change, renewable energy, water resources, food supply, and health will further impact rural policies for years to come. So, how do rural people deal with these issues so they can manage change while maintaining and improving their quality of life?

According to the United States Department of Agriculture (USDA ERS, 2008) rural regions in the United States contain 21% of the population and comprise 97% of its land area. In Canada, rural areas are 99% of the land area and contain 20% of its population (Statistics Canada, 2006). From these statistics you can surmise that rural areas of North America have a very low population density per square kilometer.

In the European Union, 56% of the population is living in rural areas that encompass 91% of the land area. It has a much higher rural density than North America, largely due to economic and cultural support for agriculture and to enhance tourism (ENRD, 2010). South Asia, on the other hand, has approximately 70% of its population living in rural areas, of which 69% is suitable for agriculture. It is one of the rural regions in the world with the highest density of population per square kilometer; and typical of developing regions where the rural population has the highest levels of poverty, with farming systems that are among the most susceptible to climate change and economic problems (Weatherhogg *et al.*, 2001).

Rural issues vary a great deal around the world, and while this book illustrates the principles of rural design through the work of the CRD in the Midwest region, design thinking – integrating knowledge across disciplines to solve difficult social, technological, and economic problems – is a process that can be applied worldwide.

## Rural design: a new way of design thinking

Rural design, as a new interdisciplinary design discipline, can help rural communities manage change through the lens of spatial arrangement, and in the process provide a link between science and society to improve rural quality of life. Rural design and urban design are similar in that both embrace quality of life. Rural design is, however, fundamentally different from urban design in seeking to understand and embody the unique characteristics of open landscapes and ecosystems where buildings and towns are components of the landscape, rather than defining infrastructure and public space – as in urban design.

Urban planning deals with public policy and statutory issues affecting the public realm and use of the land. Urban design requires an understanding of urban economics, political economy, and social theory and mainly deals with the way public places and the public realm are experienced and used. A model example of urban design is the building design that Louis Sullivan created for a bank in downtown Owatonna, Minnesota constructed in 1908 (Figure 1.1). Here the bank building (perhaps the finest example of place-making architecture in America) is clearly following the property line, shaping the edge of the street, and flanking and framing a corner of the central town park in this beautiful rural city on the prairie. Larry Millett in his book, *The Curve of the Arch*, describes how the park was the focal point of the downtown and: 'It was to this pleasant little park that Sullivan may well have come one day, probably in early October 1906, to create the outlines of a masterpiece' (Millett, 1985). To me this wonderful building is the epitome of how urban design and urban architecture shapes the public realm to define city.

Rural design, on the other hand, is the spatial arrangement of rural landscapes and the buildings within them. It is best exemplified by thinking of buildings and rural towns as objects within the larger open landscape. Like the simple wood grain elevator (Figure 1.2) standing tall in the open prairie of northwestern Minnesota as an icon for agriculture; or this modest wood, metal roofed harvest shelter (Figure 1.3) in a vineyard in Napa Valley, California almost hidden in the surrounding fields of grape vines. In both situations the buildings are clearly isolated as objects in a field just as the field is one of many in the rolling prairie or valleys of the open landscape.

1.1
A bank in the rural town of Owatonna, Minnesota designed by Louis Sullivan. Constructed in 1918, it is an example of urban architecture shaping public space and public realm. Here the building flanks the downtown Central Park creating a beautiful and timeless work of architecture and urban design, with form following function, climate, and place.

Introduction

1.2
Tall grain elevators in rural
towns throughout the Midwest
are as common as church
steeples, reflecting the
agrarian economy of the land.

Rural character and definitions of rural places have scales and relationships
to the natural and cultivated environments that are entirely different from those
that urban design has in its relationship to urban environments. This difference
requires rural designers to have an understanding of the cultural landscape as well
as the natural landscape of the rural region within which they are working.
Cultural landscape has been defined by an ethno-ecologist as 'the dynamic physical relationships, processes and linkages between societies and environments' and
'how societies perceive the environment and the values, institutions, technologies
and political interests it places on it that result in planning and management goals
and objectives' (Davidson-Hunt, 2003).

Human and natural systems are dynamic and engaged in continuous cycles of mutual influence and response. Rural design provides a foundation from which to holistically connect these and other rural issues by nurturing new thinking and collaborative problem solving. As a discipline, rural design can address contemporary problems while continuing to evolve as research-based evidence is accumulated. The principles and methodologies of rural design can be utilized anywhere because it is by definition rooted in the nature and culture of place.

The assets of a community are often hidden to its citizens, and rural design provides a civic engagement process and geo-spatial mapping that uses community workshops to review alternative scenarios to see the likely results of different decisions. The guiding ethic of rural design is not to impose a vision or solution on a community, but to:

- Provide the tools, information, and support that rural communities need to address their problems;
- Help rural citizens manage change caused by economic, cultural, or environmental reasons;
- Assist in connecting the dots to create synergy for environmental wellbeing, rural prosperity, and quality of life;
- Clearly envision and help citizens achieve the quality of rural future for their community that they deserve.

1.3
The vineyard shelter in Napa Valley, California rises like a hill out of the field, echoing the hills behind. It is a working building in the agricultural landscape reflecting functional purpose and fit with rural character.

Designers share a common trait in that we love to solve problems and create solutions. Problems excite us, and rural regions around the world have many problems. This book, in addition to being an introduction to the emerging new design discipline of rural design, also reflects my architectural background and discovery of the radical changes taking place in rural areas of North America and how I grew to realize that a new rural design discipline dedicated to resolving rural issues could have a positive impact on those changes.

I first started to write about the architecture of agriculture and the design of working buildings in rural landscapes with a grant from the Graham Foundation for Advanced Studies in the Fine Arts. That effort was based on my work as a professional architect involved in the design of interpretive facilities involving animals. These included a new zoo in Minnesota, the first northern climate zoo in the world designed to be open year-round, exhibiting animals in their natural habitat; several animal interpretive centers for both domestic and wild animals; and several animal agriculture research facilities at universities in different parts of the country. Simultaneously I was teaching architectural design in the School of Architecture and Landscape Architecture at the University of Minnesota and had organized a number of studio projects that involved students in the design of animal agriculture facilities and multifunctional educational buildings located in small towns in rural Minnesota.

The studio projects included presentations by academicians and experts involved in animal agriculture, who discussed rural issues and the profound changes that were taking place. I was aware of the poor quality of design in most contemporary farm buildings and other structures related to agriculture – however, I was not fully aware of the influences that created those buildings. We learned that because of economic conditions, there were fewer farmers and larger farms, resulting in the construction of large livestock buildings that all looked the same with many more animals than found in traditional historic barns. And we learned that these changing economic and social conditions were negatively impacting rural quality of life.

While researching historic barns, other agricultural buildings, and specialized contemporary buildings constructed for dairy, swine, and poultry, I began to realize that the issues impacting rural regions of North America were much broader and more comprehensive than I had realized. Global economics were impacting a wide range of agricultural, social, cultural, economic, health, and environmental interests. Rural areas were experiencing profound demographic shifts, less population, lack of jobs for young people, and limited access to high-quality communication, education and health services. Social conflicts resulting from various ideas about sustainability and the size of farms and farming methods contributed to the dilemma.

Rural citizens were looking for a way to manage change, and it was apparent that design schools and the design professions had generally ignored rural issues and rural America. Since there was no academic program in rural design anywhere like there was for urban design and planning, and with the approval of the deans of two colleges, I organized and founded the CRD at the University of Minnesota. Based on those experiences, the focus of the book later shifted to become an introduction to the new design discipline of rural design.

## The Center for Rural Design

The CRD, with shared sponsorship by the College of Design and the College of Food, Agricultural, and Natural Resource Sciences at the University of Minnesota, is the first in the world that brings design as a methodology to improve quality of life for rural communities. As founder and director of the CRD, I have gained broad knowledge working with a wide range of design colleagues and research scholars on a number of sponsored research projects with rural communities in Minnesota. Because of those experiences I began to understand the multidisciplinary nature of sustainable rural environments and the creative and innovative thinking necessary to plan and develop strategies to take advantage of new agricultural economics, environmental concerns, and impacts of change – all related to the global economy.

Rural design is a process for engaging rural people in the shaping of their future rural environment, and a methodology that can bridge the gap between science and society to resolve rural problems. It provides a new way of holistic thinking about and finding ways to resolve rural problems while delineating opportunities to deal with the many global challenges facing rural regions in North America and the world.

Most often the academy approaches rural and agricultural issues from the science side. They are generally approached along economic, transportation, water, social, agricultural food and fiber production, environmental protection, or healthcare lines. Rural issues have inherent connections and assets that are often overlooked because they are often addressed singularly – at institutional or political jurisdictional scales – when the problems and the opportunities for a solution are actually larger, multidisciplinary, and multijurisdictional.

In North America most rural areas are experiencing loss of population, an aging infrastructure, and inadequate transportation as well as poor access to high-speed internet, quality education, and healthcare. This is exasperated by fewer economic options, environmental degradation from changing land-use patterns, and declining quality of life – especially for young people. Global climate changes will further impact the function and character of the agricultural landscape. These impacts along with food supply, food security, and water resources are international sustainability issues that will bring dramatic changes to rural social, economic, and environmental landscapes around the world – particularly in responding to the rapidly growing world population that may double by 2050.

Carbon sequestration, for example, is an important component of national and global responses to climate change due to greenhouse gases (Miller, 2009).

What is the kind of rural landscape and land coverage required to have a positive impact on controlling carbon, and what is the character of its form? What research is necessary to understand implications of farming practices and climate conditions determining soil productivity, water quality, and human, animal, and environmental health? How can the world's limited land resources be better utilized to feed the growing world population and how can the economies of rural people be improved in the process?

A critical need exists for an effective, innovative, and creative means to engage these problems, challenges, and opportunities at the scale in which they occur. Rural design is a way to bring a community-based interdisciplinary problem-solving process to meet these challenges at all landscape scales. Rural design can integrate all of the knowledge, tools, and management skills available without confinement to disciplinary or political boundaries. Through evidence-based design it can provide visualizations that are sustainable and improve quality of life for rural citizens today without compromising the ability of future generations to meet their needs.

In his book, *The Next Hundred Million: America in 2050,* Joel Kotkin (2010) outlines a bright future for America, with its evermore diverse population bringing new ideas, technological innovations, and cultural expressions while responding to radical transformation. While most of this new population will live in cities or suburbs, he goes on to discuss the great central rural region of the United States and its opportunity:

> The Heartland, consigned to the fringes of American society and economy in the 20th century, is poised to enjoy a significant renaissance in the early 21st. Not since the 19th century, when it was a major source of America's economic, social, and cultural supremacy, has the vast continental expanse been set to play so powerful a role in shaping the nation's future.
>
> (Kotkin, 2010)

Kotkin's perspective is based on estimates that the diverse population of the United States in 2050 will be home to at least 400 million people – roughly 100 million more than today – and because of its unique demography and land assets the United States has the potential to emerge as the most affluent, culturally rich, and successful nation in human history (Kotkin, 2010).

It is important to designers and others involved in rural issues to visualize the connections that the design process can bring to help link science and society. The diagram (Figure 1.4) used by the CRD illustrates the relationship rural design and its design process brings to both science and society as a means to bridge the gap. As a problem-solving process, rural design can improve quality of rural life when it:

- Helps rural communities understand the character of the landscape within which they live, work, and play to make informed land-use, architectural,

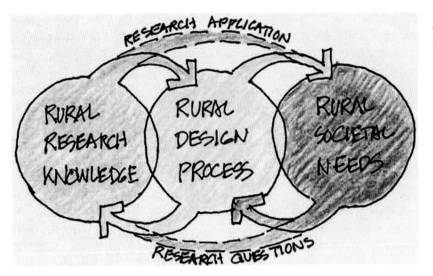

1.4
The connection that the rural design process can make between rural science and rural society. This diagram is used by the CRD to explain the foundation for evidence-based rural design.

and aesthetic decisions that enhance economic development and protect the environment;

- Connects social, artistic, cultural, technological, climate, and landscape character to better define rural regions and people's understanding of it to create a strong shared sense of place;
- Promotes sustainable entrepreneurship, production, and economic development for rural regions and communities by outlining ways to improve human, livestock, crop, and ecosystem health;
- Integrates research and practice across the many disciplines involved to meet rural societal needs, while gaining new understanding and provoking new research questions.

The CRD provides a broad interdisciplinary design approach to the visual and functional arrangement of cultural and cultivated landscapes working in harmony with natural resources. By being dedicated to innovation and creativity, the process of rural design can articulate and find solutions to rural social, economic, and environmental issues worldwide.

## Global issues and impacts

Many recent books by a variety of authors have done an excellent job of making the world aware of the global issues and impacts of climate change and the need for carbon-neutral and net zero-energy development. Others have discussed low-impact development and organic farming, rural health, and food production and processing, and all of the authors know much more about those issues than I do. This book recognizes these excellent intellectual efforts and impacts, and instead focuses on the emerging new discipline of rural design and its knowledge base as a way to address rural issues and shape rural futures.

Rural architecture and landscapes around the world inspire me, and I hope this book will instill students and professionals with a passion for rural design as a new design discipline. Through its practice it can bring rural citizens creative, innovative, and practical suggestions as to how design can improve their rural quality of life. While the book is oriented toward academia, students, and design professionals, it contains useful information for a wide range of people involved with rural communities including public officials, government agencies, and non-profit entities. The book outlines the theoretical base for rural design that seeks ways to connect issues and encourage synergy among stakeholders to create optimal solutions. It discusses the urban/rural edge, rural landscapes and their character, and outlines strategies, techniques, and methodologies used in the practice of rural design.

The book argues for a new way of design thinking about rural regions and design relationships to rural regions in states and provinces and nations through-out the world. For rural design to be effective and relevant, this new discipline must be founded on solid research, and practice must be based on data-driven evidence that will result in transformational changes (Thorbeck and Streng, 2009).

The rural design principles outlined are based on my experiences and observations from architectural practice and research projects at the CRD, and what I have learned from many colleagues in a wide range of disciplines concerned with rural issues. But the book is only the beginning and the legacy of rural design is yet to be realized. That will start to happen when rural design becomes a standard design curriculum program in universities to educate and train designers and leaders to address the full spectrum of issues impacting their rural regions.

This personal process of discovery has made it clear to me that the issues impacting rural environments worldwide are global issues offering exciting opportunities for rural citizens, regions, states, and nations to utilize rural design to shape their rural economies and environments for a healthy and prosperous future. In an opinion piece in *Yale Environment*, Jonathan Foley (now director of the Institute on the Environment at the University of Minnesota) outlines some of the issues of climate change and the pending global crisis in how land is used – particularly for agriculture – and how the world can feed its rapidly expanding population that may double by 2050. He writes:

> Although I'm a climate scientist by training, I worry about this collective fixation on global warming as the mother of all environmental problems. Learning from the research my colleagues and I have done over the past decade, I fear we are neglecting another, equally inconvenient truth: *that we now face a global crisis in land use and agriculture that could undermine the health, security, and sustainability of our civilization.* Our use of land, particularly for agriculture, is absolutely essential to the success of the

human race. We depend on agriculture to supply us with food, feed, fiber, and, increasingly, biofuels. Without a highly efficient, productive, and resilient agricultural system, our society would collapse almost overnight. Meeting these huge new agricultural demands will be one of the greatest challenges of the 21st century. At present, it is completely unclear how (and if) we can do it.

(Foley, 2009)

According to the Institute on the Environment, agriculture is a major producer of greenhouse gases contributing to climate change and it uses a great deal of available water for irrigation. Land is finite, we need food, and we need to preserve the environment. Responding to and developing solutions to these global issues is critical for feeding a rapidly growing world population while maintaining the ecosystem integrity of rural landscapes worldwide.

These challenges provide opportunities for creative and innovative land-use solutions to: slow climate change while resolving food supply and food security; provide renewable energy from solar, wind, and biomass; provide options to deal with water resources and water quality; and seek solutions that integrate human, animal, and environmental health. Rural design as a new design discipline can assist rural people to integrate issues, link issues to actions, and make wise long-term land-use decisions – decisions that protect the rural environment while promoting rural economic development and enhancing rural quality of life.

The time to act is now.

# Chapter 2

# Rural heritage

When mankind first developed the skills to grow plants and raise animals for food and fiber, a revolutionary change in human settlement took place. With the advent of farming an entirely new way of life emerged. In hunting-and-gathering societies people were always moving around pursuing food, but with farming people stayed in one place and worked with the land. No longer required to constantly relocate to find enough to eat, the early farmers selected a site for growing food, used animals to help them in their work, and designed structures to protect themselves from the elements and for storage. It began a new human relationship with nature and animals.

## Ancient roots and European origins

From earliest history when people started to grow and harvest food on the land, they generally settled in one place and created settlements. With animals they could till the soil to produce crops, transport things to trade, and begin to acquire material goods. Some animals were bred for farm labor and others to provide food and clothing. Farming created a working partnership between humans and domestic animals, and the homes and working buildings that they constructed for animal care became the genesis of functional architecture. Staying in one place, rather than constantly moving around, meant that people had more time to enjoy their new location, socialize with their neighbors, and create society.

In a discussion about early Roman sites, Frank E. Brown, the late eminent scholar in classical archeology and history, whom I met at the American Academy in Rome, indicated that the Roman farmer was just as likely to be an architect as any other early Roman, and that the Roman culture of shaping spaces around rituals is how they organized rural agricultural environments just like they organized urban environments. Farming is based on acquired knowledge, seasonal changes, local patterns for planting and harvesting, cycles in the breeding and care of animals, and family traditions of working with the land. These evolved over time into rituals, and it was these rituals that shaped Roman society and agriculture. Brown described it this way:

> The architecture of the Romans was, from first to last, an art of shaping space around ritual. It stemmed directly from the Roman propensity to transform the raw stuff of experience and behavior into rituals, formal patterns of action and reaction. From the dawn of their history we find the Romans feeling, thinking, and acting ritually. Together or singly, they sought identity and fulfillment in the performance and creation of fixed, habitual forms of conduct. This was the inherently Roman way of reducing the chaos of experience to manageable, human measures. It was the root of Roman custom, Roman tradition, Roman discipline, and Roman law. It was in the form of ritual that the specifically Roman values manifested themselves.
>
> (Brown, 1961)

There are not many sources that illustrated what rural life might have been like in the Roman era, but there are a few excellent mosaics in North Africa that illustrate rural life in the second century. A mosaic from a Roman villa in Tunisia – the Liberii Villa – provides one of the few glimpses of rural living (Figure 2.1). The mosaic was first published in a 1957 book, *The Social and Economic History*

**2.1**
A beautifully detailed Roman mosaic from the second-century Liberii farm villa in Tunisia, depicting a barn and a variety of rural scenes of life on a farm.

Rural heritage

*of the Roman Empire*, where the author described the mosaic and rural life in North Africa:

> In the centre of the picture we see a barn, in the doorway of which stands a man, probably a shepherd, leaning on a long staff and looking at an approaching herd. In the side-wall of the building are three windows and a low door; against it rests a plough. Towards the building moves a flock of goats, sheep, and cows, while two dogs run in the opposite direction across the fields. Above the flock, a man ploughs a field with a team of oxen. Near the building are a tent and a primitive well, from which a man has just filled up a semicircular trough to water a horse. Another horse is tethered to a stake between the well and the barn. Towards the right a man dressed in a heavy cloak drives a donkey. This central picture is surrounded on three sides by scenes portraying the various occupations of the owners of the estate and their workmen. On the left three men elegantly dressed and mounted on beautiful horses attack and kill a lioness. At the foot are depicted other hunting scenes. On the right of the central picture we have scenes of rustic life. A shepherd in the fields playing his pipe under an olive tree; near him his flock of goats, one of which is milked by a shepherd; while on the right a negro slave gathers olives from a tall tree.
>
> (Rostovtzeff, 1957)

This beautiful mosaic, now part of the Bardo Museum in Tunis, illustrates a small barn with a loft organized around a central axis similar to the basilica form that the Romans used for many of their important public buildings reflecting ritual and hierarchy in Roman architecture and society. The barn with its central aisle and animal stalls on each side functioned well for organizing the tasks required for caring for domestic animals. With its symbolic connection to the rituals of society and agriculture, the basilica form became the prototype for livestock facilities and agricultural buildings throughout the Roman Empire.

The basilica form worked well for organizing agricultural function while expressing a spatial connection between the rituals of farming and rituals of worship. Roman architecture had developed with new building technologies (utilization of reinforced concrete and the arch) to create large indoor spaces as gathering places for civic functions. Since religion and politics were closely integrated, the great public spaces the Romans developed were used for functional purposes while expressing faith in the gods. This quest to connect with a higher being impacted buildings for agriculture just as it did for important public buildings. It is a legacy that expanded throughout the Roman world and a theme that Christianity capitalized on and transformed.

The basilica organizational form was used and embellished by monasteries during the Middle Ages for worship as well as buildings for livestock, and they became showplaces for animal husbandry. A prime example of the monastic barn is the great thirteenth-century Coxwell Tithe Barn in England, located midway between Oxford and Swindon (Figures 2.2 and 2.3). Its basilica form is clearly expressed on the exterior and interior, and is similar in character and structural concepts to the Gothic cathedrals constructed throughout Europe in the Middle Ages. Landowning farmers throughout Europe wanted spiritual assistance in farming so they followed its paradigm, and the basilica form continues to this day in the design of barns as well as churches.

2.2
Exterior view of the Coxwell Barn in England. One of the great medieval monastic barns based on the Roman basilica organizational form that influenced barn construction all over Europe and in North America.

2.3
Interior of the Coxwell Barn, illustrating structural and axial similarity to the basilica form used in the construction of Gothic cathedrals throughout Europe.

Over time, each European country developed its own farming traditions, so that by the nineteenth and twentieth centuries farmsteads in Sweden were constructed of sawed wood lumber that was abundantly available in northern Europe. An aerial photograph (Figure 2.4) illustrates a spread out swine farm, with multiple narrow buildings each serving a separate function for breeding, birthing, raising, and growing pigs. Because of the wide discrepancy between summer and winter climate in Sweden, the barns are narrow to capture daylight and maintain temperatures so critical in hog operations. Set in and among trees, the farmstead has a direct visual and practical connection with the material the barns were constructed from. The trees shade in the summer, yet allow the winter sun to warm the red-painted buildings.

They are quite different from the tightly organized farmsteads in the flat land of the Netherlands where the land is limited and land uses very tightly controlled (Figure 2.5), or in the mountains of Austria where house and barn were often connected using heat from the animals to keep their living quarters warm while allowing easy access to the animals for care and feeding (Figure 2.6).

Climate, landscape, soils, topography, availability of arable land, and accessibility of water all influenced how the farmstead and its working agricultural buildings were designed and constructed. They reflect each country's functional rituals of farming, its architecture and its way of life, just as other cultural traditions were manifested in division of labor, clothing styles, music, food, drink, dance, and family.

2.5
An integrated dairy farm in the Netherlands, showing the close relationship between barn and house on the flat Dutch landscape. It is in a country with very tight land-use controls and zoning regulations to preserve agriculture.

2.6
A farmstead near Zell am See, Austria constructed in the mountains above the valley with attached house and barn.

## English landscapes and influence on America

Since the United States was originally established as a British colony, England influenced the character of rural landscapes the most. This influence is seen most clearly in New England, with its farms and the many small towns established to support agriculture. Although the primary method of construction in Europe in the seventeenth and eighteenth centuries was masonry, in America the availability of wood and its use in the construction of buildings created the unique visual character of the New England countryside, with stone being used mostly for foundations and fences.

In his book, *The Making of the English Landscape*, W.G. Hoskins (1955) outlined the culture of the English landscape which had a pronounced visual

impact on early settlements in North America. He describes the evolution of the
rural landscape in England by the shaping of land over time through the construction of ditches and earthen hedges on each side of the property lines, with
large open agricultural fields in between (Figure 2.7). The space between the
hedges was used for circulation and movement of goods and animals.

The earliest farmers in England lived in small villages and moved out into
the fields to tend crops and animals. Often the villages incorporated a village green
(some with ponds) as the community gathering place. Later in the eighteenth
century, by government decree through 'enclosure commissioners' the fields were
divided into smaller strip parcels with detached homes and barns as family
farmsteads. Hoskins describes the resulting character of the English landscape we
see today:

> Such was the landscape created by the enclosure commissioners . . . a
> landscape that is the product of various forces over a space of four hundred
> years. So, behind every generalization, there lies the infinite variety and
> beauty of the detail; and it is the detail that matters, that gives pleasure to
> the eye and mind, as we traverse, on foot and unhurried, the landscape of
> any part of England.
>
> (Hoskins, 1955)

Memorial Day on the Village Green
Camden, ME 5/28/01

This tradition of self-sufficient farmsteads in the country with small towns for services was the paradigm that shaped early rural villages and rural development in North America. A good example of a New England village is the church and village green in Camden, Maine (Figure 2.8) where landscape, adjacent river for power and transportation, architecture, and community are represented as a connected ideal.

The English traditions that shaped America were the result of hundreds of years of development – from early Celtic times to Roman Britain to Anglo-Saxon settlement to Tudor and then Georgian England. It was the act of parliament under George II that shaped the English landscape we know today, and it became the model for early North America. After the American Revolution, with its strong emphasis on individual property rights as outlined in the Constitution, citizen farmers and the democratic ideal defined the culture of the rural landscape and the rural villages that supported it.

## Immigrants' dream

Longstanding agricultural and social traditions were brought to America by emigrants from all over Europe in the eighteenth and nineteenth centuries. Although many urban people came to America, most were from rural areas. The problem in much of rural Europe at that time was the highly restrictive land controls and lack of a methodology for new families to become landowners to start new homesteads. Usually only the oldest son inherited the farm, and with the availability of land in the United States at little or no cost, particularly following the Homestead Act of 1862, the Midwest became the place for young and adventurous men and women from Europe to go and start a new life based on agriculture.

During the settlement period, the immigrants' dream was to own the land on which they lived – and where land was available was where they went. The growing population of the United States slowly expanded westward across the prairie as land became available. The rural landscape we see today is the result of the synergistic melding of individual farming skills and experiences from their country of origin with the traditions and experiences of others from different countries.

The emphasis on individual property rights was more pronounced in the United States with its new Constitution, whereas Canada continued to follow British laws, with more government control of land use. The sense of freedom from government control of property and the more diverse climate made the United States a magnet for immigration. Norway was second only to Ireland with the highest percentage of population that emigrated to America, and many Norwegians settled in the Upper Midwest, including my grandparents.

Even though the immigrant experience was similar throughout the United States there are regional variations based on climate and tradition. On the East Coast, farming was mostly controlled by landowners and tenant farmers, and in the South landowners on large estates were using slavery as property and as a labor force. That methodology changed slowly, dividing the country into north and south, and wasn't resolved until the American Civil War and the abolition of slavery.

Across North America there are many variations in agriculture, farming methods, and types of farms and there are many books that describe their rural heritage in great detail. For this book I am using the Midwest rural landscape as an example – because it is the region that I am most familiar with and because it is where immigration from northern Europe was strongest during the nineteenth and early twentieth centuries. Figure 2.9 is a map of North America, prepared by the CRD for the First International Symposium on Rural Design held at the University of Minnesota in 2010. It illustrates the breadth of the three great ecosystems and watersheds that converge in Minnesota and extend across southern Canada and most of the northern part of the United States.

An excellent description of the difficulties that immigrants coped with as they carved out a homestead and created a farm in the Midwest is recorded in

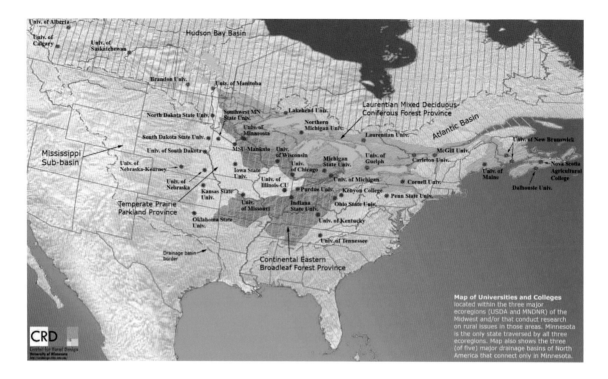

Map of Universities and Colleges located within the three major ecoregions (USDA and MNDNR) of the Midwest and/or that conduct research on rural issues in those areas. Minnesota is the only state traversed by all three ecoregions. Map also shows the three (of five) major drainage basins of North America that connect only in Minnesota.

remarkable diaries covering forty-seven years that Andrew Peterson, a Swedish emigrant to Minnesota in 1850, wrote about life on his farm in Carver County. Years later, the diaries were picked up by Vilhelm Moberg, a Swedish novelist who used them as the background for a famous trilogy of novels about Swedish emigrants to America. An article about the diaries in *Minnesota History* describes the difficult work Peterson had to do on his farm:

> The back-breaking work of grubbing trees and tree stumps and clearing land for cultivation continued annually. So did the planting of apple grafts, sowing of grains, planting and cultivation of corn, harvesting, threshing, fall plowing and planting, corn picking, winter butchering, manure hauling, cutting of cordwood for sale, construction of a new home and barns, fencing, road making, and participating in regular church and school activities. The census of 1860 valued Peterson's real estate at $600 and his personal property at $200. By 1864 Peterson clearly was becoming a successful farmer, thanks in part to increased diversification which insured a multiple income as well as subsistence. He produced wheat, oats, barley, corn, alfalfa, potatoes, rutabagas, vegetables of all types, sugar beets, many varieties of apples, pears, grapes, plums, cherries, gooseberries, raspberries, strawberries, currants, maple syrup, molasses, wine, eggs, butter, cream, milk, cattle, swine, sheep, geese, poultry, cordwood, logs, and no doubt other products not mentioned in the diary.
>
> (Qualey, 1972)

2.9
A map prepared for the First International Symposium on Rural Design in 2010, illustrating the three ecosystems that converge in Minnesota and extend throughout much of the USA and Canada. The map also identifies the many universities within the ecosystems with faculty invited to the symposium.

Andrew Peterson was a typical immigrant who started a new life in Minnesota where land became available. Because of his personality, skills, and passion for farming he become a leading horticulturist as well as successful diversified farmer. His diary is one of the few that recorded life on the prairie and his Minnesota farmstead is now on the National Register of Historic Places with the hope that it will become an interpretive farm.

It was Thomas Jefferson in the eighteenth century at Monticello in Virginia who epitomized the American agrarian ideal of linking architecture and site, inspired by the art of agriculture. Jefferson, following his aristocratic background, designed his farm around the Palladian notion of the villa as the center of farm life. William Howard Adams in his book, *Jefferson's Monticello*, writes 'perhaps it was Jefferson's enlarged American sense of space that translated Palladio's "Monticello" into a Virginian mountain on a scale quite different from the small Italian hills Palladio had in mind when he wrote his treatise' (Adams, 1983).

The American architect Frank Lloyd Wright, on the other hand, was born and raised on a dairy farm in the rolling hills of western Wisconsin, where his Welsh family settled in the 1800s. He had an innate attraction to farming and the land, but it was later – after moving to Chicago to work with Louis Sullivan, joining the Prairie School, and starting his own architectural firm – that his idea of a place-oriented American architecture was formed. This was expressed in building designs where he emphasized connection to the land, with horizontal architectural stratifications in stone, brick, and wood. These forms were similar to the limestone outcroppings along rivers and valleys in Wisconsin shaped by melting glaciers – valleys that he had explored as a boy.

The search for a new kind of architecture for America became the hallmark of Wright's individualistic style. Vincent Scully Jr., the noted architectural historian at Yale, wrote in a 1960 monograph:

> Wright was the heir, in architecture – and regarded himself as being so – of a tradition, in part Jeffersonian, which had previously found its best expression in the works of Melville, Whitman, and Mark Twain. That is, he tried, though in abstract form, to echo the shapes and dominant rhythms of the landscapes in which his buildings were set.
>
> (Scully, 1960)

The largest influx of people to America were farmers, and they carried with them their practical experience and skills in animal husbandry, barn types, construction methods, and farming practices. Upon arriving and homesteading in the new land, they experienced a new situation and had to quickly learn American business practices and adjust to the soil types, climate, and economic situation in the area where they settled. As a result, any study of farmsteads in North America is a study of the immigrant experience and the making of the new world.

As they located land and established a homestead they had to quickly construct some kind of house to live in. Many were constructed out of mud on

2.10

Sherping Farmstead in western Minnesota. This enormous historic barn, sitting on a hill, is one of the largest in the state. With the small, but ornate symmetrical farmhouse below it portrays a successful farmer in the nineteenth century.

the prairie, and others of hand-hewed logs where timber was readily available. The barn was critical to survival and it received the greatest attention. The barn, as a livestock shelter and storehouse for feed for the long winter months, was essential for a successful farm operation. It was certainly the largest building on the farmstead, but later, as farmers became more prosperous, the farmhouse emerged as the aesthetic showplace. The historic Sherping Farmstead in northern Minnesota near Fergus Falls illustrates both sides of this phenomenon, with the carefully crafted ornate house as the family gathering place, and up on the hill the great basilica barn.

While the homes expressed fashion and social status, it was the barn that exemplified the spirit of place. Ralph Waldo Emerson wrote about his love for barns: 'I like to have a man's knowledge comprehend more than one class of topics, one row of shelves. I like a man who likes to see a fine barn as well as a good tragedy'. To me a beautiful barn or farmstead that is at home with its landscape is a thing to admire, and I have always been fascinated by this unique building type where humans, animals, and landscapes interact. When farmsteads were constructed and maintained with neatness and care the farmers who lived there were considered good farmers, as landscape architect Joan Nassauer discovered in her research on the perceptions rural citizens in southeastern Minnesota had regarding agriculture environments (Nassauer and Opdam, 2008).

The farmstead, with its prominent house and massive barn became a picture of the idyllic, rural way of life. The Schiltgen Farmstead (Figure 2.11), formerly a large dairy farm (now a horse farm) adjacent to the village of Lake Elmo in Washington County, Minnesota, has been carefully maintained by grandson, Peter Schiltgen, with neatness and care exemplifying this perception. The farm today is still a source of community pride and an icon for the Twin Cities suburban community.

These farmsteads illustrate an architectural attitude about traditional farm buildings that combines a sense of appearance and style with clear operational

Schiltgen Farmstead on the
edge of the historic village
of Lake Elmo, Minnesota,
which has been beautifully
maintained by the Schiltgen
family. The farmstead is the
focal point and iconic symbol
of the historic rural village in
the Twin Cities metropolitan
area.

function connected to local building materials, landscape, and climate. They reflect uniqueness of place and pride in farming as a lifestyle. Figure 2.12 shows a simple stone barn with addition in northern Iowa constructed with local building materials, which expresses this ideal with careful attention to architectural detail.

American barns reflect the cultural background and experiences of their builders by using an architectural language of formal symmetry, asymmetrical composition, and contrast. Since these were farmers without formal training in design or architecture, they often had to develop their own visual order, using barn-construction manuals and materials found on the land. The result is often a combination of styles, reflecting prevailing ideas, new labor-saving practices, and

2.12
A handsome stone barn in
northern Iowa built with
readily available materials
which immigrants from Europe
knew how to use. It is typical of
how the art and skills of the
farmer influenced farmstead
design and construction.

2.13
This beautiful stone and wood barn in northern Illinois illustrates transitions over time, from a gable roof with heavy timber structure to a gambrel roof with cut lumber, and two different silos reflecting changing barn-construction technology.

the knowledge, whimsies, and aesthetic sense of the farmer. A good example is shown in Figure 2.13. This dairy barn in northern Illinois was constructed in multiple phases, and the transition from gable to gambrel roof construction is clearly expressed and artfully balanced.

## Farmsteads

In the Midwest, diversified farming practices focused on the farmstead – a collection of house and working buildings, including the barn, chicken coop, hog house, machine shed, granary, and well house – informally organized around a courtyard for functional purposes. My paternal grandmother emigrated from Norway to North Dakota in 1903 and later, after my German grandfather died in the great flu epidemic of 1918, she moved with six children to northern Minnesota and bought a farm near her brother who had arrived earlier from Norway. A recent aerial photo of the farm (Figure 2.14) illustrates its functional organization typical of a Midwest diversified farmstead arranged around a working courtyard that functions as a circulation and family gathering place.

This simple organizing principle of arranging functional buildings around a courtyard allows for direct movement between buildings, providing a place for farming operations such as harnessing horses to work in the field, hauling and loading hay in the barn, or a softball game at a summer family get-together. In the Midwest, the majority of farmsteads were established in the latter half of the nineteenth century and early twentieth century with three basic working building types in addition to the house: (1) barns to house animals and store feed through the winter; (2) granaries to store and protect grain, corn, and other commodities until they went to market; and (3) sheds to protect, repair, and maintain machinery and buildings. Often the farmsteads were in areas remote from rural towns and their service establishments, requiring the farm to be a nearly self-sufficient

and sustainable enterprise. As sustainable farmers they had to be carpenters, electricians, plumbers, blacksmiths, butchers, horticulturists; take care of cows, horses, pigs, and chickens; plant and harvest crops; and bring cream and grain to town to sell.

The unique design principles that these self-supporting farmsteads seem to have in common are:

- They are conceived as a unified complex that directly relates to and fits into the character of the land and its topography, soils, climate, prevailing winds, and regional farming traditions.
- They are adjacent to a road network for delivery trucks, hauling grain, milk collection, and access to towns and nearby railroads.
- They utilize natural ventilation, based on the local climate, for ventilation, drying and preservation of feed, and proper ventilation for animal health; and with high ceilings and double hung windows for human comfort.
- They represent an architecture that is a combination of locally available materials, regional construction techniques, prevailing animal husbandry practices, labor-saving functionality, and minimal cost to build, operate, and maintain.
- They consist of subtle complexities, idiosyncrasies, and contradictions in their architectural character, as the builders responded to specific needs and their own innate sense of proportion and design.

The quality and variety of farmsteads from around the country reflects where immigrants came from and their farming background and experience. A

2.15
A large gable-roof bank barn in eastern Pennsylvania, viewed from the earth bank providing access to the hay loft. It is on the National Register of Historic Places and typical of large dairy barns constructed in that region in the 1880s.

large bank barn in eastern Pennsylvania (Figure 2.15) illustrates the large scale to which wooden multiuse gable barns could be constructed. The earth is banked up on one side to access the hay loft, and the opposite side has an overhang to protect doors and windows that open into the animal holding area on the ground floor. This red-painted historic wooden 'basilica' barn with white trim is carefully designed and constructed with symmetry, and capped on top with a decorative ventilation cupola.

An Amish farmstead near Lancaster, Pennsylvania (Figure 2.16) has a gable-roofed barn with a cluster of additions and buildings that have been altered and changed over time to accommodate better ways to feed and care for animals without electricity, even though the Amish today will often use generators to power

2.16
This farmstead in Lancaster County, Pennsylvania is typical of many Amish farms with its simple and functional architecture. As a working farm today it provides a living history glimpse of common farming practices in the late nineteenth and early twentieth centuries.

**2.17**
An historic vineyard farm in Napa Valley, California with wooden house, barn, and water tower carefully composed and constructed as functional working units for living, housing animals, and growing and harvesting grapes for the wine industry.

equipment. This Amish farmstead settles into the rolling Pennsylvania countryside with a gentle, integrated architecture.

Out west in California, the linear composition of buildings on a vineyard in Napa Valley illustrates its functional purpose for growing and harvesting grapes for making wine. The house, barn, and water tower are carefully constructed of wood as independent, but architecturally related buildings of equal importance, and distinct use.

The decorative details of a horse barn on a large historic farmstead in Nashville, Tennessee (Figure 2.18), or the now demolished horse barn at the historic Fergus Falls State Hospital in Minnesota (Figure 2.19) show skillful wooden

**2.18**
A large wood horse barn in Nashville, Tennessee reflects the important status of the horse on this historic farmstead. Constructed with craftsmanship and detail, it is functionally organized with multiple locations for loading hay, doorways for horse handling, and dramatic cupolas for natural ventilation.

2.19
No longer standing, this large wood horse barn was constructed at a State Hospital in western Minnesota near Fergus Falls. The beautiful carpenter gothic style illustrates the hierarchy of the horse in animal agriculture through its fine architectural details and craftsmanship.

construction craftsmanship. And through their architectural detail illustrate the important place of the horse in farm animal hierarchy. For as long as humans and horses have had a working relationship, barns constructed for horses are always more decorative and stylistically important than barns for cattle, swine, or poultry. This barn-building tradition reflects the unique relationship between humans and horses over the centuries for work, transportation, and pleasure.

The farmstead is a functional compound where humans and animals live and work together for mutual benefit. Understanding its integrated character is fundamental to understanding why the buildings were constructed the way they were. As a family unit they depict the cultural, ethnic, and construction knowledge and skills of the people who built them. The immigrants' experience of melding their heritage with the way things were done in America to survive and prosper is what created the unique character of the cultivated agricultural landscape – as well as the creation of the many small towns that developed along transportation routes to support farming.

A study of ethnic settlements in Wisconsin in the 1880s by Jon Gjerde (1985) indicates the combination of social and economic influences the immigrants carried from the west coast of Norway (like the desire and dream to become a landowner in America) and the historic cultural practices (like building with wood and self-reliance) that shaped the character of buildings on the land as they adapted to the American way of doing business. It was this combination of influences that created the unique architectural and functional character of farmsteads and the unique character of the many small towns that developed to serve farming in the countryside. Gjerde quotes an immigrant who wrote back to his family in Norway in 1852 about settlements in America, 'It is not true that Norwegians or other national groups retain their old ways believing they are the best. He who hangs on to the old ways when they do not pay will lose out. He must learn anew' (Gjerde, 1985).

Saving labor in both animal husbandry and crop farming has always driven farmers to be innovative. A number of round dairy barns (Figure 2.20) were constructed in Minnesota because they minimized the labor required to move hay from the loft to the animal stalls during the long and dark winters. Their construction cost was greater due to the extra cutting and fitting of lumber, so most farmers stayed with the traditional basilica form. Farmers have always been prone to utilize new barn-construction technologies that cost less, such as prefabricated roof arches, which became readily accessible in the 1930s, as seen in the barn and farmstead in Door County, Wisconsin shown in Figure 2.21.

Carpentry skills and the availability of lumber were very important aspects of construction on farms in the Midwest. The early barns were constructed of wood, hand-cut and hewed from forests near the farmstead. Later, the

**2.20**
This round barn in southwestern Minnesota is still in use and typical of round barns constructed by farmers to save labor in feeding, care, and milking of dairy animals.

**2.21**
An arched-roof barn in Door County, Wisconsin. This simple barn used prefabricated wood arches and balloon frame wood construction techniques, which became readily available in the early 1930s.

standardization of cut lumber dimensions and the development of balloon framing and the availability of publications illustrating building ideas and construction techniques changed the kinds of working buildings that were built. However, the better the carpenter, the better the barn, corn crib, machine shed, or house. Yet it was the immigrants' knowledge of working with the land and their innate understanding of animals, climate, and soils that provided a learned response to topography, wind patterns, and watershed when locating buildings. It is this knowledge, connected with their cultural background, which allowed each farmstead to take on its own unique character.

As time went on, farming systems became more standardized, and a variety of other working building types were constructed in the rural Midwest landscape. With the arrival of the railroad, the grain elevator, for example, was developed to store grain purchased from the farmers until it was sold. These early grain elevators needed to be strong to resist wind and the outward force of stored grain, and were generally constructed as a series of compartments with walls of 2x4 or 2x6 wooden planks laid flat, nailed together, and covered with corrugated metal panels. Figure 2.22 shows a cluster of such elevators along the railroad track in the rural town of Hallock in northwestern Minnesota.

Feed mills were also essential to rural farms and communities and were initially located along rivers to use water as power to operate them. Later, with the availability of electricity, they were constructed in small towns along the railroad tracks, such as the one in Gaylord, Minnesota shown in Figure 2.23, where the mill was combined with the grain elevator to grind feed for animals as well as storing grain.

2.22
A string of tall, free-standing grain elevators along the railroad tracks on the Minnesota prairie is a powerful sentinel and symbol of working agricultural buildings in the prairie landscape.

Rural heritage

Over time, the small town elevator on the prairie accumulated a number of additions to become the largest building complex in the community. It could be seen from miles away, such as the elevator complex along the railroad tracks in the small prairie town of Ada in northwestern Minnesota, shown in Figure 2.24. From a distance these elevators are often silhouetted on the horizon as modern equivalents of the way the great Gothic cathedrals are perceived in the rural countryside of Europe.

More specialized structures to serve agriculture began to appear after agricultural research at land-grant universities developed new fertilizer systems to

increase crop yields. Figure 2.25 shows a cluster of contemporary fertilizer tanks along the highway in northern Minnesota. These are similar to bulk fuel tanks found in small towns throughout the Midwest.

## Buildings for agriculture

Other buildings to serve farm families and settlements include country churches. The church in Polk County in northern Minnesota (Figure 2.26) served as the focal point of its agricultural and ethnic community. There is another church in northern Iowa that was built in 1840 to serve farm settlements in two townships (Figure 2.27). To avoid favoring one township over the other, the church council decided

to locate and construct the church with the township line running down the middle. Cooperation and collaboration between the two townships eliminated tension and improved quality of life. Ingrid Semmingsen in her book about immigration from Norway writes about the church becoming

> a focus in the life of the local society: always filled at services and a meeting place after services. Even if all of them did not come to hear the minister, they could meet people and discuss other matters like horse trades, road work, hiring thrashers, or just hearing the day's news.
>
> (Semmingsen, 1978)

A different type of building is the corn crib. It fulfilled the farmer's need to protect and store grain from mold, vermin, and other pests until it could be taken to market to receive the highest price. Figure 2.28, showing a handsome round structure constructed of masonry on a farm in southwestern Minnesota, illustrates the importance of the granary on the farm. In his book about the corn crib, Keith E. Roe describes its importance: 'Farmstead architecture of all types has been characterized by the practical, of course, and the corncrib is the essence of utility. Yet folk architecture, including corncribs, is not without innovation, even decoration' (Roe, 1988). These working buildings, which developed as a small, but integral part of historic farmsteads in the Midwest, have today – as massive metal bins – become the most visually dominating buildings on the farm.

In addition to the round metal grain bin, other new types of construction which have become standard in the contemporary landscape are pole-barn or post-frame buildings (named after their construction method, which are based on chemically treated wood posts set into the ground). Metal wall and roof panels are then attached with screws, providing an inexpensive weather-tight facility. Figure 2.29, an interior view of a confinement-type dairy barn, illustrates this

2.28
The corn crib is one of the important buildings on a farmstead, and this handsome masonry structure was constructed to resist vermin and mold. Today corn cribs on farmsteads are generally pre-manufactured metal cylinders.

2.29
Interior view of a typical metal-skinned, chemically treated wood post-frame confinement-type dairy barn. Often called 'pole barns' this construction typology is typical of animal agriculture, with barns designed and constructed specifically for the economics and type of animal agriculture on the farm.

construction type commonly used for animal agriculture. These metal-skinned buildings all have a similar look and do not reflect location or place in the landscape, thereby contributing to an impersonal and standardized image of what many refer to as 'factory farming'. This industrial impersonality leads many people to perceive them to be unkind to animals, even though university research and farming practices indicates that this is not so.

Two barns in southwest Minnesota (Figures 2.30 and 2.31) illustrate confinement-type animal housing with two different types of feed storage: a swine barn where the hogs are confined indoors and fed from birth to market with automatic feeders lined up on the outside; and a long horizontal dairy farm with a cluster of adjacent purple silos for storing feed.

**2.30**
A typical metal-skinned confinement-type swine barn with flanking feed bins, designed for raising hogs.

**2.31**
A dairy barn with purple Harvester silos is a familiar scene along rural highways in the Midwest. The slender tall cylinders, standing perpendicular to the long horizontal barn, creates a strong architectural composition.

These pole-barn-type buildings are commonly used for animal agriculture and many other uses in the rural landscape and small towns throughout the United States. As a building type, they have no connection to place and are considered by many to be a visual scourge on the rural landscape when compared to traditional building types. There are exceptions, however, including the handsome small swine building on a farm in southwestern Minnesota, shown in Figure 2.32. With its scale, window proportions, and crisp details, it fits into the farmstead, feeling quite at home on the open, flat prairie.

A new building that has recently appeared on the Midwest rural landscape is the ethanol plant, such as the large complex in southern Minnesota, shown in Figure 2.33. The economics of agriculture is always changing, and farmers and rural communities are attempting to accommodate and adapt to change to

2.32
This simple, small swine barn with adjacent purple silo is one of the few contemporary pole barns that illustrate strong composition and good architectural proportions in a simple and direct way, proving that 'less is more'.

promote economic development. With rising costs for gasoline, many ethanol plants using corn (a food product) were quickly constructed to take advantage of this opportunity, with many economists attributing the recent dramatic rise in food prices to this diversion of a food crop to a fuel source. The rapid influx of these plants all over the Midwest has driven up the price of corn, and many plants are now having financial difficulties because of market fluctuations. New research is underway to convert these facilities to produce biofuels from native plants and prairie grasses, thus opening up a new form of agriculture that will also improve environmental biodiversity.

Other types of agricultural construction for energy that seem to fit well into the rural prairie landscape, without diminishing the landscape's aesthetic, are wind turbines and photovoltaic solar collectors. The large turbine (Figure 2.34) in an open field in northwestern Minnesota is an icon that can be seen for miles. While at Saint John's Abbey and University in central Minnesota (Figure 2.35) a large array of solar collectors along a crop field provides power for the campus.

2.33
A contemporary ethanol plant in southwestern Minnesota reflects a purely engineered approach to a new kind of building in the rural landscape. Using corn to create ethanol fuel, they are impressive in their size, but seem strange on the open prairie. They need a design concept that fits with the landscape.

2.34
A lone wind turbine in a field with horses, beside the highway. This is typical of thousands of large 300-foot tall structures springing up throughout the Great Plains. They are harvesting the wind to create renewable energy and seem to fit well into the prairie landscape, where the wind blows quite steadily.

2.35
An array of photovoltaic solar collectors adjacent to agricultural fields at Saint John's Abbey and University in Collegeville, Minnesota. They were constructed to harvest the sun, providing renewable energy for the campus.

The wind blows a lot on the open prairie of the Upper Midwest, and along Buffalo Ridge in southwestern Minnesota several thousand turbines have been constructed with the rolling prairie, crop fields, and grazing cattle below. One can expect to see thousands of additional turbines built along the windy Minnesota/ Dakotas border as the distribution of electricity from rural areas to urban markets becomes easier and the nation continues to advance renewable energy. To me these giant structures function together with the agricultural landscape below without aesthetic harm. Perhaps there is a romantic connection with the traditional windmill on early farmsteads in the Midwest that reflects an ancient method of working with nature rather than against it. In my opinion, harvesting the wind and sun is an agricultural commodity just like raising corn or soybeans or animals in the rural landscape. Wind turbines and solar collectors will become visible expressions of landscape character in rural regions where the wind blows and the sun shines.

## Indigenous people and the land

I cannot overlook the impact of indigenous peoples and what they have contributed to our understanding of the natural environment and their important heritage in the North American landscape. The cultural history of indigenous peoples includes beautiful and expressive artistic interpretations of the natural world, as well as a variety of highly symbolic architectures, with a wide range of building types and environmental settlements. In his book, *The Sacred In-Between: The Mediating Roles of Architecture*, Thomas Barrie (2010) provides a very interesting discussion about human manifestations through architecture to connect earth with the sky to define and articulate place in the world. He describes the animistic beliefs of indigenous people who are closely connected to their natural surroundings and the ritual architecture they created. Shaping the earth became the first architecture of ritual, and for some Native Americans the earth symbolized home (Barrie, 2010).

There is no architecture that more strongly illustrates this earth connection and a closer integration with geography than cliff dwellings and pueblos in the southwestern part of the United States. A settlement by the Salado people is preserved at the Tonto National Memorial, east of Phoenix, Arizona. Located up on the side of a hill, under a cliff overhang, it illustrates how the dwellings were constructed and how the Salado lived. They inhabited the region for over 200 years, disappearing for reasons unknown in the early 1500s. At the Tonto site, two cliff dwellings have been preserved, with the lower ruin the most accessible, located under a natural ravine high on a steep hill. The Salado people farmed in the valley below along the Salt River, with fields that were cultivated and irrigated creating an abundant food supply.

The lower ruin originally consisted of nineteen rooms, with access only from a ladder which made it easier to defend. Figures 2.36 and 2.37 illustrate the site

**2.36**
Exterior sketch of the Tonto
Cave Dwelling east of Phoenix,
Arizona. Constructed by the
Salado indigenous people,
who lived and farmed in the
valley from AD1300 to AD1500,
the site is now a National
Monument.

**2.37**
Interior sketch of the Tonto
Cave Dwelling illustrating the
arrangement of rooms under
the rock overhang and a
view toward the valley where
farming was done. It illustrates
a blending of cultural and
natural landscapes.

today, with an exterior view of the lower ruin under a rock outcropping and an interior view of different rooms. The sketches capture the sense of living in the open, but being protected from the elements and marauding tribes. This historic site is a good example of indigenous peoples settling in an area where they could connect with and work with nature over a number of generations, raising families, growing food for sustenance and fiber for clothing, and engaging in trade with other tribes and nations.

In a book about indigenous people and the connections between the cultural landscape and the natural landscape, *Culture and Conservation: The Human Dimension in Environmental Planning*, the authors (McNeeley and Pitt, 1985) describe indigenous people and their traditional relationships with the environment, and each other, that are always unique to the ecosystem within which they live. They argue that environmental planning today should pay closer attention to the cultural context within which the planning occurs and involve indigenous people in the creation of plans for a region to take advantage of their considerable knowledge of local ecosystems. McNeeley and Pitt feel that by doing so, it could lead to more effective implementation of those plans.

The more societies integrate cultural and natural landscapes into their thinking about rural environments and the relationships between urban and rural people, the better equipped they will be to manage change and guide future development that is ecologically sustainable and culturally harmonious. Rural design is an interdisciplinary and systemic way to connect rural issues together to nurture new design thinking and planning on a cooperative and collaborative regional level.

When rural heritage is linked with rural future the process of rural design can create synergy by finding opportunities to shape the rural landscape and the character of its architecture to improve quality of life. Rural design is a way to manage change, and when rural heritage, climate, and place-making are at its core, beautiful buildings and landscapes can occur. Rural regions that have the greatest sense of place illustrate a strong design relationship between human and natural landscapes, agricultural heritage, climate, and geography. These places were not designed to be the way they are. They evolved over time, yet we can learn from their character and the heritage they have, and utilize rural design as a process to create future rural environments with a strong sense of place and high quality of life.

# Chapter 3

# Rural character

Geological and cultural history shaped the landscapes of the world. Since I live and work in Minnesota it is helpful to explain the historic forces that created the Minnesota landscape and how its rural character is directly connected to this geological and cultural history. By understanding how the landscape was formed, students and professionals can better understand rural design as a process, methodology, and art that can be used anywhere in the world. They are more likely to develop creative and innovative solutions for shaping rural futures when rural character is integral to the process.

## Geological forces

The landscape of Minnesota was shaped by nature, with ice and fire. The most recent glacier receded approximately 11,000 years ago, and the glacial material deposited by the melting glaciers molded the rolling landscape and created the rivers and lakes we see today. As the forests from the east returned into the state, fires roared across the prairie from the west and where they met the struggle created the mixed prairie and woodland transition ecosystems running diagonally across the state from northwest to southeast.

As a result of this phenomenon, Minnesota is the only state traversed by three ecosystem provinces – the Temperate Prairie Parkland Province, the Continental Eastern Broadleaf Province, and the Laurentian Mixed Deciduous-Coniferous Forest Province. The state also has three great drainage basins – extending north to Canada through the Red River to Hudson Bay, east through Lake Superior to the Atlantic Ocean, and south through the Mississippi River to the Gulf of Mexico. These waterways were the first transportation routes for people and goods, bringing early immigrants into the region. Later the railroad and road networks provided most of the transportation while opening up rural lands for agriculture and settlements, creating the system of cities, towns, and trade areas that still function today.

## Cultural forces

For centuries the indigenous people who lived on the land were involved in shaping the environment through the rituals and patterns of living they practiced. The process of shaping and using the landscape, such as using fire as a tool for clearing of forest understory to grow food or using cliffs as buffalo jumps for mass killing of buffalo, assisted indigenous people in providing food and fiber for themselves. Transporting it for trade has a long and rich history and is an integral part of the cultural heritage of North America.

Because of the extensive fur trade that existed throughout Canada and the northern part of the United States, there was peaceful interaction between Europeans and indigenous people, with intermarriage and settlements at forts established by the fur companies, throughout the northern territories along waterway routes.

Over time, as the United States and Canada evolved as independent nations, new territories were being added and surveyed, opening up land for homesteading. Established in 1785, the Public Land Survey System (PLSS) was used throughout most of the new territories that were added to the United States. It divided the land, on north/south and east/west axes, into sections one mile square. The east coast of the United States, however, mostly retained the British system of 'metes and bounds' which usually described property lines based on topographic or geographic factors and human understandings. In either system, it required a public record-keeping system to ensure ownership and transfers of title. Except for the French-based 'river lot' system used in some parts, Canada applied the Dominion Land Survey grid, which is similar to the PLSS and is used throughout most of the western parts of the country.

In 1858 Minnesota became a state, and the counties, townships, and most of the small rural towns that developed were organized around the PLSS, providing services to farmers and pioneer immigrants in the agricultural countryside. Villages were usually established where country roads and railroads bisected or along rivers where the natural terrain provided a way to navigate across. These transportation systems created development opportunities for railroads and land speculators and they quickly took advantage of early timber and agricultural industries and expanding immigrant population. By 1890 the people who settled in Minnesota were equally divided between foreign and United States sources. Sixty percent came from German-language areas of Europe, 20% from Scandinavia, and the remainder mostly from Ireland, Canada, and Bohemia.

During the period 1870–1920, pioneer immigrants had settled the entire Lake Superior region westward across the prairie to the Rocky Mountains. This part of America's northern heartland (encompassing the western and northern parts of Wisconsin, all of Minnesota, North and South Dakota, and Montana) has the most extreme climate and is most remote from the east and west coasts. Yet, by 1920 over 5 million people were living in this Great Plains region, with the twin cities of Minneapolis and St Paul as the dominant business and cultural center.

Although fully occupied, the Midwest region remains as one of the least densely populated parts of the world's developed nations (Borchert, 1987).

In Minnesota, as in most of the United States, townships were abstractly defined by the PLSS. Townships generally totaled 36 square miles, but some had less if they bordered a large lake or state boundary, and one-mile-square sections could be subdivided into smaller parcels for individuals to claim. The Homestead Act of 1862 granted a quarter section (160 acres) of public lands to a head of household. If the family established a residence and improved and cultivated the land for a continuous period of five years they acquired the property for a price of $1.25 per acre, in five annual installments. Because of the relative open countryside in the Midwest, roads usually followed along section and township boundaries to provide farmers with access to markets and supplies.

Figure 3.1 shows a good example of the homesteading process. It is an advertising circular, the 'Fosston Map' of 1896, that was widely distributed by the General Land Office, Washington, DC, announcing the opening of land ceded from the Red Lake Indian Reservation in northern Minnesota for settlement on May 1, 1896. The map indicates how the land was surveyed and encourages prospective homesteaders to come by train, where to stay, and venture out to potential sites to scout the land and make a claim:

> Immigrants coming from Southern Minnesota or Iowa, or South Dakota, should either come to Fosston over the Great Northern Railway, by the way of Crookston, or else over the Northern Pacific by way of Detroit, and from there on foot or by stage. The trip across White Earth Reservation is almost worth the while of the sixty miles on foot from Detroit to Fosston. To those coming in their own wagons it is best to pick one or two objective points like Sauk Center and Alexandria or Fergus Falls, and from them come on a straight line to Fosston. It is not at all necessary to go to Crookston first. Look up your lands first and when the time comes go to the land office to make your entry.

The map provides only a limited amount of information to immigrants, yet the desire to own a piece of land and start a new life in a new country was a great incentive. This desire encouraged many European families who could afford to do so to sell what they could, pack their belongings, and travel to America to start a new life.

## Immigration to America

My maternal grandfather came to America in 1893, with his parents and five siblings from Norway, traveling by train through Canada to northern Minnesota. He was like thousands of other immigrants from Europe. He and his father brought with them their boatbuilding experience from Norway and they began

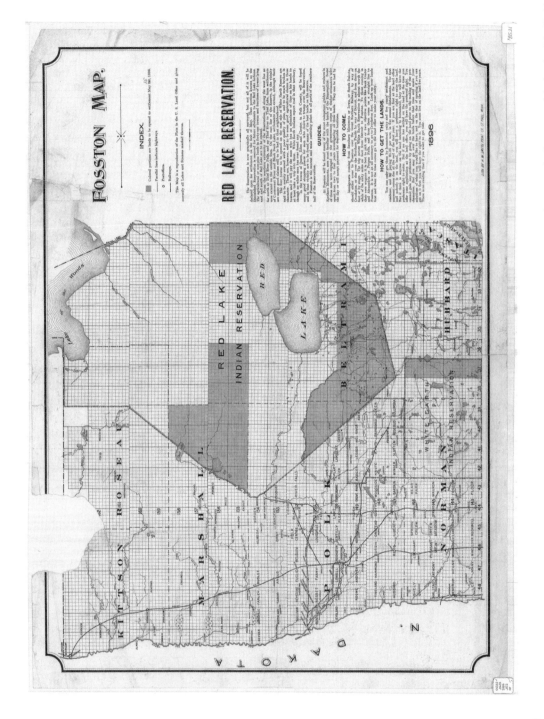

3.1

The Fosston Map of 1896, with instructions for immigrants to come to this area in northwestern Minnesota and claim a homestead, after some of the lands of the Red Lake Indian Reservation were ceded to the United States. The instructions indicate that if you made a homestead entry, constructed a residence, lived on the property for five years, and paid $1.25 per acre in five annual installments, the land was yours.

3.2
My Norwegian maternal grandfather's steamboat 'Lilly' anchored for the winter on the Red Lake River in northwestern Minnesota, adjacent to his 160-acre homestead. Starting in 1897, the steamboat was used to haul freight from the river town of Thief River Falls to the Red Lake Agency in the Red Lake Indian Reservation. That era ended when the railroads were extended.

life in Minnesota by constructing steamboats and providing transportation along the Red Lake River from Thief River Falls, an immigrant settlement located at a transportation hub, to the Indian Agency at the Red Lake Indian Reservation.

In 1904, my grandfather and his 17-year-old wife homesteaded along the Red Lake River, assembled a sawmill, built a house, and began to carve out a farm. He continued to operate the steamboat in the summer and later constructed a store and post office on the property to serve other homesteaders. Figure 3.2 shows the steamboat in winter, anchored along the frozen river, with the small wood-frame home, barn, sawmill, and log outbuildings, constructed in the wilderness.

By 1914, because the railroads now provided an alternative for transportation, he abandoned his steamboat and original homestead along the river and moved twenty miles south to a farm he purchased in Hangard Township. This was in the northern part of Clearwater County, near the southern edge of the Red Lake Indian Reservation. Here he constructed a house and barn from timber harvested on the land, and began a new career as a dairy farmer, logger, and carpenter on the flat prairie and mixed forest. They had twelve children, and one of his nine daughters married my father.

My grandparents' story is similar to that of so many other immigrants who settled in Minnesota and around the Midwest. Using the skills they brought with them, they melded with the land and other immigrants to earn a living, create a community, and did their part in the ongoing process of building a nation. The small diversified farmsteads that they and thousands of other immigrants created have largely disappeared as farming methods changed and specialized farming became prevalent, but their legacy has forever imprinted the landscape. One can only admire the strength of their family ties and the hard work they performed as families to create the agricultural landscape that continues today.

## Landscape patterns

Park and wilderness area boundaries also followed the PLSS grid system rather than natural features. It is the grid system that accounts for the checkerboard pattern of the Midwest rural landscape, seen most clearly from the air. It is interesting to fly over the region and observe the seemingly unending checkerboard pattern of farming and roads only to discover the rivers and lakes traversing it – providing a natural break in the rigid pattern. Many of the small towns that were established are located along places where rivers could be crossed, or where railroads and roads did. This juxtaposition of a rigid geometry on top of a natural landscape created the unique geometry and form of the Midwest and its landscape character.

In most parts of the country, 'townships' are political entities, but in others they were merely a means of subdividing land for sale. Counties are comprised of townships, with county seats as governmental centers, and the combination of county, townships, and villages provided a tax base for public education and the construction and maintenance of roads. An 1895 map of Minnesota (Figure 3.3) clearly shows the orthogonal organization of the state, with townships and counties as political divisions, and rivers, railroads, and roads as the forms of transportation.

By 1895, the railroads with main lines and branch lines, stretched from the Twin Cities of Minneapolis and St Paul across the entire northern regions of the United States. The governmental organization of counties, townships, towns, and roads following section lines still today delimits land-use decision making. Even though the needs of many of these entities have changed dramatically due to economic, demographic, and agricultural changes, they are the political jurisdictions in America that regulate land uses.

In Europe each country has its own rural economy and landscape that reflects its climate and its political, cultural, and economic heritage. In the Netherlands, for example, which has a high population density and must reclaim land from the sea to meet its food needs, the rural landscape is tightly controlled and zoned for specific uses. In Norway farming is highly subsidized as a way to encourage tourism by keeping people living and working on farms, maintaining the desired character of the rural landscape. China, on the other hand, regulates urban life and rural life very tightly in a manner that creates huge economic contrasts between urban 'city citizens' and rural 'farm citizens', with apparent little regard for environmental impact. Although that may be changing in rural areas as the government works to consolidate farmers' land to create connected properties to improve income; and the development of new rural villages to provide improved housing and infrastructure with a better quality of rural life while preserving the environment.

In Italy, the rolling rural landscape is still largely characteristic of the Middle Ages, with farmers living in towns on hilltops and agriculture located in the valleys. In contrast to their stone-building tradition, many more recent buildings have been constructed with an industrial aesthetic, looking like they could be

3.3 (opposite)
A map of Minnesota from 1895, illustrating the orthogonal influence of the PLSS in defining townships and counties in the Upper Midwest.

anywhere. There have been some recent studies at the Spatial Engineering Division of the Department of Agricultural Economics and Engineering at the University of Bologna which have addressed this issue. The authors outline a connection between research and the design process to significantly transform the quality of new buildings in the Italian rural landscape. They argue that one has to understand traditional Italian architecture to design contemporary agricultural buildings that have a harmonious relationship with their location. To them the architectural quality of rural buildings pursues the wider goal of landscape quality, and both historic and contemporary architecture is integral to defining rural cultural/social values (Tassinari *et al.*, 2007).

In the United States, rural regions in each state reflect their unique environmental characteristics and the experience and traditions of the immigrants who settled there and how they developed their farms and rural communities. However, one issue that was almost universal was immigrants' strong cultural resistance to the land-use controls common in the European countries they had left. It was the freedom to be pioneers – working with local soils, topography, and wind patterns and the available transportation systems – that most determined where communities developed, where farmsteads were located, and how architecture was designed and constructed. Nevertheless, there is a common element that links the cultural landscape with climate and the natural and agrarian landscape as a basic principle of rural design.

## Rural character defined

Defining rural character is a primary aspect of rural design. It is found in a combination of natural and human landscapes and the perceptions of people who live there. According to geographer John Borchert, the varied settlement patterns of the Upper Midwest reflect individual decisions by immigrants who came here because of famines, social and political movements, conflicts, and tyrannies in many corners of the world. The region, therefore, is a product of the confluence of global natural and human forces (Borchert, 1987).

Classic definitions of rural character regularly allude to agricultural heritage in North America:

*   Living in area characteristic of farming or country life. (wordnet.princeton. edu/perl/webwn)
*   Rural areas are sparsely settled places away from the influence of large cities and towns. Such areas are distinct from more intensively settled urban and suburban areas, and also from unsettled lands such as outback or wilderness. People live in villages, on farms and in other isolated houses. (en. wikipedia.org/wiki/Rural)
*   Refers to an area with mostly farmland and little human population, or characteristics of farming and county life. (www.ecohealth101.org/glossary.html)

Or, the definitions are based on the concept of exclusion:

- A term to describe something which is not of an urban center. (www. mostreferred.com/resources/glossary-r.html)
- All areas not classified by the Census Bureau as urban are defined as rural and generally include places of less than 2,500 persons. (www.ntia.doc. gov/ntiahome/fttm99/glossary.html)
- Areas outside the boundaries of urban areas. (www.fhwa.dot.gov/ environment/sidewalks/appb.htm)

A more recent definition was put forth by Jean Richardson (2000), based on her experiences working in Vermont, where she proposed a combination of perception and physical form in an effort to clarify the question of what is rural. She defines rural as:

- Agriculture and forestry, at large and small scales;
- Open lands that are a working landscape of farms and forest, or large areas of forest or other vegetated regions with scattered settlements;
- Communities are scattered with relatively low densities of population over a large area with open land in between. This includes small towns as well as larger regional urban centers that serve rural areas;
- The region may have characteristics of both rural and urban areas, particularly at the urban/rural edge where rural characteristics pre-dominate;
- The resident population believes that the mix of land uses is rural to them.

(Richardson, 2000)

Even though immigrant history is varied, most of the new immigrants to the United States came from Europe, and they were mostly white. However, the background of people living in rural areas in North America has become more diverse over the last few decades; thus, the definition of rural has also become more diverse. Despite individual perceptions of what constitutes rural character it is apparent to the CRD that however rural character is defined, it is the land-scape character that attracted people to rural regions in the first place and continues to attract people today as a lifestyle of choice (Roos and Kinney, 2009).

Thomas Jefferson advocated the agrarian state as the political ideal for America and epitomized the image of the educated, publicly engaged farmer. America developed as an agrarian nation, and the farmer and the farm were at the core of it. Jefferson 'confided to a friend that if heaven had given him a choice of a profession or calling, it would have been as a gardener and farmer' (Adams, 1983). It was this agrarian vision that immigrants from Europe and elsewhere carried into settlements throughout America.

In the Upper Midwest, small rural towns were often located six to eight miles apart along primary roads, a pattern based on the round-trip distance that a farmer with horse and wagon or buggy could easily accomplish in one day. The small towns provided the basics farmers needed for their operations, including the grain elevator and mill, creamery, grocery store, blacksmith, banks, school, physician, hardware store, pharmacy, and – in the twentieth century – the supply of fuel. This close relationship between landscape, farmstead, and town was, and still is, a core value in rural areas of the Upper Midwest and around the country.

'Rural landscape character' is a land-analysis procedure used exclusively by the CRD as a means to identify and explain the human perception of the landscape within which rural people live and work. The procedure, which uses a geo-spatial database, was developed by landscape architecture Professor David Pitt at the University of Minnesota, based on the work of R. Burton Litton (Pitt *et al.*, 1995). It has been developed for a wide range of rural landscapes and is an excellent methodology to explain the nature of place to citizens living in that place. It covers human perception issues such as:

- How human perception of place and the aesthetic sensibility of the land-scape are formed.
- How the interplay of land cover and landform affect the landscape's biophysical function.
- How geological history and climate shape a region.
- How a recognizable sense of the region that can be spatially defined is created.

Primarily through the work of Senior Research Fellow Steven Roos, a land-scape architect who specializes in computer graphics and geo-spatial Geographic Information Systems (GIS), the CRD uses the work of Pitt, and defines rural landscape character at three scale levels in which environmental attributes are encountered by participants:

(1) The *regional* unit, which defines a large homogeneous geographic area of similar landform and similar land cover containing a similar sequence and character of human experience. The rolling farmland of the Upper Midwest (Figure 3.4) with small ponds and drainage patterns left from melting glaciers is an example of a landscape feature that defines a region;

(2) The *setting* unit, which is a sub-region within the regional unit. It can range widely in size or shape, but has the distinct feeling of interconnected human activities, like farmsteads in and among fields (Figure 3.5), that gives a distinct sense of being within it;

(3) The *character* unit, which defines specific places within the setting unit with recognizable detail, such as a farmstead (Figure 3.6) with its planted windbreaks, gardens, home, and cluster of agricultural buildings around a working courtyard in the gentle, rolling countryside.

3.4
Rolling farmland and fields
in southern Minnesota,
illustrating a landscape
*regional* unit.

3.5
Farmland and farmsteads in
southern Minnesota,
illustrating a landscape *setting*
unit, typical of a place within
the regional unit.

3.6
A dairy farm in southern
Minnesota, illustrating a
landscape *character* unit,
typical of a special place within
a setting unit.

Rural landscape character is, therefore, fundamental to the methodology for defining a region's land assets and the values citizens put on them, and for using them to create a vision for their future, based on those values. The computer drawings (Figures 3.7 and 3.8) show examples of rural landscape character. Using geo-spatial analysis prepared by the CRD, the drawings were produced to help citizens in an eight county region in southeast Minnesota, bordering on the Mississippi River, understand the character of the landscape within which they live. They illustrate topography and land cover as two of the primary features of regional landscape unit.

## Rural policy

Subsidies for agriculture are a policy tool that governments use to preserve regional agricultural systems. For example, subsidies to farmers in remote areas of Norway preserve their traditional agricultural landscape for tourism, while subsidies to farmers in the United States are meant to maintain production by covering fluctuations in market prices. The utilization of subsidies can become an internal political problem if it is perceived as being unfair by promoting large-scale

3.7
A GIS map for eight counties in southeastern Minnesota, along the Mississippi River, illustrating generalized land cover.

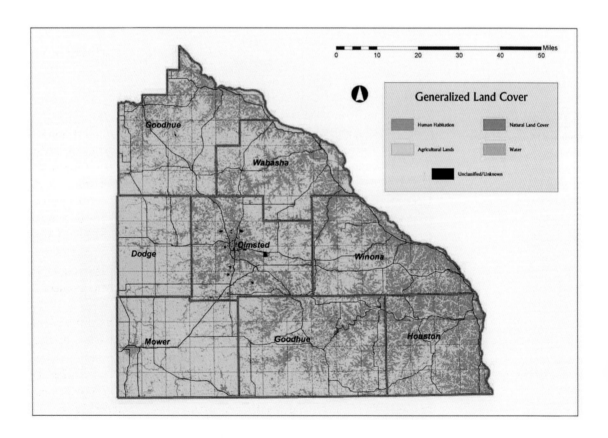

Rural character

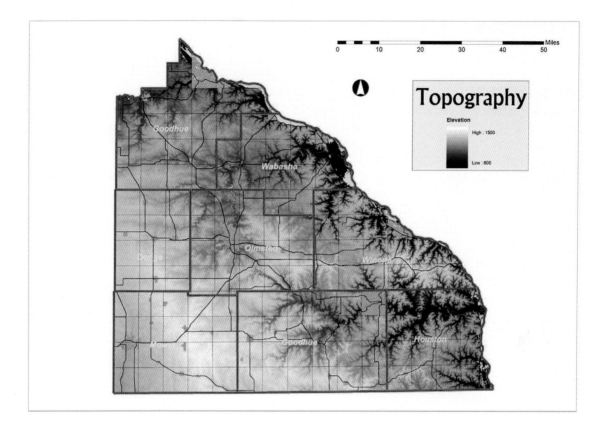

3.8
A GIS map for eight counties
in southeastern Minnesota,
along the Mississippi River,
illustrating topography.

mono-cultural farming that often raises environmental, economic, and food safety issues because of a lack of diversity.

However, if subsidies are used properly to promote ecosystem services or landscape amenities they can help create incentives for farmers, as opposed to the current system of solely awarding increased production, as is done now in the United States. China is looking at ways to subsidize farmers who provide vegetables to Beijing to cover their increased transport and marketing costs if they move further away from built-up urban areas. Today, these farmers want to be very near the urban market and yet their farming methods with plastic green-houses and small animal enclosures result in a rather unkempt landscape. By planting crops closer to built-up urban areas and moving the vegetable farms further out (with appropriate subsidies) it would greatly improve the aesthetic of high-rise living at the urban/rural edge (Zhang *et al.*, 2010).

Rural design can help shape rural policy by outlining landscape patterns and new agrarian landscapes that promote multifunctional character while addressing economic and cultural issues. Rural policy has many different aspects – social, economic, and environmental – and will only be effective as a fair system when the policies are considered as part of a national and global objective dealing with climate change, land use, health, and food for a rapidly expanding world population.

## Forces changing rural landscapes

Since the 1960s the character of farming in the Midwestern landscape has changed dramatically due to the shift from a rural economy to an urban economy, and the effect of more efficient farming methods and global competition. Global issues, particularly the economics of climate change and the need to provide food for a rapidly growing population, will have a large impact on the character of rural landscapes. In Minnesota it is anticipated that climate change over the next 100 years could increase the average temperature by 3.8–5.8°C, causing major shifts in the makeup of the forest land cover. In addition, rising temperatures can lead to invasive species and diseases and to different crop and livestock production, which can fundamentally adjust the economic and social foundations of rural people. Global economics and competition and the need for safe and secure food; renewable energy from solar, wind, and biomass; and the ecological need for diversity – they will all create shifts in agricultural production, transportation, and landscape patterns.

According to the Minnesota Pollution Control Agency, the state is already experiencing impact from climate change to its ecosystems, natural resources, and infrastructure (MPCA, 2007). They indicate that:

*   During the summer, public health and quality of life will be negatively affected by increasing heatwaves, reduced air quality, and increasing insect and waterborne diseases;
*   Increased precipitation in winter and spring, more heavy downpours, and greater evaporation in summer will lead to more periods of floods and drought;
*   A longer growing season may increase the potential for greater crop yields; increases in heatwaves, floods, droughts, insects, and weeds will present increasing challenges to managing crops, livestock, and forests;
*   Native species are very likely to face increasing threats with pests, diseases, and invasive species moving in from warmer regions.

Because of the three ecosystems traversing the state, Minnesota is particularly sensitive to changes in climate, and there are new efforts to recognize the implications that global climate change may have on the economy, environment, and quality of life. Perhaps it is this sensitivity to climate that explains why people in Minnesota seem so obsessed with the weather. It's not so much that we live part of the year in a very cold and snowy place – it's that our climate is so extremely variable.

A critical need exists for an innovative and creative means to deal with these problems at the scale at which they occur and where they can be most effective. Rural design can bring multidisciplinary research and design tools, without regard to jurisdictional boundaries; and can provide rational choices to help reconcile the social, economic, and environmental issues that influence how land is used and the quality of life it determines.

Traditional views of farming and the rural landscape are not consistent with the realities of agriculture today, yet farming is still an inherent part of American culture and heritage and the economy. In the United States most people live and work in urban areas with minimal knowledge of where their food and fiber come from. In the 1950s most people lived or had relatives living on farms and knew more about food production, and the small diversified family farm was an essential aspect of rural vitality.

Today, the global nature of agriculture and its economics for producing and processing food, bio-technology, and the growing gap between urban and rural people in understanding agriculture are having major impacts on farming practices, rural land use, and the design of buildings constructed to support farming operations. How rural regions in North America and around the world respond and adapt to these pressures remains to be seen. It is clear from discussions with academics in China, South Africa, and Norway that the issues are very similar. It is the political and cultural climates that create the largest variables. Time will tell how vital rural environments in the future will be, but it is essential that they work as well as possible.

## Managing forces of change through rural design

America developed as an agrarian society, and images of the rural landscape, towns, and farmsteads were widely published for the urban audience by Currier & Ives in calendars and post cards. These images still remain as the vision of rural architecture and landscape in the minds of most urban dwellers. Traditional farmsteads up until the 1950s functioned as self-contained, ecologically balanced, sustainable enterprises, supplying most of the things required for daily living. What could not be provided on the farm was purchased in the small towns and settlements which had developed to serve farmers and function as centers of government. These small towns also provided schools, shopping, a variety of legal and medical services, and a place to sell farm commodities like cream to the creamery or grain at the elevator.

Sustainability today is generally defined as a balance of economic, environmental, and cultural concerns, and rural America was very well fitted to that concept. In the early part of the twentieth century it was the industrialization of America and the construction of factories with smokestacks and industrial waste that created most of the environmental degradation. As time has gone by, climate change due to greenhouse gases has emerged as a major global concern, and agricultural systems worldwide have been determined as a major cause of the change.

The economic and technological changes taking place in agriculture and rural America have had a dramatic effect on the shape and character of contemporary farm buildings and the appearance of the rural landscape. Changes in animal agriculture, resulting in fewer farmers and larger farms, have had a major impact on quality of rural life. Many old barns and farm homes throughout the Midwest have been demolished, blown down, or are standing empty and deteriorating as farms have consolidated. As William A. Gabler wrote about abandoned farms in his sad book, *Death of the Dream: Farmhouses in the Heartland*: 'When all living things are removed from the farm, it becomes difficult to see how it worked and what the product was, and interpreting farm life from the abandoned buildings is like trying to determine the daily behavior of an animal from its fossil skeleton' (Gabler, 1997). Since the publication of that book many of these abandoned structures now have crops growing or cattle grazing on top of their remains.

The landscape character of rural regions is still the same, but new housing is being constructed in many areas with scenic value by retired urban dwellers desiring a rural life style. This demographic shift is creating conflicts – between farmers who are expanding their operations and new non-farming residents – over manure odors, dust and noise from equipment operation, and other large-scale farming practices. People who choose to live in rural areas need to understand the character of farming and the character of the landscape within which they live and work, just as farmers need to explain and adjust their sustainable farming practices to accommodate concerns from new and diverse neighbors.

A project by the CRD to deal with this issue, 'Environmental Practices on Dairy Farms', involved working with the Minnesota Milk Producers Association and Minnesota Department of Agriculture. The project created a more specific methodology for dairy farmers to protect the dairy industry from public concerns about large-scale dairy operations, herd expansion, and odor, as well as protect the environment from manure management and runoff. The project resulted in a comprehensive methodology that dairy farmers could use to analyze their farm and operations and rank them to see how sustainable they are.

This project extensively used geo-spatial technology to develop and portray four component models: surface water, ground water, habitat, and social sensitivity. Each is, in itself, a synthesis of subcomponent models and together they formulate the 'Environmental Quality Assurance' model. It provides the dairy industry with a tool to identify areas of environmental concern in their region, with suggestions to achieve a higher degree of environmental stewardship while enhancing the economic base (Roos *et al.*, 2003). (See case study in Chapter 6.)

## Aesthetic issues

A frequent criticism of current construction for animal agriculture is the appearance of animal facilities. In the past, local materials such as stone and lumber were the primary building materials on the farm, following established and clearly understood traditions of animal care and farm management. Today, because of lower cost and larger numbers of animal, most animal agriculture farmers in

North America commonly use pre-engineered building systems for a wide range of agricultural building needs.

Although the layout of these animal facilities is based on animal science research, with animal care being the highest priority, the public perception is that they all look the same – without any visual connection to the character of the landscape or climate within which they are built. This impression influences negative public opinion about animal farming and is partially the reason for strong public concern about confinement-type housing on dairy, swine, and poultry farms. They look like factories and their appearance questions the quality of animal care. Also, the technology that is incorporated into these animal facilities changes very rapidly and the durability of this type of wood construction is challenged due to the physical and chemical agents present (De Belie *et al.*, 2000).

One of the techniques recommended by the CRD to counter public perception of confinement-type barns as being harmful to dairy animals, is to always graze the cows that are 'dry' outside, near public roads, so that citizens can see that the cows are not always indoors. Seeing domestic farm animals in the rural landscape (Figure 3.9) is also an aesthetic issue that influences tourism and visitors' perception of the quality of animal farms in the landscape.

Cows in the open landscape are also an economic and social issue, and the dairy industry in California advertises this image very strongly on national television. University economic studies have indicated that rotational free-grazing of dairy cows produces better and more nutritious milk and contributes more to the local economy than a large, confinement-type dairy and grain-fed cows. Usually smaller in size (100 cows or fewer), they can carry the organic label and obtain higher prices. With cows in pastures, manure management becomes a much easier way to handle the odor issue from an ecological perspective. On the other hand, many larger dairy farms (250 cows and more) are becoming even

3.9
Cows in a field – an icon that typifies animal agriculture and the rural Midwest landscape.

larger, to provide more milk at less cost to consumers. All of the social, environmental, and economic consequences and the continuing ability to provide inexpensive fresh and safe foods for rapidly increasing populations are yet to be fully understood or resolved.

The character of land uses along the urban/rural edge is also rapidly changing. Many small farms near urban areas, but outside of municipal sewer and water systems, are being sold to developers who construct housing on 5-, 10-, or 20-acre lots, thereby contributing to urban sprawl and loss of land for agricultural production (Figure 3.10). Since many small farmers are aging and want to sell, this wasteful land-development scenario has removed a great deal of prime agricultural land from production, pushing local food farmers further and further away from city centers. As food production becomes a more critical issue in the near future, preserving land for agriculture will become more important.

One method for dealing with the loss of agricultural land is to use more creative zoning strategies, such as the scenarios (Figures 3.11 and 3.12) prepared by the CRD to illustrate zoning alternatives for agricultural areas. The strategies ranged from small-scale zoning to overlay districts. Each scenario provides different methodologies for determining land use, based on landscape character, and includes identifying optimal areas for new residential development, farmsteads, environmental areas to be protected, and areas for agricultural enterprise development. They were intended to illustrate new ways to guide rural land decisions that harmonize land use with landscape character.

Livestock farming has been particularly affected by changing economics and movement toward specialized and larger farms, requiring new forms of barns to raise and care for increasingly larger numbers of animals. Dairy farms today often have several hundred to several thousand milking cows housed in a single

**3.10**
New low-density housing development in rural areas near a major metropolitan region. While providing for retirement of the farmer, the selling of land eliminates forever its use for agriculture.

3.11
A CRD diagram of a land-use
scenario, illustrating different
zoning for rural areas as a
means to guide and manage
land-use decisions to preserve
natural and scenic areas.

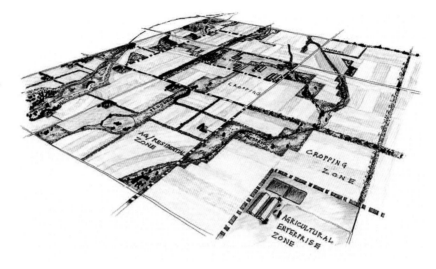

3.12
A CRD diagram of a land-use
scenario, illustrating an overlay
land-use concept for rural
areas, reducing the potential
social conflict.

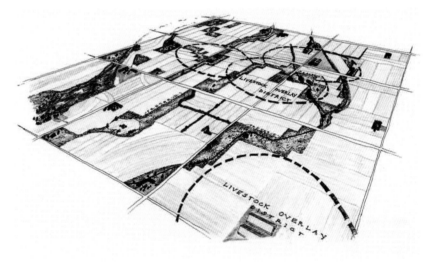

building, and farms for swine and poultry have multiple barns arranged like military barracks in the open landscape. Traditionally, immigrant farmers built barns and other farm structures following generally recognized patterns in the region where they settled, which in many cases, were published in manuals. These manuals covered a wide range of architectural types, ranging from homes to barns, along with the millwork, material, and construction techniques required to build them.

Today lumberyards and building-system manufacturers structurally engineer, fabricate, and construct these structures – often called 'pole barns' – for a wide range of uses throughout rural America (Figure 3.13). These buildings, with metal wall and roof panels, appear as though they could be built anywhere with no apparent connection with the local landscape, climate, or region where they

are constructed. There is nothing inherently wrong with this construction system – it just hasn't yet evolved into architecture with sustainable meaning and connection to climate and place.

What is it about traditional farm buildings that make them so interesting? Who built them and when? Why were they constructed the way they were? Was there an aesthetic idea that created the form, or was it strictly practical and functional? Is it architecture? I think the strong attraction people have to barns and other working buildings in the rural landscape is based on family roots, immigrant history, and identification with place.

To me the most interesting thing about old barns and farmsteads is that they all seem similar, yet each is different. The barns' proportions, materials, and colors, and the care with which they were built, reflect the builders' personalities. When you see a beautiful barn and farmstead, it feels right with the landscape, works with the climate, and uses building materials and traditions from the region. These barns and farmsteads transcend functional purpose and become architecture.

Although a number of historic barns, farmsteads, and individual buildings in small rural towns are on the National Register of Historic Places, working farm buildings in the agricultural landscape have not been generally discussed by architectural historians except as vernacular objects. The appearance, construction, and landscape fit of these working buildings, reflecting function, climate, and place, deserves significant architectural and theoretical study, just as churches, banks, and schools in rural towns have been studied.

If we are to preserve those qualities of the rural landscape that we admire so much, then we need to develop a decision-making process for land uses, and construct buildings that result in positive impacts on the visual, social, economic, and environmental character and values of rural life. A community-based process of design thinking about architecture, agriculture, and planning at the urban/rural edge and into the rural landscape is a collective way of preserving and enhancing the best of rural landscapes, small towns, animal buildings, and rural culture. Tourists like to visit an area for the same reasons people like to live there, and seeing a rural character reflecting creative and innovative ways of integrating sustainable agricultural buildings into the landscape reflecting place and climate will contribute to a positive perception.

## Contemporary working buildings in rural landscapes

There are architects designing buildings in small rural towns, such as schools or banks, but not many are designing working buildings for agriculture. There are some good examples of contemporary agricultural buildings with timeless character. They have been designed and constructed with form, material, and architectural idea reflecting functional purpose, heritage, and fit with the landscape of their rural location. The following projects are some from around the world that illustrate well the relationship between buildings and landscape.

### *Bodegas Salentein, Valle de Uco, Mendoza, Argentina*

ARCHITECT: BORMIDA & YANZOW

Although winemaking is an ancient form of agriculture, this is a vineyard in the twenty-first century, where working buildings and the landscape come together in a spectacular and exciting way. The Bodegas Salentein winery in Uco Valley near Mendoza (Figures 3.14 and 3.15) is a place that is carefully designed and staged to reflect the great tradition of winemaking in Argentina. It does so by bringing a reverence for winemaking, regional agriculture, and place-making to create a visitor experience of peaceful and sustainable connection to its rural landscape.

The Mendoza architects write that the idea was to:

> create not only a modern winery and viticulture destination but also to develop a concept with sound cultural roots that would help to sustain the region and its people. From the beginning, Bodegas Salentein used an environmentally friendly design that emphasized the use of local stone and celebrated the natural landscape. Its architecture offers a modern interpretation of old techniques typical of the Cuyo region. The result is a contemporary, yet strongly Andean presence . . . the construction was based on a landscaping axis that is one kilometer long and links the chapel, the park, the winery, and museum. The axis is conceived as a line of cultural landscape amid arid nature summarizing and integrating the two

3.14 (opposite top)
Bodega Salentein in the
Uco Valley near Mendoza,
Argentina. This winery is a
special place, integrating
building and landscape
surrounded by vineyards with
the Andes Mountains in the
background.

3.15 (opposite bottom)
The chapel at Bodega
Salentein, located at one end
of the central circulation spine
with the winery at the other
end and Kilka Museum in the
middle.

environments typical of rural Mendoza: the desert and the agricultural oasis.

(Bormida & Yanzow)

The complex creates an unforgettable portrait of the Andean landscape, linking architecture and agriculture. When I visited the winery in 2009, I recorded my experiences in some sketches (Figures 3.16 and 3.17) that illustrate the powerful presence of the Andean landscape and my perceptions of how this bodega connects to place and climate.

Bodegas Salentein is not alone in the Mendoza region for connecting to place and climate. Zuccardi Winery is also exceptional, with an incredible restaurant in and among the vines. However, Uco Valley is special. Each of the three bodegas I visited (Salentein, O. Fournier, and Andeluna) have a unique expression and architectural character, but with a common passion and respect for place-making, and pride in what they grow, make, and offer to the world. Those three wineries, with the Andes Mountains in the background, alone made the trip to Argentina worthwhile.

3.16
Sketch of Kilka Museum, in the center of the 1-kilometer-long winery complex.

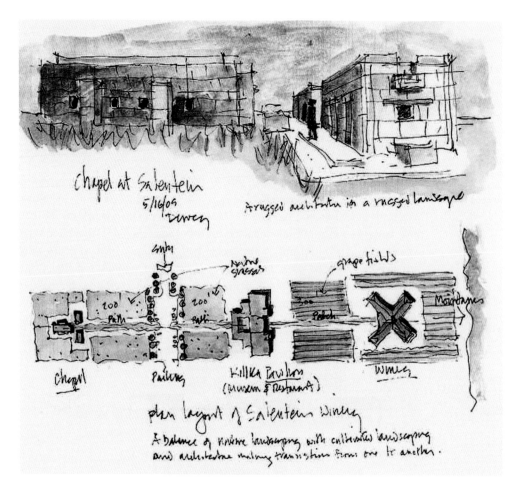

## Purina Farms, Grey Summit, Missouri

3.17
Sketch of the chapel and site layout of Bodega Salentein.

ARCHITECT: THORBECK ARCHITECTS

The Ralston Purina Company first commissioned the Minnesota architect to design a 'Farm at the Zoo' exhibit for the St Louis Zoo, on ten acres of adjacent land. When the land became politically unavailable the company shifted its focus and asked the architect to design a Visitor Center (Figure 3.18) at their research farm in Grey Summit, Missouri (45 miles west of St Louis). It is called Purina Farms and is designed around the animal/human bond as a theme to interpret, illustrate, and enhance the relationship that humans and animals have developed over the centuries and the special role animals play in our lives.

The design is based on wood-frame vernacular Missouri farmsteads and homes constructed with porches that are found in the St Louis region. It utilized two existing barns on a sloping site with 12 feet of grade change. The complex is centered on a working space between the barns forming an outdoor courtyard with an amphitheater as the focal point (Figure 3.19). It was designed with

**3.18**
Purina Farms Visitor Center from the entry road, with new Pet Center and remodeled barns, and pasture for horses and cattle.

**3.19**
Purina Farms courtyard with outdoor amphitheater and live animal barn in background. The Visitor Center emphasizes the human/animal bond interpreting the long-term working partnership between humans and domestic animals.

interpretive exhibits, live animals, and animal demonstrations in the amphitheater to help an urban population understand livestock farming, pets, and the unique bond between humans and domestic animals, dogs, and cats.

It is one of the few interpretive centers in America that tell the story of humans and animals and how they have worked together for mutual benefit. The complex allows urban visitors the opportunity to experience a farmstead and provides little-known facts about common farm animals (such as: pigs were trained to hunt when dogs were not allowed in the royal hunting grounds in England; a horse has larger eyes than a whale or an elephant; and poodles were originally bred as retrievers). Its wooden architecture and agricultural character provides a Visitor Center that expresses uniqueness of rural Missouri heritage, climate, and place.

### Tigh na Dobhran (House of the Otter), Isle of Skye, Scotland

ARCHITECT: STUDIOKAP

The architects, located in Glasgow, described their concept for this small holiday house (Figures 3.20 and 3.21) located in the township of Fiscavaig, on the western side of the Isle of Skye, as an architecture that:

3.20
A small holiday house on the Isle of Skye in Scotland, emerging out of the rolling island landscape near the sea.

Rural character

**3.21**
The holiday house, gently sitting on posts, floats above the ground – with no disturbance of the natural landscape.

deliberately eschews convention due to its unusual site. Indeed on first visiting the site it was difficult to see how any proposal could succeed if it disrupted a landscape that did not lend itself to intervention. The decision to lift the building off the ground on small piloti released the design from convention and allowed it to relate to the wider context – the views to the north and the sun from the south. The form of the house deliberately narrows to the north, reducing its surface area, and leans into the weather. The entrance bridge lifts one off the landscape and immediately upon entering one is connected with the view through the fully-glazed elevation to the north. The other windows are secondary and draw light into the two-storey volume. Simple timber construction reinforces the character of the house as a visitor in the ancient landscape.

(StudioKAP)

The house is on a remotely situated farmstead, surrounded by rough pasture just below the tree-line. The project reflects a number of projects by StudioKAP on the Isle of Skye that are 'distinguished by three particular factors: very limited budget, very difficult site access, and a very small contractor'. Although not an agricultural building, the project is significant because of how it gently connects with the legacy of rural place, creating a sensitive spiritual relationship with the rural landscape. It sits upon, but does not disturb the natural environment.

## *Agricultural Management Center, University of Minnesota, Crookston, Minnesota*

### ARCHITECT: THORBECK ARCHITECTS

This project is located on one of the flattest places on earth – the bottom of the ancient Lake Agassiz in northwestern Minnesota, created by the melting of glaciers 11,000 years ago. Located on the northern edge of the University of Minnesota Crookston campus, the cluster of buildings reflect the prairie, with long horizontal lines. The building complex consists of a classroom/laboratory/administrative wing attached to an indoor riding arena and horse stable, an adjacent cattle/sheep barn, and future machine storage and swine barns. The buildings utilize post-frame wood construction, with metal siding and roofing panels in a color and texture that connect with historic campus architecture while reflecting traditional Midwest barn architecture in a contemporary manner.

Figure 3.22 shows the main building of the complex. Utilizing the most common form of structural and material system currently being used on farms in the Midwest, the project design is significant because of its fit into the horizontal prairie as an icon for agriculture. With common metal panels on the exterior walls and roof, and simple wood siding, steel trusses, and skylights on the interior of the arena (Figure 3.23), it becomes an architecture where the ordinary becomes extraordinary.

**3.22**

Agricultural Management Center on the University of Minnesota Crookston campus, reflecting its functional purpose as a horse stable for agricultural teaching and research, and its horizontal architectural connection with the flat prairie of northwestern Minnesota.

3.23
Interior view of the
horse-riding arena at the
Agricultural Management
Center.

## *Sheep Farm, Northfield, Minnesota*

ARCHITECT: LOOM ARCHITECTS

This project (Figures 3.24 and 3.25) is proposed for the reconstruction of a sheep barn near Northfield, Minnesota that was tragically destroyed by fire. The Minnesota architect based the design on traditional arch-framed barns to provide a new sheep-raising facility for producing cheese and meat, while providing a place for traditional religious rituals with sheep. In addition, the design accommodates educational tours and the sale of cheese and meat products. This is a wonderful example of traditional barn form being restated to create a new contemporary tradition in the rolling rural landscape of southern Minnesota. For this project form follows function, climate, and place.

## *Animal Education Center, Milton Hershey School, Hershey, Pennsylvania*

ARCHITECT: THORBECK ARCHITECTS

The Milton Hershey School was founded in 1903 by Milton Hershey (also founder of the Hershey chocolate company) as a school for orphan boys from urban areas. Today the school is home to approximately 2,000 boys and girls from disadvantaged families who live in surrogate homes on the campus. This project is an

3.24 (opposite top)
Winter view of a proposal for
reconstructing a sheep farm
in southern Minnesota that
was destroyed by fire. It is
an architecture based on
traditional Midwest barns
design, but assembled in a
unique and powerful way.

3.25 (opposite bottom)
Close-up view of the sheep
farm proposal, emphasizing
the wonderful historic human
relationship with raising sheep.

integral part of the Agricultural and Environmental Education (AEE) curriculum of the Milton Hershey School fostering agricultural and environmental literacy with life and career skills development. The Animal Education Center complements existing horticultural and environmental facilities, providing contextual experiential learning for students aged 5–18.

The school originally intended for the architect to design an integrated facility as an 'Animal and Dairy & Foods Processing Center' that would provide students the opportunity to appreciate human relationships with animals, study and conduct research in dairy animal science, engage in food processing, while learning about economic interdependence and governmental and social interaction through practical hands-on work experiences. That project was intended to provide a consolidated working farm for education, including new housing for dairy, horse, swine, beef, sheep, goats, and poultry, along with an indoor riding arena, classroom building, and planetarium. Later the school abandoned this effort as too costly and decided to move forward with the design of a smaller Animal Education Center (Figures 3.26 and 3.27).

An existing 1860s stone farmhouse is being remodeled for offices, student club room, and classroom. An addition provides for a classroom/laboratory and housing for small and large animals. The project's design is intended to connect the historic past of the Milton Hershey School to the future. The new addition reflects the need, due to global climate change, to design and construct buildings that are net-zero energy and carbon-neutral. The proposed design accomplishes this through an integration of geothermal, solar, and wind energy with a number of energy-conservation details, while using metal panels for the walls and roof that could be a LEED Platinum project (see Chapter 5). It provides exciting new spaces for animal agricultural education and thinking about the future of animal

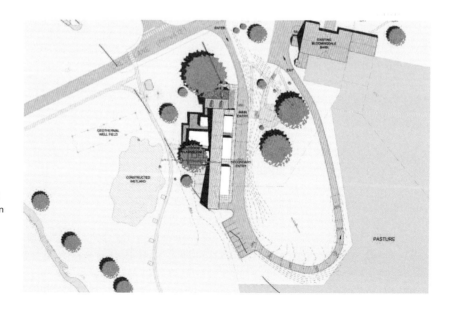

3.26
Site plan of proposed Animal
Education Center at the Milton
Hershey School in Hershey,
Pennsylvania showing the
existing house and barn with
a new addition for 5–18
education and hands-on
learning.

agriculture, while the existing historic stone house firmly anchors the facility to the legacy of the site and the Milton Hershey School. It is a building that learns as well as teaches, providing an experiential instructional strategy to enhance student achievement in all academic areas through first-hand experiences that: provide an authentic context for learning; foster improved agricultural and environmental literacy; and facilitate development of life and career skills.

## Mitchell-David house, Connecticut

### ARCHITECT: BURR AND MACCALLUM

This vernacular house (Figures 3.28 and 3.29) expresses its historic precedents in a contemporary manner at the edge of an agricultural field. The New England architects work as a team, and Andrus Burr described the way they operate and approach design this way:

> We are heavily influenced by the architectural language of farms, of early New England industrial architecture [mostly pre-twentieth century], and by the architecture of the Shakers who combined both farm and industry. I myself grew up on a dairy farm in the Berkshire Hills and I've never lost my fascination with those forms. The Mitchell-David house leans more toward the nineteenth-century industrial vernacular, the long dormer over the living room, the projected window in the very highest gable, and the large paned windows in several areas which resemble industrial steel sash windows. In addition, the house is made up of several parts – living room and bedroom 'tower', master bedroom building, and garage/guest room building – rather like both agricultural and industrial structures. New England had many wood framed mills with clapboard siding which sat very comfortably with their wood framed residential neighbors. The six-paned 'barnsash' windows recall both agricultural and industrial precedents. This architectural vernacular was appealing to our clients who like New England architecture, but didn't want a grand formal house and preferred the feeling of loft living.
>
> (Andrus Burr)

The significance of the Mitchell-David house is that it is a fine example of rural architecture that connects to place and historic tradition. It is a New England residence reflecting the character of the region within which it is located. It feels quite at home, integrated with its site and the architectural legacy of the New England landscape.

## *Straitsview barn, San Juan Island, Washington*

ARCHITECT: THOMPSON & ROSE

This project (Figures 3.30 and 3.31) is one of many designed by Massachusetts architect Maryann Thompson that has a strong relationship to the encompassing landscape. It reflects her philosophy of designing buildings that 'resonate at a visceral level with anyone who interacts with it. Issues of the landscape and its relationship to architecture are at the center of our design thinking and our work embraces a variety of interactions with the land and site.'

Constructed as part of a working farm on a site overlooking the Olympic Range across the Strait of Juan de Fuca, the barn reflects traditional western barns in the region constructed by using wood in a variety of contemporary and sculptural ways to serve functional purpose. The barn accommodates a farm office, wood and machine shops, veterinarian space, and a space for a variety of large-scale equipment and machinery storage. The shape of the building deflects the prevailing northeastern winds off of the Pacific Ocean, sheltering the adjacent working courtyard. Its architecture reflects the unique landscape character of

3.30
Exterior of the Straitsview barn, gently nested in and among pine trees, which fits well into its regional landscape, with wood timbers and materials from the region.

**3.31**
Interior view of the Straitsview barn and its beautiful wood structural expression.

island living, forming a beautiful and functional relationship with climate and place.

## Somis hay barn, Somis, California

ARCHITECT: STUDIO PALIA FEKETE (SPF)

This unique hay barn in southern California (Figures 3.32 and 3.33) has a character that combines traditional horse stalls on the interior with an insulating skin of baled hay on the exterior. The Los Angeles architects describe the concept as

> based on the ever-changing color and positioning of the hay as cladding. When stacked in the winter it is green, and as the season unfolds the hay turns yellow. Both factors keep the façade forever in a state of evolution. The building is a metaphor for life, death and birth, common seasonal themes in an agrarian society.
>
> (Studio Palia Fekete)

**3.32**
Somis hay barn on a foggy day. This is an extraordinary structure, designed to change with the seasons by storing hay on racks on the outside surrounding the horse stable.

**3.33**
Interior view of stable in Somis hay barn, which truly reflects an architectural philosophy of less can be more.

With natural ventilation through clerestory openings and the large roof sheltering stacked hay, the barn illustrates, in a very simple, clear, and contemporary way, how function in the feeding and care of animals can provide a fresh new form in a rural setting that is beautiful and meaningful.

## Form follows function, climate, and place

Rural architectural and landscape character has many design interpretations. Some are based on science, some on tradition, and some are aesthetic. But all are important and when defined as an integrated phenomenon through the multidisciplinary process of rural design, architecture and landscape design can contribute greatly to the human emotional experience of rural climate and place.

Architect Louis Sullivan framed the concept of 'form follows function' in an article on tall buildings, first published in 1896 by *Lippincott's Magazine,* where he wrote:

> It is the pervading law of all things organic and inorganic,
> Of all things physical and metaphysical,
> Of all things human and all things super-human,
> Of all true manifestations of the head,
> Of the heart, of the soul,
> That the life is recognizable in its expression,
> That form ever follows function. This is the law.

In an interesting and informative book about architecture without architects, Bernard Rudofsky (1977) discusses vernacular architecture and its roots in human existence and connection with place. He argues that architecture is an art that transcends utility, quoting Churchill's dictum that 'first we shape our buildings, then they shape us'. Rudofsky believes that it is vernacular architecture that most clearly reflects human connections and relationship with the land, quoting Louis Sullivan's desire to design buildings connected to place: 'The world is filled with Knowledge; it is almost empty of Understanding. For let me tell you, Knowledge is of the head, Understanding is of the heart.'

Writing about Louis Sullivan and his influence on American architecture near the end of the nineteenth century, Leonard Eaton (1972) describes Sullivan as a programmatic innovator and the first American architect to study the relationships between architecture and society, and the first to evolve a true philosophy of architecture. He describes the philosophy that guided Sullivan as poetic and religious. The bank that Louis Sullivan designed in Owatonna, Minnesota is truly regarded as one of the great works of architecture in America. When constructed in 1908 it reflected the past, present, and future of the region all in one beautiful, creative, and innovative idea.

Today, because of global issues impacting the future of human life on this planet, Sullivan's architectural dictum might want to be modified to: Form follows function, climate, and place. This elaboration more clearly reflects the importance of designing buildings to become an indigenous part of the place within which they are constructed. It demands that sustainable buildings be shaped to work with the landscape and nature's opportunity for ventilating, heating, and cooling. This is an approach that can lead the way as the world moves toward zero-energy and zero-carbon in the design and construction of buildings and the shaping of rural landscapes.

# Chapter 4

# Regional vision

According to many estimates, the population of the United States is expected to increase by 100 million by 2050, to approximately 400 million people. This growth will place new stresses on rural and urban environments, challenging the United States to be even more entrepreneurial and innovative in building new homes, communities, and businesses to sustain the larger and more diverse society. Joel Kotkin, a distinguished social thinker has predicted that the vast majority of the US population growth will be Asians and Hispanics, and that this ethnic diversity will positively affect the country's relationships with the rest of the world. Kotkin goes on to predict that this growth will take place in a variety of places, from inner city to suburban and exurban towns and into the vast under-populated 'heartland' region of the United States (Kotkin, 2010).

This projected surge in growth will impact the landscape and reshape the national geography. In rural regions affordable housing, renewable energy production, new ideas for recreation, expansion of animal agriculture, and new rural industries are exciting opportunities to integrate and coordinate development in the rural landscape, while preserving food and fiber production and the scenic value of the rural landscape. These are issues of important public concern, and new ways must be found to make room for new production and processing technologies while ensuring rural environmental, cultural, and economic health.

During the same time span, the Institute on the Environment at the University of Minnesota has predicted that the world's population will double by 2050. In addition, they have studied the sources of greenhouse gases and determined that agriculture uses 40% of the world's land area, consumes 70% of the water, and produces 35% of greenhouse gases that impact climate change. How land is used and food produced in the future is both a regional and global issue, and will require coordinated and collaborative planning and decision making that reflects the issues of climate change and population growth. These, and other related issues of water and renewable energy can only be effectively addressed at the regional level, but at the same time it must be reviewed, discussed, and planned from a global perspective.

Rural design is a methodology to accomplish effective change when citizens are involved in the decision-making process and a multidisciplinary regional perspective is utilized. It is most effective when scientific evidence impacting rural environments is objectively presented to rural communities in the planning and design process. Geo-spatial scenarios that illustrate future choices and their potential impacts will be critical to citizen understanding of the issues and viable options available.

While this book discusses issues related to regions in North America, the principles of rural design can be effective worldwide. The CRD uses the lens of spatial organization and design to organize and put into practice the work of research disciplines to identify and solve rural issues and problems. As a result of projects at a wide range of scales, the CRD has found that economic development is more possible and has greater potential when land assets are looked at regionally. It believes the regional perspective is equally important to foster collaboration and cooperation on a multi-state and international basis to address global issues such as climate change, renewable energy, water resource protection, and food security. 'Regional' is defined as any land area that is perceived as a common landscape with shared human and natural assets and economic opportunities – albeit at multi-county or multi-state levels.

Knowledge and a data-driven rural design process are critical to understanding the opportunities and options for rural regions as they struggle to manage change. It brings a regional perspective, crossing political and disciplinary jurisdictions, to provide a new way of thinking about rural problems and the challenges and opportunities facing rural regions in North America – and indirectly the world. These challenges include potential global impacts resulting from climate change, issues of food supply and food safety, renewable energy, and ecological understanding.

In a paper, 'Ad hoc rural regionalism', published in the *Journal of Rural Studies*, Hamin and Marcucci (2008) present an argument for a new regionalism theory to foster a specific conceptualization of region. They argue that one result of globalization is that the definition of 'region' must be of sufficient scale to interact effectively in the global economy.

In a Chicago Council on Global Affairs paper, *Past Silos and Smokestacks*, (Drabenstott, 2010) the argument is put forth that regional partnerships must cooperate and collaborate to compete in the global economy, and that multi-county regions must be organized to combine forces to create new businesses and job opportunities. The paper goes on to declare that traditional rural areas have followed only one path to economic development and that is to try and recruit new businesses. This tradition follows through in county boards and city councils, often resulting in communities competing with each other rather than working together. It argues that a new model is needed that emphasizes regional action crossing political boundaries and building upon the local assets of the region.

A paradigm based on regional cooperation, innovation, and leveraging strengths is critical to create a new rural Midwest economy for the twenty-first century.

## Thinking regionally

Leaders in many rural regions feel strongly that the realities of today's global economy – with most people living in cities, fewer farmers, and larger farms – is a fact of rural life contributing to the decline of small rural towns, townships, and counties. However, they believe that it is of paramount importance to have a new way of thinking about the opportunities and challenges facing rural areas.

Rural design is a methodology to organize, plan, and paint a vision for future growth and prosperity in a rapidly changing global marketplace. For a recent public meeting about rural design Jonathan Moore, a graduate research assistant in architecture at the CRD, created a drawing of southwestern Minnesota (Figure 4.1). It illustrates a way to look at a multi-county region without political boundaries to help citizens focus on their fundamental geographic and historic regional assets.

The Southern Minnesota Initiative Foundation (one of six in the state of Minnesota established by the Minneapolis-based McKnight Foundation to promote regional thinking and economic development) focuses on regional issues in eighteen southern Minnesota counties. It has, through regional focus group workshops, identified five key strategies as being critical to regional growth:

- *Promoting diversity* by embracing a broad definition that includes religion, age, lifestyle, ethnicity, and socioeconomic status in order to expand

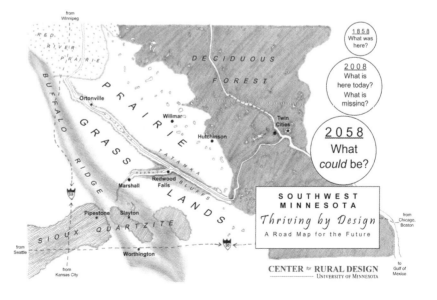

**4.1**
Drawing created by a graduate student for a CRD meeting with a regional planning commission to discuss rural design and how a region can be interpreted without jurisdictional boundaries.

leadership capabilities, celebrate and share traditions, and ensure collaboration among key leaders and stakeholders.

- *Marketing/branding* the region by creating a regional marketing entity to conduct research, promote the region, and focus on regional economic advancement. This entity would identify the region's distinctive selling features/assets; create a marketing plan for targeted audiences; tell positive stories about the region; and train people, groups, and communities how to promote shared messages.

- *Combating out-migration* by educating young people and their parents, educators, and counselors about career opportunities in the region, and aligning training and education with incentives to attract young people, such as scholarships and loan forgiveness.

- *Educating* businesses how to recruit workers and develop a marketing campaign about career and lifestyle opportunities available in the region in order to attract, retain, and develop a quality workforce. Formulate a regional economic development strategy, free of competition and boundaries within the region, with incentives to attract young people to the region, such as lower mortgage rates, scholarships, internship opportunities, and mentorship opportunities. Directly related to recruitment is the need to create affordable housing options that are integrated into the fabric of the community.

- *Creating a collaborative regional database* that includes information on amenities and job vacancies and provides collaboration opportunities between employers on jobs for spouses, along with a methodology to keep it up to date.

The Southern Minnesota Initiative Foundation, along with a sister group, the Southwest Initiative Foundation, was instrumental in developing the Partnership for Regional Competitiveness as a network of organizations, businesses, and government agencies working together to create a strategic economic development plan on a region-wide basis. The first project involved thirty-eight counties in southern Minnesota, and through research by the Rural Policy Research Institute in Columbia, Missouri industries were identified as southern Minnesota's core strengths:

- The three established industries are agriculture and food, manufacturing, and health care.
- The three poised to be most promising are bioscience, renewable energy, and high technology.

The key to any regional partnership is identifying opportunities and the critical mass necessary to forge partnerships to compete in the global economy; and the ability of the region to foster innovation and entrepreneurship. It is critical that the definition of the region be carefully established to enhance collaboration and cooperation. The CRD suggests that regardless of the size of a region, a shared natural environmental feature such as an eco-region or watershed, rather than political boundaries, might be a better way to define landscape assets and economic opportunities, because all people and lands within it are similarly affected. This way of thinking is sometimes called 'bioregionalism' as a way to organize and coincide political boundaries for mutual benefit.

A recent conference at the Federal Reserve Bank of Minneapolis sponsored by the Center on Institutional Cooperation (a collaborative of the Big Ten Universities and the University of Chicago) focused on moving the Midwest forward economically (Mahon, 2008). From the conference it was revealed that over the previous ten years every state in the Midwest had had a lower rate of output growth than the nation as a whole. One of the speakers, Richard Longworth, senior fellow at the Chicago Council on Global Affairs, discussed the fact that while the Midwest is geographically and culturally one region, it is politically fragmented by its multi-state structure, and this fragmentation prevents real movement forward. He went on to call for greater cooperation by Midwestern universities to create a think-tank or 'Midwestern studies' department to help spur greater economic and political cooperation across Midwestern states (Longworth, 2008).

Longworth's comments could be applied equally to the fragmentation of counties, townships, and towns in the sub-regions in each state of the Midwest landscape, most of which were defined in the 1800s. Rural design is a way to think regionally and it can be utilized at the broad multi-state level as a way to cut across political boundaries. It is this type of regional focusing and planning that rural communities need to ensure a sustainable future, determine how the land is used, and create an ability to compete in a global economy.

The Center for Regional Competitiveness, at the University of Missouri Rural Policy Research Institute, has declared that the rural Midwest needs a new paradigm to transform its economy and has outlined a strategy to help rural communities think regionally to compete globally. The director of the Center has put forth an argument that the rural Midwest needs to build upon its traditional strengths – among which is its fertile land, its hardworking people, its liveable communities, and its central location in the nation. The proposal identified four things that the Midwest needs to do to meet the imperatives of the global economy:

- Help rural communities and counties to think regionally to compete globally by functioning through a regional scale appropriate to the population density, rather than competing locally.
- Focus public investments on transforming economic opportunities by concentrating public dollars on projects that unlock a region's unique economic potential while leveraging returns from private sector investments.
- Spur both innovation and entrepreneurship by engaging the regional research potential of public universities to translate research and innovation into economic progress in rural areas.

- Change the business culture and recycle wealth by encouraging home-grown companies and recycle its wealth into new companies with new mechanisms.

(Drabenstott, 2010)

Missing from the list of issues, however, is the need for planning and design tools to understand and define rural regions, and create the economic opportunities their land assets can bring to their region. Rural design, as a design and problem-solving process, can help rural communities understand opportunities for economic growth and improved quality of life. Thinking regionally can help define a number of shared cultural and environmental issues while simultaneously supporting economic development and job growth, including pride in place, climate, and quality of life.

## A regional vision

A shared community vision for the rural landscape must be based on their landscape assets to enhance quality of life, accommodate population expansion, and improve agriculture, while protecting the ecological integrity of the landscape. A shared understanding and consensus on the values placed on those assets is crucial to a community's prosperous future. Rural design is a way to bring design thinking to rural land use and other issues, and it is most effective when it can help find the linkages and connections that nurture economic, environmental, and social progress. Design is fundamentally a problem-solving process and a way of design thinking about an issue by analyzing, speculating, evaluating, and recommending.

To protect farming and achieve a healthy regional future with regionally grown, safe, affordable, and adequate food, it is important to nurture public confidence in stewardship traditions – on the farm, in small towns, and across the region. The nation needs to recreate a broad stewardship and entrepreneurial tradition based on design thinking while responding to changing technologies and issues of renewable energy production, climate change, new food production systems, communications, and transportation.

The recent construction of a large number of wind turbine farms (Figure 4.2) in southwestern Minnesota along Buffalo Ridge (a high ridge where the wind blows steadily year round) illustrates some of the rapid changes taking place. Managing and locating wind turbines and transmission lines, along with solar energy and biomass gasification in the rural landscape, requires regional and cross-jurisdictional thinking inherent in rural design.

The aesthetic relationships between the visual and social quality of the rural environment and the economics of rural communities and agriculture needs to be better understood, and strategies need to be agreed upon in order to encourage farmers and rural communities to build for the future in a way that

**4.2**
A cluster of wind turbines
in southwestern Minnesota,
with agricultural crops below.
This growing phenomenon to
harvest renewable energy from
nature is increasingly seen in
the rural Midwest landscape
and around the world,
particularly in rural regions
where the wind blows steadily.

preserves and enhances the beauty of the rural landscape, quality of life, and economic vitality.

Rural communities need to work together to clarify their assets, determine what is rural and what is agricultural, and identify what they value the most about the character of the landscape so that they can decide what they wish to preserve and what can be exploited. Paradigms are needed to illustrate what the rural environment can be like and how the urban/rural edge can be defined to help rural farming and non-farming communities make intelligent choices. A computerized geo-spatial graphic system that presents environmental characteristics in a manner that rural citizens can understand, trust, and use is a very helpful tool. It can be very effective in explaining rural character to build regional cooperation and collaboration. This technology needs to be advanced so that it can illustrate in three dimensions and become readily available to rural communities.

An example of cross-border regional planning at the township scale is a project the CRD is currently working on. It consists of a four-township (144 square miles) project within Scott County (one of seven in the Twin Cities metropolitan area) that might become a paradigm for dealing with multi-jurisdictional cooperation at the urban/rural edge. It is a project that will explore a collective vision of rural character in the four townships, which today are mostly agricultural but will change over time as new residential development takes place. (See case study in Chapter 6.)

The project's goal is to gain broad public and political support to preserve and protect the environmental/cultural functions of the townships, by understanding the perception residents have and then translating the desired rural character into an appropriate pattern of development and development types. The result of the project is to formulate a set of design guidelines and a design pattern book to guide development toward the most sensitive environmental outcomes while maintaining a rural character that is attractive to current and future residents.

Figure 4.3 illustrates this concept and shows four different ways, at the same residential density, the townships might incorporate new residential development while preserving rural character and agriculture. One is to organize new residential development along township roads leaving existing prime agricultural lands to continue food production; the second organizes residential development around and along the perimeters of the township road network leaving land in the centers for agricultural uses; the third clusters residential development in a corner of each of the townships, leaving the remainder for agriculture; and the fourth (and most radical) is for the townships to cluster all residential and other development in the middle of the four townships, thereby creating a new rural village.

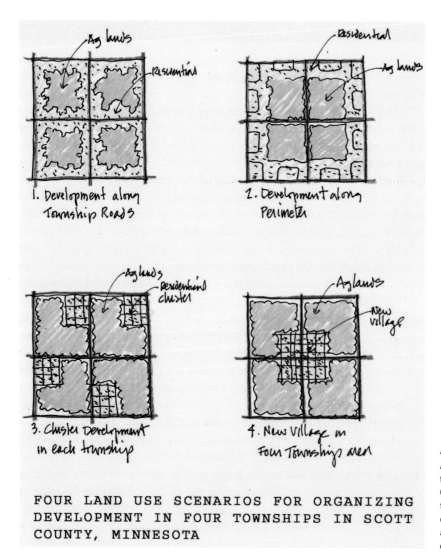

1. Development along Township Roads

2. Development along Perimeter

3. Cluster Development in each township

4. New Village in Four Townships area

**FOUR LAND USE SCENARIOS FOR ORGANIZING DEVELOPMENT IN FOUR TOWNSHIPS IN SCOTT COUNTY, MINNESOTA**

4.3
A CRD illustrative diagram for four townships in Scott County, Minnesota, showing four different scenarios for development while preserving agriculture and rural landscape character.

Regional vision

The project, through community design workshops, is defining what citizens mean by 'rural' and the final decision by the township boards and the county commissioners will depend on citizen's definitions, preferences, and values for the rural landscape. Where and how development is done and the architectural development it represents should reflect the unique character and climate of the region and its sense of place on the planet.

## Regional landscapes

Understanding the rural landscape is critical to rural design. In his book, *The Rural Landscape,* John Fraser Hart (1998) describes the three principal components of any rural landscape as: (1) the landforms and geometric shapes as seen on the surface of the land; (2) the vegetation and the trees, shrubs, and grasses that cover the surface; and (3) the structures and the varied kinds of functional buildings and road systems that people have added. The form of the landscape on the surface mostly reflects the geological history that made it, however the vegetation varies depending on climate and the soils' ability to grow living things. The structures are the buildings constructed for agriculture and in the villages to serve people. To the Fraser Hart list I would add a fourth component of the transportation system, consisting of the many networks (water, roads, railroads) of how people have moved and continue to move to grow food and fiber, make a living, and build community. Historically, Fraser Hart says, the agricultural systems in a region determined how the land was used, the population it could support, and the kinds of structures required to cultivate the land to produce food and fiber. As the demand for food increases, the systems agriculture utilizes will become increasingly important.

The cultural beliefs, values, patterns of behavior, and technical competency of the people who live there have greatly influenced the character of the rural landscape around the world. Rural people who live on the land and depend on it for their livelihood will use their skill and knowledge to carefully use and preserve it. Many of the buildings constructed in the rural landscape utilized materials that were readily available and labor-saving, and when discussing the aesthetics of these buildings Fraser Hart notes that:

> Most people are motivated by functional, not aesthetic, considerations when they erect a structure, and most ordinary human structures must be understood in terms of their functions. They are not intended as works of art, and any artistic quality they may happen to possess is unconscious, accidental, and incidental. People do not intentionally erect structures that are ugly, but neither do they erect structures because they are beautiful – they erect them because they need them, not because such structures will beautify the landscape.
>
> (Fraser Hart, 1998)

The surface of the land we see today is a result of geological history, the erosion of running water, and the vegetation nurtured by weather and climate and soil. Because of its three ecosystems, Minnesota contains in one state much of the landscape diversity of herbs, grasses, shrubs, and trees found throughout the Midwest and southern Canada. Landscapes are interconnected regions with watersheds and plants reflecting climate and geography, and any discussion of rural design that incorporates a regional approach must recognize this interdependency.

In a paper about transforming the rural economy in the Midwest, Mark Drabenstott (2010) outlined five actions that he feels are critical to a new framework for rural development: (1) the twelve states comprising the Midwest should unite in a call for federal action on regional development to transform rural economies through competitive advantage and innovation; (2) leaders in state governments in the Midwest should seamlessly join together to make the region the most innovative and entrepreneurial place in the world; (3) align education to support new regional initiatives and find ways to translate research and ideas into strategic plans as a bridge to society; (4) take steps to ensure businesses' innovation and access to capital are synonymous; and (5) nurture non-profit organizations as catalysts to provide and train leadership and support new rural development initiatives.

It is important that the Midwest region states organize and speak with one voice and function as a champion for regional thinking, and I think the land-grant universities in the various states should take the lead in organizing such a Midwest endeavor. They can utilize their ongoing strengths – in public health and disease prevention, traditional crop and animal agriculture, rural design and geo-spatial analysis and documentation, natural ecosystems, renewable energy, environmental and global warming mitigation, and habitat restoration – to respond to new and expanded areas of land-based research by integrating human, animal, and environmental health with agriculture and land use.

The small diversified farm that was so prevalent in the Midwest landscape has slowly disappeared since 1960 as agricultural economics encouraged fewer farmers and larger farms. In a sad book about the changing rural landscape, William A. Gabler ends his summary on vanishing farmhouses in the southwestern Minnesota prairie with these thoughts about the nature of the agricultural landscape:

> The classic farm was not a permanent ideal whose form could be perpetuated indefinitely, but rather a structural species evolved through adaption to a specific set of economic conditions . . . that exploited the virgin land. There was nothing built there before the farmers came, and nothing built there since that time really belongs to the region. The realization of the dream consumed the basis for the dream, and the next dream has not yet been formed.
>
> (Gabler, 1997)

People living and working in rural regions need a new rural dream. A dream based on a shared regional vision for the next fifty years that builds the institutional capacities of townships, cities, counties, and states to improve their ability to integrate community values and sustainability in the comprehensive planning process. A vision that will capture community values and then integrate those values into a collaborative planning process that works for different situations, needs, and degrees of change, leading to a regional way of thinking and action.

## Regional thinking worldwide

The CRD has been nurturing connections with scholars from around the world who are involved in rural issues – doing research, proposing land-use changes, defining social constructs, and developing land management ideas. The projects have been led by academic leaders in their respective universities and institutes or departments, reflecting a high standard for applying evidence-based design to rural issues in their global regions. Below are some examples of those rural design efforts.

### *Redefining the Beijing region*

China has the world's largest population at 1.34 billion in 2010, and it is projected to reach 1.47 billion in 2032, according to the National Bureau of Statistics of China. Because of concerns that the loss of farmland may endanger food security, the central government of China is emphasizing cropland protection, and issued the 'Land Administration Law of P.R. China' in which the provincial governments were asked to prevent further loss. For each piece of cropland lost for urbanization, an equivalent must be created elsewhere.

To adjust to this requirement, the Beijing People's Government created in 2003 the 'Urban Master Plan of Beijing (Years 2004–2020)'. The plan proposes to adjust cropland based on the spatial arrangement of the city and to combine the protective zone of prime cropland with planning of green belts and ecological corridors to limit the irregular sprawl of the city. Beijing has many urban problems, including traffic congestion, water shortage, lack of green space, increased heat island effect, and air pollution. The proposed plan for Beijing, however, looks at the city from an urban perspective and lacks the detail on the spatial distribution of the various components of agricultural production (Zhang *et al.*, 2010).

The issue in Beijing is typical of urban planning around the world, and by omission argues for the idea of rural design to simultaneously look at the rural side of the urban/rural edge. In a paper, 'The spatial planning of agriculture in Beijing: Towards producing a more livable city', Professor Fengrong Zhang, director of the Land Use and Administration Research Center at the China Agricultural University in Beijing, along with other colleagues in the Department of Land Resources and Management Sciences (Zhang *et al.*, 2010) propose a different organization of agricultural rings that could be a model for other major cities in China. To succeed however, they realize that the government, urban and rural planners, private industry, and farmers must work together to ensure food security while enhancing livability.

The paper outlines five aspects for reorganizing the agricultural rings: (1) granting ecological and resource subsidies for crop production that has significantly positive ecological and water-saving effects; (2) increasing agricultural infrastructure and land consolidation for creating scenic rural areas; (3) supporting investment in pollution remediation projects and reusing animal waste for fertilizer; (4) strengthening agricultural technologies and product monitoring and testing systems for farm products; and (5) promoting the modernization of agricultural operations.

The study was sponsored by the Natural Science Foundation of China and, in the paper, Zhang proposes a spatial arrangement for agriculture around Beijing with four rings radiating outward from the city center (Figures 4.4, 4.5, and 4.6). The inner-city ring is focused on urban beautification with flowers and grasses; then a city-skirt ring with fruit trees, grain crops, and vegetable and grass – a ring without intensive agriculture; then a suburban plain ring for efficient, intensive

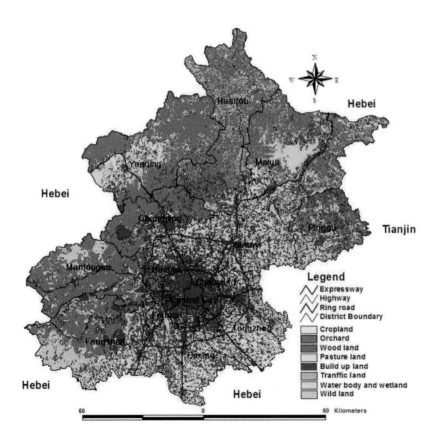

4.4
Map of Beijing, showing existing regional organization and agricultural and natural landscape zones.

**4.5**
Map of Beijing, showing
existing food-growing areas
for field vegetables, wheat,
maize, and greenhouse
vegetables.

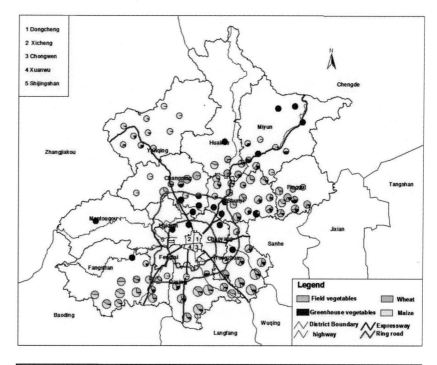

**4.6**
Map of Beijing, showing
proposed rings around the
city: (1) Inner-city ring for
urban beautification;
(2) City-skirt ring for green
landscape; (3) Suburban
plain ring for efficient
eco-agriculture; and
(4) Mountainous region ring
for ecological-conservation
characteristic agriculture.

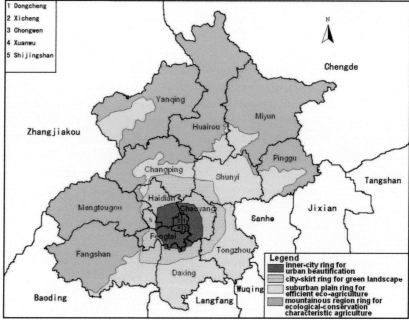

vegetable and grain production; and lastly the mountainous regions for ecological conservation and the production of specialized agricultural products.

The proposed spatial arrangement of the landscape character surrounding Beijing steps away from the existing ring pattern that has been functioning since

1826, and recommends a new spatial arrangement to balance the land resources and the city's spatial structure with the socio-economic development of Beijing. The authors recognize that the proposed plan emphasizes benefits to the greater public and, as a result, farmers who are negatively impacted by the new arrangement should receive government subsidies or compensation for any economic loss.

The paper argues that by developing 'modern urban agriculture' for Beijing it will not only develop the production and tourism functions of agriculture to increase farmers' incomes, but also utilizes the agricultural and ecological landscape to make Beijing a more comfortable and beautiful living environment (Zhang *et al.*, 2010). Their argument is that rural landscape character, agriculture, and rural environmental issues – and their relationships to urban settlement – should have a large influence on land-use and planning decisions related to large metropolitan regions.

## Cross-border collaboration in Northern Europe

A paper (Joenniemi and Sergunin, 2008) published by the Barents Institute of the University of Tromsø, located in Kirkenes, Norway near the Norwegian-Russian border, describes cross-border experiences in Northern Europe to stimulate cooperation and collaboration for economic development between cities located around the Baltic and Barents Sea regions. This bonding concept has been developed around 'sister' cities located on each side of a state border, and has evolved into the establishment of the City Twins Association (CTA) in 2006.

Currently fourteen Northern European cities are associated with CTA, including two in Russia. The cities have found that by working together they have a stronger image and brand that can be marketed throughout Europe. When applying for funding in joint projects and sharing experiences in problem solving they turn the negative aspects of being on the outer edge of a state into a joint asset. In addition to local, regional, and national funding, financing has come from regional and international financing institutions such as the Nordic Investment Bank and the European Investment Bank. The CTA is now looking at establishing a new financial institution, the Northern Investment Bank, that will focus on mutual projects between Russia and other Northern European countries.

The paper describes a number of twin-city cross-border efforts, including: (1) Tornio and Haparanda across the Finnish-Swedish border, which started in 1987 and has developed into a very strong bicultural community with the border as a connection rather than division; (2) the Russian cities of Narva-Ivangorod and Imatra-Svetogorst which were formerly part of the Soviet Union with a river between them, and are now situated at the Estonian-Russian border. They have had to rebuild public infrastructure after the political change resulting in a number of joint activities and projects involving culture, tourism, employment, spatial planning, and simplified border-crossing; and (3) Kirkenes-Nikel across the Norwegian-Russian border near the most northern part of Europe, which recently signed a memorandum outlining their intentions to develop joint projects in the

4.7
Northern Europe map of
cross-border twin-city
collaborations near the Barents
and Baltic Seas.

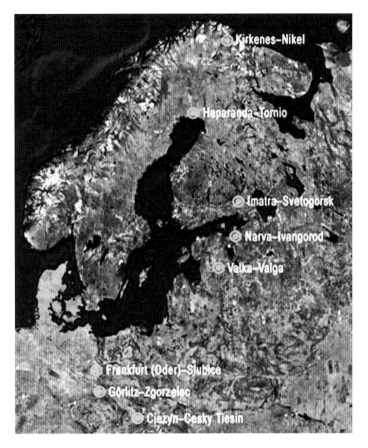

spirit of CTA. A map of Northern Europe (Figure 4.7), prepared by the Barents Institute, illustrates the cross-border twin-city collaborations currently being developed.

The authors point out that some of the cities that have joint agreements have succeeded in creating considerable dynamics around border assets, despite histories of conflict, economic problems, and different politics. In other cases the different and divergent issues are still making it difficult for some cities to exploit the opportunities provided by cooperation and collaboration.

While the model of networking and international contacts is improving economic development, it is a slow process, but with a bright future. The broad experiment in cross-border relationships is constantly changing and adapting to new issues and interests to expand and enlarge the land area of the region impacted by the relationship. In the future, the relationships provided by the twin-city concept will expand and evolve into regional corridors for economic development (Joenniemi and Sergunin, 2008).

The cooperative association between Tornio (Finland) and Haparanda (Sweden) is of special note because it has proven to be very successful. In 1987 the two cities developed a very explicit strategy across the Torne River at the

border between the two countries, and as a result the two cities (Figures 4.8 and 4.9) have moved from marginal towns on the remote edge of their countries into a vibrant regional centre. Tornio was established on the western side of the river by King Gustav II in 1621. Later, in 1809, it came under Russian control, and Sweden established Haparanda in 1842 as a new town to replace it on its side of the river. Tornio is the larger of the two, but the two cities had never worked together even after Finland became an independent nation after World War II.

In 1960, the two cities shared in the construction of a common swimming pool and this cooperative effort slowly developed into an interregional organization called 'Provincia Bothniensis', started in 1987. The association, based on mutual trust and a common vision, has created cooperative relationships dealing with a number of practical problems impacting both cities. These range from joint hospital and postal services, employment agencies, educational facilities, and common library and fire-fighting capability. A new central city core is being created, and they have attracted investments and new businesses (including a new IKEA store). This has been made possible by redefining the market and cultural region as a cooperative cross-border initiative which neither could have accomplished alone.

Even though it has taken a while for cooperation to develop, in the long run the border connects the two cities rather than divides them from each other. People, goods, and ideas flow across the border almost without restrictions. The border is the most frequented in the Nordic countries, with more than 35,000 crossings each day.

Dennis Zalamans, in an article related to *Northern Experiments: The Barents Urban Survey 2009*, described the steps the two cities have taken as 'acting small and thinking big' and as a result of their cooperation they are now the focal point of a new large regional area that includes parts of Norway and Russia. Discussions between the two cities are ongoing about their future, and may lead to the establishment of one common town. If this takes place it will be the first in the world (Zalamans, 2009).

In another article in the same report, Aileen Espiritu (2009), who was originally from Canada and is now director of the Barents Institute, described some

**4.8 (left)**
Street with contemporary buildings, with shops on the ground floor and apartments above in the central area of Tornio, Finland.

**4.9 (right)**
The historic City Hall and modern Haparanda Hotel in Haparanda, Sweden.

4.10

The city of Kirkenes, Norway in the summer, with a view of the harbor and the downtown area which was reconstructed after World War II. It is today partnering with the Russian city of Nikel across the border.

of the cultural difficulties in reshaping identity in the region. She describes the very strong masculine identity of Kirkenes (Figure 4.10) that was constructed around iron mining in the nineteenth century, and later through German occupation during World War II and after during the Cold War period, with many male military people.

As a landscape that was highly industrialized it was a frontier to be confronted, and the character of the region is still strongly masculine, even though today the number of men and women is roughly equal. As a newcomer to the city and to Norway, she looks on the region through the lens of an outsider and has concluded that the masculine character of the region as it was in the nineteenth century still persists today even though Norway and Norwegians regard themselves as an egalitarian society (Espiritu, 2009).

### Dimensions of place and space influencing the health of rural people: A view from Canada

*Professor Judith Read Guernsey is director of the Rural Centre at Dalhousie University in Nova Scotia. She has been involved with a number of other scholars and researchers in a variety of studies about rural health in Canada. The following notes describing their findings were compiled by her for this book.*

There is increased recognition by health researchers and policymakers of the importance of aspects of local settings and places in shaping people's health experiences. This recognition arises from the realization of remarkable differences in health disparities and life expectancies within local regions which implicate local social and physical environmental factors. Aspects of local settings which have been suggested to influence health include:

- Physical features of the environment shared by all residents in a locality;
- Availability of a healthy environment at home, work, and play;

- Services provided publicly and privately to support people in their daily lives;
- Sociocultural features of a neighborhood;
- Reputation of an area.

There is also consideration for spatial patterning and diffusion of physical and biological risk factors:

- Psychosocial impacts of pollution as well as the physical health outcomes may depend on the community context – and that social construction of hazard may be significant to interpretation of physical environmental risk;
- Models of infectious disease transmission over space;
- Structure of settlement hierarchies (geographic theories).

While variations in rates of infectious and chronic diseases between countries have historically been used by epidemiologists to identify risk factors as possible explanations (e.g. diet in Asian countries and their high rates of stomach cancer, high fat intake in North America and Scandinavia and heart disease), systematic analysis of these factors has only emerged within the last decade or so. This is due in part to newly available GIS technologies and to more advanced geo-statistical methods, hierarchical equation modeling, and the convergence of health geography disciplines with epidemiology and demography. There is also recognition of two possible classes of explanations:

- Compositional explanations – different types of individuals, their genetic inheritance, behaviors, and interaction with their environments and these differences account for differences between places;
- Contextual explanations – features of social or physical environment (pollution, physical facilities, infrastructures) which influence the health of those exposed to it.

Further interest in this issue has been enhanced by new theoretical approaches in thinking about the health of populations versus treating individual sick people, and the economic benefits gained by societies in adopting such approaches. As noted, the difference between these two approaches is a 'high-risk' approach (treating susceptible individuals at high cost) versus 'attempts to control the causes of incidence of disease' (at low cost per person). A significant driver in adoption of this population health approach has been the rapidly escalating costs of health care in countries where a national health insurance system financed by taxpayers is in place (i.e. Canada, United Kingdom, northern Europe). This has led to the focus on the factors that are termed 'determinants of health' (i.e. the upstream, structural factors present in society that seem to create or break down barriers to health).

Further extension to this thinking has been the articulation that people live within a range of settings – largely governed by where people live, work, and play.

There are local settings (homes, community neighborhoods) which are governed by local municipal and county government policies, regional settings (states and ecosystem biomes), and national and international settings (climate change, trade pacts). When one thinks about settings that influence health according to this hierarchy, one recognizes that for most people it is the local setting (homes and neighborhoods) which has the greatest direct influence on people's health. It is at this level that processes as well as safe and secure access to resources (food, transportation, social resources and social support systems, education, employment, communications, quality of the physical environment) occur which are vital for health. What determines quality of access is largely dependent upon local investment in social architecture and infrastructure.

With the widespread adoption of population health frameworks that advocate for social, economic, and environmental policies and actions to improve health of populations, there is a need for more thoughtful conceptualization of how societal and environmental conditions transcend to impact individual health. Population health theorists have made progress in identifying categories of thematic determinants of health, but there has been limited development of theoretical constructs that adequately reflect the complex nature of these societal dimensions. Much of the current research activity in these areas remains focused on the expression of individual life circumstances as community-level aggregated indicators with little regard for how these factors transcend to community-level dynamics. For example, income is identified as a determinant of health. But how does income actually become a causal influence on health (get under the skin – as one of my students says)? Sociologists, geographers, and economists have provided considerable theoretical insight in this regard. But as noted in the World Health Organization report:

> Where people live affects their health and chances of leading flourishing lives. Communities and neighborhoods that ensure access to basic goods, that are socially cohesive, that are designed to promote good physical and psychological wellbeing, and that are protective of the natural environment are essential for health equity.
>
> (WHO, 2008)

Labor (human capital), land (natural capital), and capital (financial capital) have been described as the cornerstones of production, according to neo-classical economists. The addition of social capital (networks) acknowledges that humans develop social relations while engaging in activities based on market exchanges. All four domains are spatially distributed. Bill Reimer, a sociologist and Principal Investigator of the New Rural Economy project at Concordia University in Montreal, has contributed much to this discourse, in relation to these issues in Canada. For the project they have divided the entire country by census subdivision (urban and rural areas included) and stratified each area by seven indices (Table 4.1).

**Table 4.1** Rural Influence Index in Canada

| Index | Definition/Main idea |
| --- | --- |
| Economic stability | Smooth economic growth, without strong surges and recessions. Less fluctuation is preferred. |
| Global exposure and integration | Degree of international linkages and exposure to global market in local industries. |
| Social progress | Progress toward sustainable development. Balancing present requirements with future needs. |
| Local institution capacity | Capability and potential for self-reliance and effective and efficient operating. |
| Competitiveness | Capacity to achieve sustained income and employment growth relative to others. |
| Regional disparity | Differences in socio-economic status and opportunities. |
| Resource reliance | Degree of employment in primary industry. |

Reimer and other members of this large national collaboration then focused on the rural regions and described access to four types of social relationship processes (market, bureaucratic, associative, and communal) as being relevant to rural communities: (1) natural capital; (2) economic capital; (3) human skills capital; and (4) abilities capital.

Other features of the Canadian rural landscape that the group described as influencing health are:

- Predominance of natural resource reliant economies (including agriculture and fisheries) which in turn impact and are dependent upon natural resources and health of ecosystem;
- Physical environmental conditions (extreme weather events, exposure-related (heat/cold) conditions, unmonitored water quality);
- Livelihood strategies and choices (hazardous working conditions, work-related mobility due to lack of jobs, and seasonal employment, or unemployment);
- Governance structures (surveillance and control of social and environmental processes (environmental and security) and conditions) that support people in their daily lives (hospitals, doctors, schools, internet).
- Economic restructuring and demographic shifts (out-migration by those most fit and most able to leave);
- Social cohesion and resiliency (acknowledged to be stronger in rural areas – but volunteerism, like in the United States, is dwindling, due to both family members needing to work).

The population health approach in Canada transcends the traditional bio-medical perspective on health, and focuses on the interrelated social, economic, and environmental conditions that influence the health of populations over the life course. In addition to biological endowment, health is conditioned by a complex of factors related to a person's social and physical environments – and income, situated in the context of national wealth and prosperity.

To build on this broader perspective of a population's 'health', the Federal, Provincial, and Territorial governments in Canada have embarked on a national process with public health stakeholders, experts, and concerned Canadians to define public health goals for Canada. It is important to understand that 'public health' does not refer solely to public health services, but rather to 'the science and art of promoting health, preventing disease, prolonging life, and improving quality of life through the organized efforts of society'. Table 4.2 summarizes their findings.

**Table 4.2** Rural Social Determinants in Canada

| Social determinant | Rural context |
| --- | --- |
| Income and social status | • Substantially lower average incomes<br>• Higher proportion of social assistance |
| Natural environment | • Extreme weather conditions<br>• Preponderance of outdoor employment<br>• Less water and air quality monitoring and surveillance |
| Employment and working conditions | • Higher unemployment<br>• Higher underemployment – part-time and seasonal work<br>• High hazard jobs and exposures to toxic substances, particularly in resource jobs |
| Education | • Lower levels of formal education (completions of high school diplomas, university degrees)<br>• Lower levels of literacy<br>• Less access to internet, education facilities, libraries |
| Housing | • Higher proportion of substandard housing, particularly for Aboriginal populations<br>• Group homes, nursing homes, senior citizens' residences not generally available |
| Health care services | • Lack of health promotion programs, lack of diagnostic services, restricted access to emergency and acute care, large distances to services<br>• Major shortages of nurses, GPs, and specialists |

## Urban and rural connections with South Africa

The Center for International Food and Agricultural Policy (CIFAP) in the Department of Applied Economics at the University of Minnesota, St Paul and the University of Free State, Bloemfontein, South Africa and its Department of Agricultural Economics (UFS/DAE) have since 2002 been exchanging research knowledge through a Memorandum of Agreement. They are two of the leading organizations in their respective regions dedicated to research, teaching, and out-reach, and the agreement they have is for faculty and student exchange to conduct research and facilitate cooperation between the two institutions.

The UFS/DAE has experienced considerable growth in the demand for its services since the democratization of the political system in South Africa. The major source of this growth originates from other countries in Sub-Saharan Africa, as more and more professionals from these countries turn to the University of Free State for graduate studies in agricultural economics. The areas of research interest of the UFS/DAE include trade, marketing, policy, environmental and resource economics, production economics, and rural development.

They have accepted their new responsibility to develop into an institution with a strong teaching and research program which will contribute to finding solutions for Africa's many problems. The majority of its graduate students are from other African countries and most will return to their home lands as govern-ment officials or as academics. These graduates will have a profound impact on the formation of future policies and decisions in their respective regions.

This extraordinary agreement began when Professor Herman van Schalkwyk, Head of the Department of Agricultural Economics at the UFS visited the University of Minnesota to seek out a cooperative and collaborative relationship. After the meeting, van Schalkwyk and Professor Claudia Parliament of the Department of Applied Economics, College of Food, Agriculture and Natural Resource Sciences at the University of Minnesota and executive director of the Minnesota Council on Economic Education, picked up the challenge. Over the years Professor Parliament has taken many groups of students to South Africa to exchange ideas and research issues impacting rural economies.

Professor Parliament says that some of the major issues facing rural regions there are: (1) land reform to redistribute land to more black owners; (2) water resources and food supply (the Free State region is relatively dry, but varied in its landscape and climate, and new emphasis on agricultural systems needs to be resolved); (3) health, and in particular HIV/Aids prevention and treatment; and (4) wildlife management and environmental quality. Professor Parliament has given me several images of rural regions in the Free State, illustrating housing in QwaQwa, a former homeland, providing a glimpse of rural life in South Africa (Figures 4.11 and 4.12).

Professor Yandisa B. Mashalaba is a town and regional planner in the UFS Department of Urban and Regional Planning. In 2009, he was part of a group from the UFS that visited the University of Minnesota, and as part of his tour he

4.11 (opposite top)
QwaQwa Township village in Free State, South Africa, with homes on terraces. QwaQwa is one of the former homelands in the region. It is a very dry, but diversified agricultural region of the country.

4.12 (opposite bottom)
Newly constructed round house in QwaQwa, with thatched roof and concrete block foundation. The design follows traditional homes in rural regions and there is a variety of more contemporary homes nearby.

requested a meeting with the CRD. We discussed many of the rural issues in our two regions and the relationships between urban and rural life – and how the education system is organized to deal with it. He shared concern about the lack of adequate environmental policies and inequities among tribes in South Africa in how land is used.

After he returned to South Africa he sent me some information about a series of conferences that provided opportunities for planners across Africa to discuss changes that have been taking place on the African continent. The conferences were meant to find ways to deal with changing rural issues, including challenges of poverty, environment and energy concerns, resource limits, and efforts to clarify thinking regarding spatial arrangements of the land as the basis of planning.

In 2010 the 'Planning Africa' conference in Durban focused on outlining opportunities and strengthening the planning profession in Africa. The intention of the conference was to respond to global economic and ecological crises from an African planning perspective by articulating and publicizing leading planning practice and solutions across Africa. One of the sessions, 'Placing design central to urban decision making', described the current situation:

> Despite political calls for radical changes to South African towns and cities, the performance of these settlements, as containers of life, remains very poor. Cities in South Africa have been rated, in a recent United Nations publication, as the most inefficient and inequitable in the world and the quality of the public spatial environment, of crucial importance to poor people who conduct many of their daily activities in these spaces, remains ubiquitously poor.
>
> A major contributing cause of this situation is that there appears to be no shared agreement amongst professionals concerned with the built environment about the nature of the urban problem or about a vision of what it is they should collectively be seeking to achieve, In particular there appears to be little concern about qualitative environmental issues.
>
> (Todeschini, 2010)

The Province of Free State is known as the breadbasket of South Africa. The rich soil and pleasant climate allow a thriving agricultural industry, includ-ing leading the nation in the production of biofuels. The next phase of the Memorandum of Agreement exchange program is to expand its focus to include other departments at the respective universities to broaden the kinds of research and issues that can be studied. There is much that can be learned, and some of the research being done in South Africa would be a good basis for research and regional thinking in Minnesota.

## Regional thinking in Minnesota

In the 1960s the metropolitan area of Minneapolis and St Paul was experiencing rapid and uncontrolled expansion and competition between the two cities and their suburban regions. At the urging of many local government, business, and civic leaders, the legislature established the Metropolitan Council to provide guidance and coordination for growth for the seven-county Twin Cities metropolitan area to address issues that could not be adequately resolved with existing governmental arrangements. In signing the bill, then Governor Harold LeVander noted that the council 'was conceived with the idea that we will be faced with more and more problems that will pay no heed to the boundary lines which mark the end of one community and the beginning of another' (Metropolitan Council, 2010).

Governor LeVander was quite right in his statement about cross-jurisdictional planning and land-use management and it will become even more important in the near future as regions throughout Minnesota and surrounding states respond to global economic issues. Cross-jurisdictional planning is a core aspect of regionalism and fundamental to rural design. However in many rural areas around the country, as in rural Minnesota, the cities, townships, and counties are mostly left to fend for themselves.

Planning is not well synchronized or supported – particularly in relation to the townships and counties surrounding the Twin Cities metropolitan area, which are being rapidly affected by urban sprawl. Nor are most of the other regions of Minnesota working around a coordinated plan for economic development, use of land assets, and quality of life. Lacking a vision, many land-use decisions reflect the path of least resistance which, over time, creates a patchwork of individual project developments unrelated to each other and the larger landscape.

Cross-jurisdictional and community-based comprehensive planning presents numerous opportunities for the enhancement of human rights, quality of life, and economic development throughout rural areas. In Minnesota the law allows cross-jurisdictional planning by authorizing governmental units to enter into voluntary agreements to cooperatively offer services to, or perform functions for, all participating governments.

In Minnesota, counties, cities, and townships currently have the ability to create and implement comprehensive plans independently. However, the political relationships between these institutions are not equal. For example, counties oversee cities and townships, and cities (where most people live) are drivers of tax bases, leaving townships with the least amount of political clout and in some situations a greater land-to-person ratio than cities.

When it comes to animal agriculture, state and county regulations don't always connect with local township concerns. The political power imbalance results in missed opportunities, a lack of checks and balances, hard feelings between institutions, and ultimately a lack of representation for what matters most – community values and managed change.

The involvement that the CRD had with Wyoming Township (see case study in Chapter 6) located on the northeast edge of the seven-county Twin Cities metropolitan area, is a project that helped resolve potential conflict between the township and the adjacent Chisago City, the county seat. The township had gone through a 'comprehensive plan update' process required by state law, only to find that citizens did not like the recommendations because, in their opinion, they did not properly address the environmental protection and landscape character that they valued. Nor did it deal with the city's desire to annex township land and expand its boundary.

The CRD worked with a steering committee selected by the township board, and through community design workshops utilizing its visioning process, created maps that reflected values the citizens placed on their land. The revised plan was passed unanimously by the township board and became the basis for zoning amendments to help manage residential and commercial development in a way that preserved citizens' values and resolved the annexation issue with the city. This project is the kind of cross-jurisdictional, community-based comprehensive planning process that is needed – one that economically links cities and townships with counties and regions based on common interests.

This concept may seem threatening to existing jurisdictions organized around political boundaries, but through community-based planning, based on a common asset such as water, all planning and land-use recommendations are oriented around common interests. A community-based rural planning model respects political lines but emphasizes the common interests of different jurisdictions to clarify community values and shapes land-use zoning to reflect those values. It is a model that can connect cities, townships, counties, and states together to help guide land uses at the local, regional, and national scales.

Another illustration of cross-jurisdictional planning is a discussion diagram (Figure 4.13) for the City of Detroit Lakes in northwestern Minnesota and the seven small towns around it. The concept was to work together with the small towns as spatially separated neighborhoods of the larger city as a regional network. Preliminary analysis of the region by the CRD indicated that while Detroit Lakes is a major tourist destination, with hundreds of lakes surrounding it, the seven small towns around the regional city of Detroit Lakes were all struggling to survive, due to inadequate population and property tax bases to support their existing infrastructure. The conceptual idea for the Detroit Lakes region was that some of the towns might be focused toward tourism, while others are agriculturally oriented, and some might be better as bedroom communities – but all could collaborate and cooperate with the larger regional center, as connected but spatially separated neighborhoods to support and promote each other individually and collectively.

This idea had earlier been outlined by Minnesota State Economist Tom Stinson (Professor in Applied Economics at the University of Minnesota) and Minnesota State Demographer Tom Gillaspy as a way for small towns and regional centres to cooperate and work together for mutual benefit. They argue that any

4.13
A CRD diagram prepared for a
meeting in Detroit Lakes,
Minnesota illustrating
collaboration and cooperation
where the small nearby towns
function as spatially separated
neighbors of the larger
regional city for mutual
benefit.

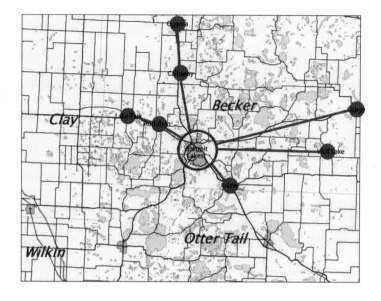

rural community's future depends on the success of the regional economy in which
it is located, not its relative success compared to its neighbors. In their paper,
Stinson and Gillaspy (2006) go on to ask what is the larger community when
rural communities function as a network of spatially separated neighborhoods
and how do you define it? Rural communities need to identify the shared demographic, economic, cultural, and environment conditions that create bonds
between the communities. Because rural communities often interact with each
other across county boundaries, they have proposed a reorganization of the state
into five rural regions and one metropolitan region (Figure 4.14). Even though
they admit the edges are fuzzy, they believe that these are the groups of counties
that are generally bonded as a region, using soil types, geology, climate, and
settlement patterns to define each region.

The CRD uses the proposals advocated by Stinson and Gillaspy when it
works with rural cities and regions to find ways to connect the dots. It is an effective tool to identify synergistic connections that can bring people and landscapes
together around mutual and shared interests and assets. For example, in planning
for the Minnesota Sesquicentennial in 2008, the CRD and the Minnesota Rural
Partnership (the state citizen organization officially recognized by the US
Department of Agriculture) proposed a project called 'Minnesota 2058 – Thriving
by Design'. It was intended as a two-year study to create a long-term regional
planning process for the state. A diagram prepared by the CRD (Figure 4.15)
illustrates a regional organization of the State of Minnesota into six rural regions
that cross township and county jurisdictions. The regions shown are shaped to
approximately coordinate with the Stinson and Gillaspy conceptual diagram, the
three ecosystems that diagonally cross the state, and the three great watersheds
that meet in Minnesota. Both diagrams (Figures 4.14 and 4.15), however, fail to
illustrate regional connections that might cross state lines.

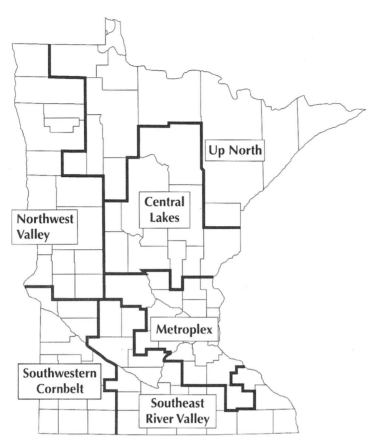

4.14
A map of Minnesota as
proposed by Minnesota State
Economist Tom Stinson and
Minnesota State Demographer
Tom Gillaspy, illustrating
potential cooperation regions,
based on county lines within
the state that have common
economic characteristics.

Nevertheless, it is the idea of regional cooperation and collaboration that is so critical to gain an advantage and become more economically competitive in a time of rapidly changing global dynamics. Defining regions based on their natural assets and characteristics is a more rational and effective means to economic gain and improving quality of life. Any boundary should be respected but uninhibitedly crossed in order to define shared assets and values while developing a strategy for competitiveness in the global economy.

## Looking ahead

What is the future for rural regions? As is in many other regions of the country and worldwide, Minnesotans are wondering what its rural character will look like in twenty or fifty years? Where will people live and work, and where will the million-plus additional new people arriving to live in Minnesota by 2030 be located? What kind of transportation and what kind of environment will the state have? Will it maintain a high quality of life with outdoor recreation and a beautiful rural landscape as well as vibrant metropolitan and rural regions? What will be

A vision map, prepared by the CRD, of Minnesota in 2058, which is similar to the Stinson/Gillaspy map, but organized around the three ecosystems that diagonally cross the state. The drawing was prepared to encourage and illustrate cross-boundary design thinking and planning for rural Minnesota.

the economic drivers and what kinds of jobs will there be, and where will they be located? How can rural Minnesota continue to compete in a global marketplace? Finally, what is the design of Minnesota and neighboring states for 2050?

This is a question that the CRD has been discussing with rural communities throughout the state to empower citizens, while considering the following important observations and questions:

- The population will increase significantly in both urban and rural regions due to immigration with a more diversified and aging demography.
- The rural landscape of each region of the state was developed with a particular economy in mind. As new opportunities and needs emerge, what knowledge base can aid the state to recognize the landscape's potential for economies of the future? Where will people want to live?

- For the economies of the future, how can rural design and a regional approach support the critical mass of people (families, young people, and elderly) needed to maintain anchoring institutions such as schools, hospitals, businesses, and churches?
- What will enable transportation (road, rail, and river) needs to be seriously considered as infrastructure – in visioning and supporting economies of the future?
- How can education be best delivered to enhance economic prosperity? How can local school districts and higher education be better connected?
- What is the relationship of small rural towns to regional centers, and what are the relationships of rural centers to the large Twin Cities metropolitan area?
- What are the land-based assets of each region that can be utilized to ensure a healthy future?
- What aspects of the unique geological and landscape character of the state's regions need to be preserved and enhanced?
- What are the opportunities for entrepreneurship and capital funding to support and enhance environmental protection, economic development, and quality of life?

The CRD recognizes and supports the increasing ethnic, cultural, and economic diversity of each region of the state and the vibrancy and resulting impacts on social and economic structures and infrastructure needs. Building upon existing county planning and policy frameworks, the CRD's projects over the past fourteen years have provided the opportunity to think about the future and how individual regions' valuable resources can translate into strategic projects and policies to enhance quality of life, promote economic development, and ensure a healthy environment. In the following chapter, the research foundation and methodologies of rural design used by the CRD in its research projects will be discussed. It is evidence-based design that is at the core of the rural design methodology.

# Chapter 5

# Research foundation

Rural design focuses the design process on the diverse environmental, social, and economic problems of rural communities. As a planning and design discipline, rural design can help resolve rural issues, and from a regional perspective it can help citizens answer questions such as:

- Can a regional economy and regional way of thinking be established and can rural people become excited about its potentials and opportunities?
- Can changing demographics and an aging population be an economic advantage?
- What is the rural quality of life and sense of place that can be promoted to encourage young people to stay and tourists to visit rural communities?
- Can animal agriculture be expanded without harming the environment or quality of life?
- Can affordable housing be developed?
- What economic criteria should regions utilize to ensure a healthy future?
- Can incentives be established to promote regional cooperation that crosses boundaries?
- Can renewable energy from biomass and carbon sequestration become an economic catalyst for rural development?
- What role do the arts and culture have in community vitality?

Knowledge-based design is fundamental to the rural design process. As such it raises the question as to what research is needed for rural design to be effective and pertinent in the rapidly changing global economy and its impact on rural environments. The First International Symposium on Rural Design was held at the University of Minnesota in January 2010, and was attended by participants from academia, government and non-profit organizations, and professionals in architecture, landscape architecture, and planning. The attendees represented seventeen different academic disciplines from twenty different universities across Canada and the United States.

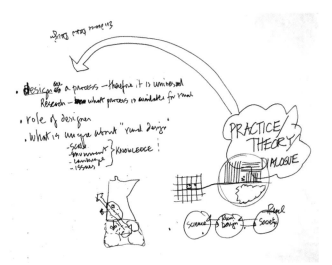

5.1
This drawing, from one of the sessions at the First International Symposium for Rural Design in 2010, illustrates discussion about evidence-based design as the foundation for rural design and a link between rural science and rural society.

The different disciplinary perspectives brought to the symposium by participants suggested a number of possibilities, focusing on systemic and holistic interdisciplinary approaches to rural issues. They agreed that rural design is an exciting new approach for meeting rural needs and resolving rural issues, with the potential to produce transformational change. They also agreed that this new discipline must be founded on solid research and its practice based on data-based evidence. Figure 5.1, a diagram sketched during one of the sessions, illustrates participants' thinking about rural design and its research base.

## Research issues

As a result of the symposium, rural design was further conceptualized, defined, and positioned as a new interdisciplinary field of inquiry and practice, capable of meeting the need for a means to address rural issues – comprehensively, scale appropriate, and effectively. Research issues discussed were quite varied, and included multifunctional landscapes, regionalism, and ecosystem health.

### *Multifunctional landscapes*

Large-scale monoculture farming has generated increasing concern about the costs to the environment and rural communities. This has created a search for landscape patterns that promote wider benefits and fewer negative impacts. These patterns require biodiversity to increase production of ecosystem services important for agricultural production as well as societal needs. They must be shaped to provide high-quality water supplies, carbon storage, biochemical cycling, biodiversity, and greenhouse gas emission reduction. A multifunctional landscape is defined by five aspects:

- Land is not all the same and policymakers must recognize and build on the differences.
- People are not all the same and to transform a landscape, people's different strengths must be emphasized to ensure their participation.
- An ecosystem is very complex and it is important to recognize that every action has a reaction.
- Every solution to an ecosystem problem brings a new set of problems.
- Problems should be resolved by utilizing the capacities and assets of the land and its people.

The discussion indicated that to achieve multifunctional landscapes, policies from both bottom up (local government efforts) and top down (e.g. the US Federal Farm Bill) are required to work together and be integrated. Rural design can, through geo-spatial computer systems, help communities visualize the results of alternatives so they can judge the various impacts on social, political, and economic concerns to make good choices that reflect their values.

The top research issues for multifunctional landscapes identified by the symposium were: (1) to develop a better understanding of the dynamics of governmental incentives and how to use them; (2) to find better ways to connect information across relevant disciplines for academic research in providing information to policymakers; and (3) that the design process must reflect community values and recognize the importance of accounting for the impact of energy costs to influence land-use practices and landscape patterns.

## Regionalism

It was clear to all participants that rural problems such as polluted water, poverty, uncontrolled growth at the urban/rural edge, degraded ecosystems, and lack of economic opportunity do not conform to political or institutional boundaries or disciplinary ones. Nor can the research and applications of solutions be defined by a boundary. One problem is that environmental data are collected on political boundaries. Another is to understand the unique natural system that gives a region its identity as well as determine who do people talk to when a crisis develops. It was pointed out that the province of British Columbia in Canada has numerous regional districts for delivering infrastructure, health, and other services and they are all defined by and function around common topography. The province of Manitoba, on the other hand, has regions that do not work well because residents cannot perceive the rather arbitrary definition of boundaries.

It was clear from the discussion that regional cooperation and collaboration will become more important as regions work to take advantage of their assets and values to compete in the global economy. How to define regions and cross-jurisdictions without upsetting local traditions, cultures, and interests is an area for further study. Rural design brings a process to enhance those connections and definitions.

## Ecosystem health

Using an ecosystem model and the metric of health to facilitate holistic approaches to solving problems is an emerging technique. Ecosystem health is defined as the integration of humans, animals, and the environment – sometimes called 'One Health'. Discussion indicated that public health still follows the definition of health being a function of environmental exposure; however, the view is shifting to thinking more globally about the health of populations. The new way of looking at public health is as a whole system including the social and political environment, allowing the ecosystem perspective to engage and improve health. Using the landscape as a way to introduce rural citizens to the issue can improve the community engagement process. Currently everyone involved in agriculture – from seed companies, equipment manufacturers, farmers, and policymakers to bankers – are basically designing the landscape without understanding the consequences. Emerging problems of climate change, food security, and energy are likely to become dominating world issues. The key issue is to determine how to integrate people, animals, and the environment, while recognizing the inseparable and entwined relationship between urban and rural areas.

## Definitions

The United States Department of Agriculture has created definitions that are useful when discussing research issues for rural regions (USLegal, Inc.).

The term 'food and agricultural sciences' means basic, applied, and developmental research, extension, and teaching activities in food and fiber, agricultural, renewable energy, and natural resources, forestry, and physical and social sciences, including activities relating to the following:

(A)   Animal health, production, and wellbeing;
(B)   Plant health and production;
(C)   Animal and plant germ plasma collection and preservation;
(D)   Aquaculture;
(E)   Food safety;
(F)   Soil, water, and related resource conservation and improvement;
(G)   Forestry, horticulture, and range management;
(H)   Nutritional sciences and promotion;
(I)   Farm enhancement, including financial management, input efficiency, and profitability;
(J)   Home economics;
(K)   Rural human ecology;
(L)   Youth development and agricultural education, including agricultural clubs;
(M)   Expansion of domestic and international markets for agricultural com-

modities and products, including agricultural trade barrier identification and analysis;

(N)  Information management and technology transfer related to agriculture;
(O)  Biotechnology related to agriculture;
(P)  The processing, distribution, marketing, and utilization of food and agricultural products.

The term 'sustainable agriculture' means an integrated system of plant and animal production practices having a site-specific application that will, over the long term:

(A)  Satisfy human food and fiber needs;
(B)  Enhance environmental quality and the natural resource base upon which the agriculture economy depends;
(C)  Make the most efficient use of non-renewable resources and on-farm resources and integrate, where appropriate, natural biological cycles and controls;
(D)  Sustain the economic viability of farm operations;
(E)  Enhance the quality of life for farmers and society as a whole.

In addition to these definitions, the CRD includes forests, regional parks, rivers, lakes and open spaces, small towns, and regional centers in its thinking about rural design and descriptions of rural character and rural landscape.

*The Bellona Scenario*, published by the Bellona Foundation (2008), an international environmental NGO based in Norway, presents a number of ideas to reduce greenhouse gas emissions by 85% by 2050. It argues that everyone must work together because no single solution can do the job alone. The suggestions include:

*  Lifestyle change to bring about a change in consumer behavior, using emission-based pricing and public awareness;
*  Efficiency in the transformation of energy and materials into products and services;
*  Renewable energy from solar, biomass, and wind to replace fossil energy;
*  Carbon capture and storage in geological formations;
*  Carbon negative energy using non-agricultural land by growing biomass for power plants;
*  Greenhouse gas reduction from waste, industry, and agriculture;
*  Land-use change by managing forests better to increase their role as natural sinks of $CO_2$.

The Bellano Foundation endeavors to identify and implement sustainable solutions to the most pressing environmental problems. They state that fossil fuel currently accounts for 80% of world energy use, and energy use is responsible for 60% of global greenhouse gas emissions, and that immediate action is required to make energy supply more sustainable (Bellona Foundation, 2008).

In the Midwest, the latest predictions are that summers will become warmer and drier, with wetter winters and springs. These new conditions will increase energy demands and provide opportunities for new human, plant, and animal diseases; increase stress on water supplies; and affect ecosystem composition with shifts in flora and fauna species. If the increase in winter and spring precipitation occurs, increased flooding and corresponding changes in hydrology will have profound effects on landscape qualities, impacting tourism and cultural identity.

These predicted changes (and those unpredicted) will require the design of new landscape patterns, infrastructure, and economic and community identities. The planning for these changes must begin immediately. Rural communities must be equipped with information and tools, including the problem-solving process of rural design, to effectively adapt to and manage change.

In his book, *The Fifth Discipline: The Art and Practice of the Learning Organization,* Peter Senge (1990) outlines the need for systems thinking as a methodology for seeing the whole and a framework for finding interrelationships. He describes five disciplines of the learning organization as: (1) personal mastery of continually clarifying and deepening personal vision, focusing energies, developing patience, and seeing reality objectively; (2) mental models as deeply ingrained assumptions, generalizations, or images that influence understanding the world and taking action; (3) building a shared vision of the future that fosters genuine commitment rather than compliance; (4) team learning that starts with dialogue and continues into genuine thinking together; and (5) systems thinking – the fifth discipline that integrates the other four (Senge, 1990).

Rural design embraces design and systems thinking because of the scale and breadth of rural issues – particularly when the issues are regionally oriented. A visualization diagram utilized by the CRD (Figure 5.2) illustrates the data-driven community design process used in its work with rural citizens to develop creative and innovative solutions that reflect community vision.

The strategies for rural design are simple, but effective when they are community-based. To have meaning for the future the strategies must include research that can result in transformational changes. These research directions and others, and the community-based design process will enable rural design as a problem-solving process to:

- Help rural communities make land-use, architectural, and aesthetic decisions that enhance their quality of life and the environment;
- Connect social, artistic, cultural, technological, and environmental issues that define rural place;
- Promote sustainable economic development for rural communities that improve human, livestock, crop, and ecosystem health;

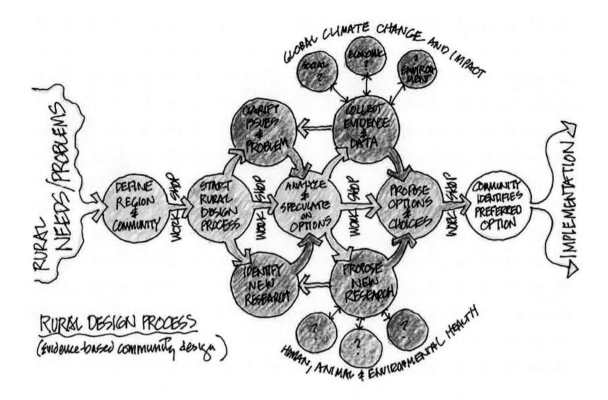

GLOBAL CLIMATE CHANGE AND IMPACT

SOCIAL ?  ECONOMIC ?  ENVIRONMENT

CLARIFY ISSUES & PROBLEM  COLLECT EVIDENCE & DATA

RURAL NEEDS/PROBLEMS

DEFINE REGION & COMMUNITY  START RURAL DESIGN PROCESS  ANALYZE & SPECULATE ON OPTIONS  PROPOSE OPTIONS & CHOICES  COMMUNITY IDENTIFIES PREFERRED OPTION

WORKSHOP  WORKSHOP  WORKSHOP  WORKSHOP

IMPLEMENTATION

IDENTIFY NEW RESEARCH  PROPOSE NEW RESEARCH

? ? ?

RURAL DESIGN PROCESS
(evidence-based community design)

HUMAN, ANIMAL & ENVIRONMENTAL HEALTH

5.2
A diagram used by the CRD to illustrate the design process that functions to connect the dots, to find opportunities for rural economic development, environmental enhancement, and improved quality of life.

• Integrate research and practice across the many disciplines involved in rural issues to meet rural needs, provide new data, and provoke new research questions.

## Sustainability challenge

Typically, most buildings designed today, that aspire to be sustainable, utilize prescriptive standards such as that developed by the US Green Building Council's Leadership in Energy and Environmental Design (LEED). The program provides a system, with third-party verification, of obtaining points for a building design at increasing levels (Silver, Gold, Platinum). However, there is no research evidence that illustrates that these LEED prescriptive standards actually result in significant energy conservation and environmental protection.

Buildings should be designed around performance metrics that are measurable to ensure energy conservation and environmental protection. As developed by the Center for Sustainable Building Research (CSBR) at the University of Minnesota, these measurable performance metrics (Figure 5.3) involve 'building metrics' (including energy, water, wastewater, solid waste, materials, and indoor

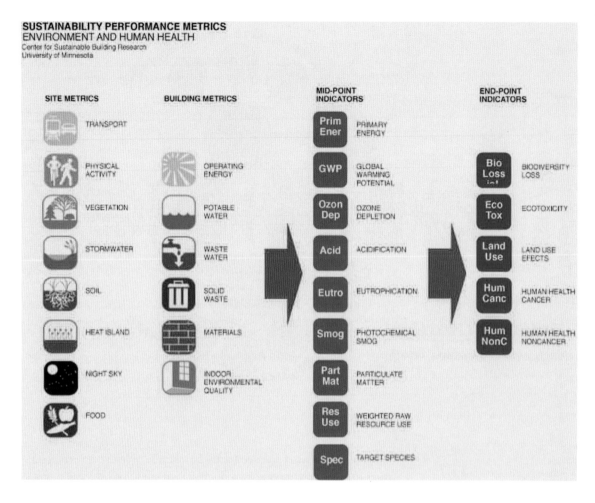

**SUSTAINABILITY PERFORMANCE METRICS**
ENVIRONMENT AND HUMAN HEALTH
Center for Sustainable Building Research
University of Minnesota

| SITE METRICS | BUILDING METRICS | MID-POINT INDICATORS | | END-POINT INDICATORS | |
|---|---|---|---|---|---|
| TRANSPORT | | Prim Ener — PRIMARY ENERGY | | | |
| PHYSICAL ACTIVITY | OPERATING ENERGY | GWP — GLOBAL WARMING POTENTIAL | | Bio Loss — BIODIVERSITY LOSS | |
| VEGETATION | POTABLE WATER | Ozon Dep — OZONE DEPLETION | | Eco Tox — ECOTOXICITY | |
| STORMWATER | WASTE WATER | Acid — ACIDIFICATION | | Land Use — LAND USE EFECTS | |
| SOIL | SOLID WASTE | Eutro — EUTROPHICATION | | Hum Canc — HUMAN HEALTH CANCER | |
| HEAT ISLAND | MATERIALS | Smog — PHOTOCHEMICAL SMOG | | Hum NonC — HUMAN HEALTH NONCANCER | |
| NIGHT SKY | INDOOR ENVIRONMENTAL QUALITY | Part Mat — PARTICULATE MATTER | | | |
| FOOD | | Res Use — WEIGHTED RAW RESOURCE USE | | | |
| | | Spec — TARGET SPECIES | | | |

environmental quality) and 'site metrics' (including transportation, physical activity, education, storm water, soils, heat island, night sky, and food).

Based on their research analysis, the CSBR have outlined the net-zero energy possibilities for human habitation in urban areas in the United States (Carmody *et al.*, 2010) involving three kinds of systems that suggest how urban/suburban development might happen in the future:

*Energy systems*

•   For both single-family dwelling and townhouse developments, a district energy system achieves the best energy performance and is potentially the least expensive.
•   It is possible to build net-zero energy single-family dwelling units using autonomous and district-oriented infrastructure systems.
•   It is only possible to build net-zero energy townhouse developments with conventional building envelopes using district infrastructure systems. To

5.3
Diagram prepared by the CSBR at the University of Minnesota, illustrating interrelated performance metrics for environmental and human health to guide the design of sustainable buildings and communities.

achieve net-zero energy performance, envelope design must have a higher level of energy savings.

- In townhouse developments, consolidated energy systems for an entire building are more energy efficient and cost effective than individual energy systems for each unit.
- Optimum energy performance is achieved with a centralized (district) HVAC plant coupled to a zoned hydronic heating and cooling delivery system in the individual housing units combined with separate ventilation.
- Operating revenues from investments in heating, ventilating, and air conditioning plants at both the dwelling and district scale significantly exceed those derived from investments in building envelope conservation.

*Water systems*

- It is possible to build single-family and townhouse developments with no off-site water, wastewater, or storm water infrastructure, using autonomous and district infrastructure systems. At a district scale, this infrastructure can be achieved for a lower cost than conventional and autonomous development.
- District water systems (potable water, wastewater, and storm water) do not require the same large up-front capital expenditures that are required with conventional systems.

*Overall systems*

- With district systems, typical development patterns change, with neighborhoods planned with and around central open spaces. In addition, there is a new flexibility in the type and sequence of development. Each new district can be designed uniquely, with appropriate housing types and densities in response to the marketplace.
- Integrated energy, water, and wastewater systems at the district scale create synergies, resulting in lower energy demand.
- Closing loops in energy and water systems at the district scale creates synergies, resulting in lower capital and lifecycle costs with better environmental performance compared with conventional infrastructure development.

Although these metrics and conclusions were developed for human habitation in urban/suburban areas they are similar to what needs to be developed for small towns, livestock and related land uses, and other agricultural buildings in rural regions. Agricultural buildings today are mostly exempt from any building code. There is a significant gap in available science-based information about animal production facilities, and research is needed that will help all segments of society cope with the issue of what is good for animals, humans, and the environment in the design and construction of animal facilities.

The Lowell Center for Sustainable Production at the University of Massachusetts Lowell was organized to promote new forms of industrial production. It defines sustainable production as: 'the creation of goods and services using processes and systems that are: non-polluting; conserving of energy and natural resources; economically viable; safe and healthy for workers, communities, and consumers; and socially and creatively rewarding for all working people' (Veleva *et al.*, 2001). They emphasize the interconnections between the environmental, social, and economic systems within which production and consumption occur.

Many of these sustainable concepts look at only one and sometimes two aspects, yet to be truly effective all of these ideas must be integrated and integral to the intellectual and research foundation for rural design. Sustainable rural environments, ranging from multifunctional landscapes and food production to renewable energy and rural economic development, are important issues in the research work of the CRD.

## A new approach to rural issues

Rural regions outside, but near, large metropolitan areas are having difficulty in controlling low-density urban sprawl with leapfrog development. This type of development outside of existing metropolitan sewer and water services, allows for one house on ten acres with individual wells and septic systems. This type of development happened because more and more young families were looking for new lower-cost housing, even though they have to drive longer distances to work and shop. The unavailability of low-cost housing loans, rising cost of gasoline for transportation, and the public costs to support infrastructure for communities with such a low density will hopefully change that phenomenon in the near future. A recent survey found that rural Minnesota families spend on average 20% more on gasoline than urban families, regardless of the cost of gasoline. Other costs of living, while lower in rural areas than in urban ones, are not low enough to counteract this added burden when gasoline prices climb and infrastructure costs are assessed against their properties. Rural residents have few practical transportation alternatives and rural households end up bearing the full cost of gasoline price increases (CRPD, 2009).

Soil types, climate differences, and unique watersheds have historically determined regional patterns for agriculture and rural development, and understanding the character and ecology of the land is critical to proper management of land resources. Understanding the ecological integrity of the landscape may become the best way for communities to understand the environment in which they live and where and how they should build. Even though rural regions may cross political boundaries, the ecological integrity of the region should become the basic planning unit for land-use planning – rural as well as urban/suburban – to guide land-use decisions that preserve agriculture, economic development, natural environment, and the aesthetic beauty of the rural landscape. Outlining and presenting these issues geo-spatially and in three dimensions is a much more effective way to help rural citizens understand the implications of their options.

Based on the CRD experience with rural communities it has become very apparent that there is a genuine desire in rural areas for new ideas and new strategies that:

- Preserve the rural landscape for agricultural and recreational uses;
- Emphasize environmental quality that improves both cultural and natural landscapes;
- Promote economic development while enhancing quality of life.

Rural design is not an easy process, but holistic and systemic methodology is a very good way to analyze problems and recommend solutions that can be implemented with strong citizen support.

By focusing on quality of life, the CRD has been involved with a variety of rural communities at different scales and landscape character to find: (1) new ways for crossing boundaries for small towns to become connected with regional centers, to the betterment of both; (2) new economic development opportunities based on renewable energy from wind, solar, and biomass; (3) new food and fiber production and processing methods which emphasize food safety at both local and state-wide levels; (4) new forms of affordable housing incorporating sustainable design concepts for energy conservation; (5) new ways to encourage the arts as an economic catalyst for design thinking; and (6) new transportation and communication possibilities to bring people back to rural areas as a workforce for the new rural economy that might be realized.

The CRD knows, from working with the Tourism Center at the University of Minnesota, that tourists like to visit a rural region for the same reason people like to live there. Rural regions that focus on creating a high quality of life are more likely to attract people. And if people like to live in the community it is more likely to encourage entrepreneurs and attract new businesses and business expansion, with related social, cultural, environmental, and economic development.

Rural design and its geo-spatial technologies can help plan, design, and resolve rural land-use and other regional issues. In the near future, as the nation becomes more and more reliant on renewable energy and food production, it will become even more critical as a means to visualize the shape of the future rural environment. Now is the time to clarify and develop curriculum programs in rural design – particularly at land-grant universities around the United States – that can educate undergraduates, graduates, and post-degree professionals to obtain necessary skills and understandings of rural design methodologies and strategies. Rural regions need designers, artists, and planners who are good at connecting the dots to encourage entrepreneurs, attract investors, and integrate wellness at all levels – human, animal, and environmental.

## Evidence-based rural design

Rural design is a multidisciplinary approach to meeting rural needs and resolving rural problems through the lens of spatial awareness and the integrated problem-solving process of design. To be effective it must be based on credible research and be data-driven as a design process. Also it must be creative and inspirational in how it interprets and outlines possibilities for rural regions to manage change and spatially organize with flexibility to meet changing global challenges.

Evidence-based design originated in medical practice, but is now appearing more often in the architectural and design fields. In their book, *Evidence-Based Design for Multiple Building Types*, Hamilton and Watkins (2009) declare: 'evidence-based design is a process for the conscientious, explicit, and judicious use of current best evidence from research and practice in making critical decisions, together with an informed client, about the design of each individual and unique project.'

Evidence-based design which creates design decisions on the best available current research evidence, is now gaining understanding among architects, planners, and landscape architects for a wide range of building types and landscapes. Architecturally, the concept of evidence-based design and its use is more likely to lead to the creation of high-performance buildings and environments. It focuses on the methods by which design professionals and their clients can create better buildings by critically interpreting the implications of credible research and careful observation of completed projects.

Rural design is much more complex than any single building, and as a process for dealing with rural issues it needs a research foundation to be effective. The rural issues and large land scales they cover are broad and multidisciplinary, requiring a rural perspective to understand the problems and develop solutions. Rural design must cross and integrate disciplines to collect data, analyse and understand its implications, and utilize that information for each individual and unique rural design project. It is a multidisciplinary design process and while based on research related to the problem, the process often results in defining new research issues.

Rural design is a catalyst for coordinating and connecting the best available evidence for dealing with rural land use and other issues. As such it cannot develop as a sub-discipline of architecture, landscape architecture, urban design, or planning. It must be a unique stand-alone design discipline with an educational curriculum and certification system for professional practice. Rural design provides a process for collecting information and working collaboratively with rural communities to understand problems and propose creative and innovative solutions that are rooted in place and climate.

Any curriculum program in rural design must recognize the unique inter-related relationships between design and planning, economics and social issues, urban and rural issues, and human, animal, and environmental health, emphasizing the importance of connection to, and expression of, unique climate and place. Jane Jacobs, the great urban planner and writer, described the importance of experiencing place this way: 'The greatest asset a city of neighborhoods can have is something different from every other place' (Jacobs, 1961). That dictum to build upon unique landscape and cultural assets is also true for rural regions and their counties, townships, and small cities and towns throughout rural North America and, by extension, worldwide. Each rural region has its own unique landscape, climate, and cultural character and it is this sense that should guide the process of rural design.

## Research opportunities

Academic research and practitioner observations are equally important to rural design and the intellectual and knowledge aspects of its methodology. These aspects are multidisciplinary, involving a wide range of academic research interests (e.g. agronomy, forestry, applied economics, rural sociology, plant and soil sciences, community development, water resources, public health, veterinary medicine, ecology, biosystems, and tourism).

New research which can explore and make the connections to provide the knowledge for design is ongoing and changing as rural regions respond to global impacts and economies. The opportunities the global economy provides for research impacting the earth's resources include issues such as:

- The relationship between rural planning and rural design is a connected one. Rural planning is often based on policy issues responding to ecological and resource protection, environmental integrity and water quality, and to functional issues of transportation, power, and communication. Rural design uses the lens of spatial awareness to make connections by creating alternative visualizations to these issues in the rural landscape. This integrated process begins with educated assumptions and a literature search collecting data to provide research evidence that, taken together, inform alternative solutions. The more knowledgeable the design team is about the implications of research the more likely recommendations will favourably impact policy decisions.

- Economic and social issues are partners with environmental issues, and balancing their importance is a critical component of sustainable rural design. Global issues of climate change, renewable energy, and food supply and security will impact the economic and social nature of rural regions, especially as the world's population doubles over the next forty years. Research can identify the impacts global issues have on local issues and the importance of resolving them for both short- and long-term economic gain.

- Urban/suburban and rural understanding must be interrelated. One cannot discuss urban/suburban design without also considering the implications of development on rural environments. Likewise, issues of agriculture and rural environments are important considerations for thinking about urban/suburban environments and human uses of the land. If prime agricultural land is taken for development, that source of growing food is lost – maybe forever. Understanding the differences between what is urban, suburban, rural, and agricultural is critical to effective urban and rural design. The design issues of urban and rural design are interconnected, but uniquely different.

- Integrating human, animal, and environmental wellness is a growing academic understanding – often called 'One Health'. It is a way of thinking that interconnects wellness issues so that food supply and distribution is connected to food security, just as human health and disease prevention is connected to animal health. Rural environments can be shaped to help eliminate the transmission of disease from wildlife to domestic animals and in turn to humans, just as they can be shaped to support human wellness with biking/hiking trails and outdoor venues that encourage exercise and connection to nature. The research challenges of One Health for shaping rural environments create entrepreneurial opportunity.

- Human health encompasses a broad range of issues and in rural areas it is often the remoteness from a major urban area with medical facilities that encourages innovation. Rural regions in Canada and the United States have been exploring the use of 'community paramedics' as a way to support rural health. The location and distance factor for paramedics is directly connected to how rural regions are designed for health. The relationship between healthcare providers and citizens' ability to pay is another crucial part of this design issue that suggests collaboration between businesses and providers in rural areas on a regional basis might be beneficial to all.

- The kinds of agriculture in any region of the United States are influenced greatly by national and state farm policies, as well as regional soils, climate, and water. These policies have contributed to the current form of agriculture that favors a selected set of commodities. An emerging research issue is the impact of agricultural policies on other functions of the rural landscape, such as land conservation, sustainability of landscape structure and natural resources, biodiversity preservation, and the economic and social viability of rural areas (Boody et al., 2005). Boody et al.'s research has indicated that economic and environmental benefits can be attained through changes in agricultural land management without increasing public costs. The multi-function agriculture that is desired will require a shift in policy to direct subsidies toward alternative incentives, such as farming systems that provide environmental benefits while fitting local situations. Rural design is a way to link the economic and social benefits of agricultural policies, based on the nature and character of the regional landscape, with biodiversity and social capital.

- Systems thinking and entrepreneurship is an important marriage to create a sustainable and economically viable rural future. This idea, along with business expansion, is an important asset that a community must consider in any economic development plan. Furthermore, it must be integrated with the region's natural assets to find opportunities. The more rural communities connect, collaborate, and cooperate, the more likely they are to open up the doors for entrepreneurs to develop and create jobs and provide economic development that is sustainable. Rural design is a way to visualize information and its availability is connected to any regions efforts towards sustainable economic development. The Center for Rural Policy and Development in Minnesota noted in a recent study that *information* is what most rural entrepreneurs and small businesses need for successful development and expansion (CRPD, 2009).

- Sustainability is, of course, fundamental to any rural design issue. In rural areas it has different ramifications because agricultural buildings are not covered by building codes. There has been very little research on the location, design, construction, and management of commercial buildings for animal production in the last fifty years, yet the way people think about their rural communities in North America has changed significantly (Jacobson *et al.*, 2009). Little attention has been paid to the design and construction of livestock buildings and their important role in maintaining a sustainable and healthy food and fiber system. The development of integrated performance design guidelines which address emerging challenges to producers and society will help lead the way for North American animal agriculture. The guidelines can assist the industry in how it locates, houses, and manages agricultural animal production (particularly dairy, swine, and poultry) to effectively and sustainably deal with local, state, national, and global issues.

- Renewable energy from wind, solar, and biomass is becoming an increasing source of energy production in North America and around the world. In northern Spain it is common to see wind turbines on the tops of mountain ridges and solar collectors in the valleys, located within and among fields of crops and cattle. The wind and sun are seen as agricultural commodities, to be harvested like the wheat or corn. When you look at rural environments with that in mind, these technologies seem quite at home with natural and agricultural environments. New advances using biological and biomass systems to create fuel and electricity are promising developments which will impact rural landscapes. This issue needs to be connected with government policies, economic development, and environmental protection to support the social, economic, and ecological impacts that renewable energy production can have on the rural future.

- Food supply and food security is of great concern when looked at from a pandemic perspective. According to the Global Initiative for Food Systems Leadership: 'Feeding the world with safe and nutritious food requires a robust food supply system. Local food production, regional food trade, and global supply chains all play a part since no country can provide all the foods demanded by its people' (Hueston, 2009). To feed future populations with healthy and safe food, the systems must be flexible, to accommodate local vagaries of harvesting crops, regional preferences for different products, and the acute shortages that accompany natural and manmade disasters. The process of rural design can help ensure robust food supply systems that function locally, regionally, and internationally.

- Water resources and water quality are global issues that will have large impacts on food production and human settlements as the planet adjusts to climate change and increasing population. Currently, about 70% of the world's annual water use is for agricultural purposes (primarily through irrigation) and providing food is critical to human survival. Rural design can assist in determining better ways to preserve water and how it is used by utilizing geo-spatial analysis to provide alternatives that illustrate different scenarios for adjustment in water use and the positive and negative aspects of each.

- The arts of a region can help define its characteristics, providing a cultural identity to the landscape and dimension of the people who live and work in the region. Research is needed to better understand the connections between the arts and community vitality for economic and social development to improve quality of life.

These research issues suggest the richness of opportunities and challenges that design thinking and the rural design process can address to provide for entrepreneurial activity and improve quality of rural life. Evidence-based design is fundamental to the rural design process and it can provide a conduit by which rural regions can clarify the issues that need to be resolved and work with science to create options that respond to those issues. Since most of the issues impacting rural regions are global, science can help articulate what can be accomplished on the local/regional scale while fitting into a large world view. Issues of climate change, renewable energy, food supply and security, water, and health can and must be simultaneously addressed at multiple scales throughout the world while meeting local needs.

## Social capital

'Social capital' is a term that refers to the resource potential of social relationships. The main premise is that integrated social groups are better able to mobilize resources to pursue desired outcomes. Similarly, in terms of community activities, an integrated community should be more effective in resolving a community issue (Agnitsch et al., 2006). More research is needed to understand and create strategies as to how diverse social groups, crossing jurisdictional boundaries, can effectively work together, using their landscape and social assets for a common good and future wellbeing.

Rural design is a community-design process (Figure 5.4) which works to create and enhance social relationships to achieve consensus on a course of action that the community can rally behind. Rural design does not profess a point of view, but rather it brings design thinking to determine the community's preferences and values; and in the process develop the social conditions under which community action is likely. The question is – Can social capital be nurtured when the definition of community extends beyond traditional boundaries? Can diverse peoples from different communities which share a common landscape come together in the process of rural design to define their assets and outline opportunities for economic development and quality of life that the individual communities cannot accomplish on their own?

The future success of rural regions is dependent on cooperation and collaboration in managing change and taking advantage of new opportunities created by global economic and climate pressures. Social and community capital are directly connected to economic development, and rural communities that incorporate design thinking and take the initiative to plan for the future are more likely to experience economic development and an improved quality of life.

5.4
A CRD community workshop in Scott County, Minnesota (see case study in Chapter 6), showing the community-based process of rural design in action.

5.5
A research field with
professors, graduate students,
and visiting farmers at a
University of Minnesota open
house for public engagement.

Positive design thinking encourages positive actions, which promote positive communities.

Knowledge about the social and artistic character of the landscape within which a community and their neighboring communities live is the key to mobilizing local and regional resources to effectively act. Today, global issues of climate change, food supply and security, renewable energy, water, and health are rapidly impacting rural regions and the rate of change has rapidly accelerated. Land-grant universities need to be more proactive in identifying the research knowledge that rural communities need to resolve (Figure 5.5) and to take advantage of global economic and climate changes before they become a detriment.

Rural design is not a research discipline by itself, but it is a proven methodology for bringing science to society by integrating research evidence and sustainable issues regarding the rural landscape with economic development and quality of life. It is the knowledge that provides the information for citizens to cross jurisdictional and disciplinary boundaries to create effective solutions to land and other issues. Rural design is a process that provides for this transformation.

# Chapter 6

# Rural design strategies

When making choices about using the land and constructing buildings in the rural landscape it is important to think and act holistically. What is the impact on the visual appearance of the rural landscape? What are the issues that need to be considered? The discipline of rural design can define the kind of architecture that links traditional barn building and farming practices and fit with the landscape, with the latest technological and economic methods of producing food and fiber and renewable energy. Rural design is based on a rural land-use philosophy that seeks a balance between quality of life, economic growth, and preservation of the natural and cultivated landscape. It recognizes the importance to all people, urban as well as rural, of respecting the unique landscape character of where one is living and working. A building on the flat prairie in northwestern Minnesota should be different from one in the rolling hills and hardwood forests of the southeastern part of the state.

The CRD vision is to reconnect people with the American landscape by raising awareness of, and appreciation for, the value of rural communities and environments. Its mission is to work with rural landscape, cultures, and communities using innovative design strategies. Rural design is most often the understanding and visualization of large open spaces, with buildings and towns as objects in the rural landscape. It is a methodology to assist rural citizens to improve their daily lives while protecting and enhancing the beauty and diverse ecology of the rural landscape for future generations to appreciate and enjoy. Rural design is a way to connect economic, environmental, and social issues for public good – and a way to ecologically view the world.

## Strategies

Over the past fourteen years, strategies developed by the CRD for dealing with rural land-use issues that seem to work best include community-based research tools and technologies. These strategies were outlined in a paper to a conference on architectural research, describing innovative design strategies for dealing with rural land-use issues (Thorbeck, 2010):

- Envisioning alternative physical scenarios for rural community response, working with steering committees and community-based design workshops to engage citizens. By collecting data and research pertinent to the issue and then preparing and presenting alternatives based on that evidence, the community becomes part of the process. Through visualization techniques and scenario alternatives, stakeholders gain knowledge so they understand the implications their choices could have on rural environments.
- Presenting a systemic and holistic point of view from an unbiased rural perspective, using an interdisciplinary and collaborative design approach. Experts from within the academic community as well as agricultural industry representatives can provide knowledge to help ensure a more positive impact on the rural economic, social, or environmental issue being studied. This integrated process can also identify new research necessary to fully understand the issue.
- Working with interactive media, both electronic and tactile, such as communicating with GIS imaging, three-dimensional models and kits of parts, drawings, and web-based and print publishing to provide multiple methods for communicating information to educate rural citizens about possibilities and opportunities for economic and community vitality.
- Partnering with communities and organizations as a whole to find the linkages and connect the dots between local and regional opportunities to identify stakeholder issues and their participation in the design process.
- Identifying regional land assets, characteristics, and relationships that large-scale communities may have in common, to encourage collaboration and cooperation for economic development and environmental protection that crosses jurisdictions, at multi-township, multi-county, or multi-state scales.

These rural design strategies outline a holistic and systemic process for connecting environmental, economic, and social issues with educational, technological, and organizational research to formulate models for a healthy and prosperous future for rural areas. They are models that can be utilized worldwide and will work well for shaping rural environments when citizens are involved and allowed to identify their preferences.

## Building codes

Currently, most states exempt agricultural buildings from any building code. Until the1950s most animal facilities that were constructed involved a relatively small

6.1 (opposite top)
Aerial view of Riverview Dairy farm in northwestern Minnesota, with 5,000 cows in a single barn building on the right and 2,500 cows in a barn on the left, and two manure lagoons in the center. Each barn has its own milking parlor.

6.2 (opposite bottom)
Interior view of animal stall and feeding lane in the larger Riverview barn.

number of animals. They were generally small diversified farms, with small buildings for a variety of animals. Since then, however, the number of animals in a facility has dramatically risen and the farms have become specialized. Although there are dairies in some parts of the country that have nearly 10,000 cows, in Minnesota there are large dairy farms that have as many as 5,000 cows under a single roof. The highly respectable Riverview Dairy in northwestern Minnesota is one of those (Figures 6.1, 6.2, and 6.3). It functions with 350 employees, of whom

6.3
Rotary milking parlor holding
84 cows in the larger Riverview
barn, which operates 24 hours
a day, every day.

50 are working around the clock, feeding and tending cows, removing manure, cleaning pens, and operating the rotary milking parlour.

The Riverview Dairy is very well managed and a showplace for large-scale dairy operations but, being exempt from the building codes, the only design criteria used in its construction were the professional responsibilities of the people involved. Many other specialized commercial facilities have been constructed for dairy, swine, and poultry throughout the state and region using pole-barn technology with large numbers of animals and people working in those buildings. Over the past several years a number of these structures have suffered severe damage from wind and snow loads.

The International Building Code (IBC) is currently used throughout North America (by most states and provinces) for animal research facilities constructed by academic institutions, which must follow code requirements for educational buildings. As a result, these academic research facilities for animals generally cost more than those constructed on farms which are exempt. Also, the code does not have a good definition of what is an 'agricultural building'. The 2006 IBC defines an agricultural building as:

A structure designed and constructed to house farm implements, hay, grain, poultry, livestock or other horticultural products. This structure shall not be a place of human habitation or a place of employment where agricultural products are processed, treated or packaged, nor shall it be a place used by the public.

The IBC does have a one-page appendix for 'Group U – Agricultural Buildings' which provides some standards regarding height, floor area, and exits, but is not mandatory unless specifically referenced in any adopting ordinance. However, even with this appendix there is no limit on area for one-story agricultural buildings when they have open yards or public ways on all sides of minimum 60 feet width.

Fundamentally, most rural buildings in rural regions of the United States, other than those in small towns and cities for human occupancy, are considered agricultural and generally exempt from the building code. Thus, there is no standard code regulation protecting the safety, health, and welfare of humans who work in those buildings or the animals that are housed in them.

The CRD is involved in research planning with faculty in Bioproducts and Biosystem Engineering, Veterinary Medicine, and the CSBR at the University of Minnesota to develop science-based performance metrics for sustainable commercial animal agriculture facilities. The project is an attempt to establish a societal shift to raise the standards and building code requirements for agricultural buildings. The project goal is to create guidelines for the design and construction of commercial animal buildings for swine, dairy, and poultry production systems in the United States. The guidelines would help optimize productivity, reduce energy consumption, maintain cost competitiveness over building life, and use more durable and environmentally friendly building components. In addition, the guidelines hope to improve the character of the rural landscape, provide more socially acceptable animal housing, improve working conditions and workers' health, and increase biosecurity to enhance food safety and food security.

To improve the design of commercial buildings for animal agriculture, farmers, builders, insurance companies, and regulators must all consider the integration of human, animal, and environmental health, as well as the structural integrity of these buildings for wind and snow loads. These are critical life safety issues, and when people are involved in daily animal care operations, buildings for animal agriculture that exceed a limited number of animal units and people should be required to meet contemporary building code standards similar to other commercial or industrial buildings.

The performance metrics and design guidelines being developed in this interdisciplinary research idea are intended to be utilized by producers and design and construction professionals as a reference for the next generation of animal production systems while considering emerging market conditions and legislative action and/or regulation of carbon trading, air emissions, manure management, and animal welfare concerns.

## Rural outreach

How Minnesota deals with major changes in farming, small towns, tourism, and the quality of rural life now will have a direct impact on the preservation and future development of rural Minnesota. The long-term economic health of the state and the Midwest region as a major global center is dependent on a holistic and inclusive community-based design approach to rural issues.

Working with university faculty, graduate students, rural communities (cities, townships and counties), and industry, the CRD has been providing this integrative problem-solving approach for over a decade. Through research-based design projects that cut across disciplines and interests the CRD promotes communication and learning in rural communities and among policymakers on possible design responses to complex rural land and community issues.

The CRD focuses on areas of public concern, primarily in rural Minnesota, which includes issues such as:

*   Integrating change at the urban/rural edge while preserving rural character and community values;
*   Empowering rural communities to actively participate in the decision-making processes affecting land use and community well-being;
*   Making room for new production and processing technologies (like renewable energy from agricultural waste) and ensuring the environmental and economic health of a region;
*   Filling an educational gap by providing support and information on rural land issues;
*   Defining regional character, based on ecological systems and relationships between large and small rural towns and communities;
*   Limiting urban sprawl and loss of prime agricultural land which impacts future food supplies to urban areas;
*   Mediating social conflict between farm dwellers and non-farm dwellers over land use;
*   Containing unmanaged change in land uses due to, for example, demographic shifts, economic pressures, spot rezoning, and the search for low-cost affordable housing;
*   Easing the sense of loss experienced by rural people due to changes affecting sense of place, purpose, and self-identity.

At the CRD we have found that regionally focused rural design principles and methodologies to manage change are critically needed in Minnesota. They can help rural communities nurture their capacity for social and economic success through a rural design approach that makes a connection between landscapes of the past and landscapes of the future. The sense of place is an intrinsic part of a person's quality of life and purpose. The personal meaning derived from having a strong sense of place is fundamental to rural architecture, landscapes, and rural design. For it is the sense of place and pride of place that the CRD has found is what people in rural cities and small towns, as well as farmers living in the rural landscape, strive to attain. It is the 'lust for rural life' that provides the passion they have exhibited in our discussions.

## CASE STUDIES OF THE CENTER FOR RURAL DESIGN

The following case studies are typical projects that the CRD has been involved with since 1997. They illustrate different rural design approaches and the rural design process at various scales, with lessons and strategies learned, and in some an epilogue as to what has happened since the project was completed.

### Rural township scale: Wyoming Township – conflict at the urban fringe (2003–2004)

Wyoming Township sits in Chisago County just beyond the northeastern boundary of the seven-county Twin Cities metropolitan area (Figure 6.4). In 2003, Wyoming Township updated its comprehensive plan, but many of the township's

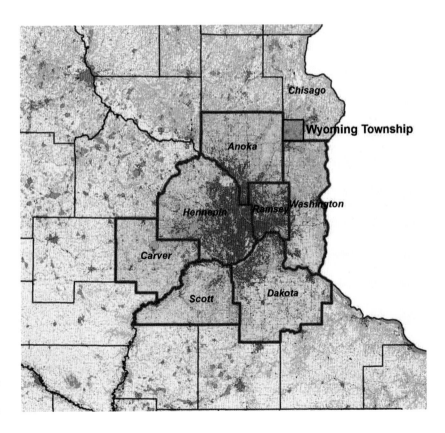

6.4
Map showing the relationship of Wyoming Township to the Twin Cities metropolitan area.

citizens expressed strong dissatisfaction with the draft update, particularly the zoning that appeared to emphasize urbanization and development as the township's future direction. Citizens were especially concerned by the zoning depiction of the transformation of US Highway 8, that runs diagonally through the township, from the scenic road they had always known into a commercial corridor.

In part, the plan was a direct result of the pressure felt by all communities at the rural/urban edge. Agricultural land was quickly being replaced by uncoordinated commercial, industrial, and residential development resulting from the Twin Cities' growing population. As in most communities on the rural/urban fringe, some residents and landowners saw this expansion as an opportunity for economic growth and financial gain. Others saw it as an inevitable force to be accommodated as best as possible. And others saw it as a frightening threat to their community, values, and culture.

Wyoming Township, like most rural communities in Minnesota surrounding the metropolitan area, has been left to its own devices to manage the growth pressures emanating from the Twin Cities. Although extensive citizen comment had been elicited in early stages (1995 and 1998–1999) of the comprehensive plan update process, the results were not analyzed for response patterns. No maps were created that reflected preferred land uses, landscape characteristics, or community values, thus the Township Board literally could not visualize what the citizens wanted. Yet, once maps were produced for the draft updated comprehensive plan, the citizens could clearly see what they did not want! The uproar was so great that the Township Board agreed to revisit the draft plan and consider additional citizen input.

A University of Minnesota extension agent familiar with both the controversy and the work of the CRD facilitated the Township Board's request for the CRD's assistance. This project gave the CRD an opportunity to research methods of community-based design. Specifically, it could experiment with methods for eliciting a community's true desires for its future through visioning exercises. Also, the CRD could for the first time incorporate the methods for using GIS pioneered by University of Minnesota Professor of Landscape Architecture David Pitt. The CRD's Steve Roos, Senior Research Fellow, had previously worked closely with him on research projects and led the mapping aspects of the visioning process.

The CRD organized the project in three phases. The first would inventory and assess citizens' values, beliefs, and priorities and the resources of the community and landscape. This information would be used in the next phase to develop design principles that would inform the creation of different development scenarios for the township. In the final phase, a preferred scenario would be identified and used to update the comprehensive plan and related zoning ordinances.

In August 2003 the Township Board created a Citizen's Advisory Committee to assist with the project. Citizens were solicited by an advertisement in a local newspaper, and the committee also included a liaison representative from the township's planning commission. An important part of any group undertaking is

6.5
The planning process ground
rules agreed to by the Citizen's
Advisory Committee.

Planning Process Ground Rules
for Wyoming Township Citizen's Advisory Committee
2003–4
(adapted from Ellen O'Niel & Associates ©)

We all have something to teach and something to learn in the process.
We are all experts.
The process of learning requires us to rethink our assumptions.
We agree to be open to rethinking our own assumptions and to hearing other people's ideas.
We will act with respect for everyone's knowledge and experience by:

· Listening without interruption or talking over each other,
· Listening without judging someone's ideas or experience,
· Sharing time and space equally with each other,
· Agreeing to disagree respectfully, and
· Describing the problem or issue, not in person.

We agree to act in ways that are in the best interest of the Wyoming Township community and move beyond our own self-interest.
We agree to listen to our neighbors in the public meetings and reflect their concerns, ideas and needs in the planning process.

to set expectations for how the group's members will behave and for the group to agree upon how it will conduct its work. Figure 6.5 shows the 'Planning Process Ground Rules' agreed to by the committee.

At a committee member's suggestion, the CRD engaged the fifteen committee members for its first exercise in a photographic inventory of their community. Committee members were assigned a portion of the township and asked to photograph those places that defined and affected their 'sense of place' about the township and also represented the township's problems and opportunities.

At a later committee meeting the photographers gathered into groups according to their assigned portion of the township, discussed and summarized their findings, and reported back to the whole committee. By clarifying for the committee members and communicating to the CRD what the members' land-use concerns were, the photographs helped define the scope of analysis for the CRD during Phase I, and the scope of planning and policy issues to be addressed.

## Phase I

In Phase I, the CRD focused on four areas: water resources, biological diversity, resources (commodity and amenity), and areas suitable for development.

## WATER RESOURCES

The water inventory looked for areas where particular land uses could affect surface water or groundwater. Sensitive areas were defined as those 100 feet around a cased well (a well whose bore hole is lined with an impermeable material), 200 feet around an uncased well, and 1,000 feet around public/municipal wells.

## BIOLOGICAL DIVERSITY

Actual biological diversity is difficult to measure because that would require a time-consuming and expensive survey of all the organisms in an area. Instead, landscape areas are evaluated based on their habitat quality, with the assumption that better habitat can support a more diverse range of organisms. The parameters analyzed to determine the landscape's potential habitat quality included its size (larger, more contiguous areas of forest, grassland, wetland, etc. are potentially better habitat), whether the same type of land cover existed as did before pioneer settlement, and how much the land is disturbed by human activity. In addition, for forested areas, the amount of core forest (i.e. forest area away from the forest's edge) was also determined, because core forest supports many species that edge forest cannot. Areas were scored on all these parameters and the scores combined to rate the habitat quality of the landscape and map it.

## RESOURCES

Any landscape contains a number of resources that have significant social value to the people who live there and in surrounding areas. These resources can be generally divided into two categories: commodity resources and amenity resources.

*Commodity resources* are landscape features or components that can be readily assigned a monetary value. These include productive agricultural land, land with mineral aggregate resources (e.g. gravel and sand) that can be used in construction materials, or land that has some location-specific value, such as lakefront property. To identify commodity resources in Wyoming Township, the above resources and existing built infrastructure were mapped. These were combined to produce a map of all the commodity resource areas in the township's landscape.

*Amenity resources* are features of the landscape that enhance the area's quality of life. Identifying and mapping some amenity resources can be straightforward. For instance, trails, public lands, and historic features are obvious amenities and were identified to create a map of recreational and cultural amenities. Other amenity resources, however, are more complex to define and identify. A concept the CRD uses in its work is 'intrinsic scenic value'. It stems from physical landscape features that interact to give visual pleasure. The CRD's method for assessing intrinsic scenic value is to measure two components.

The first is landform complexity, which is the total extent of topographic change in a landscape – all the hills, valleys, ridges, and swales – and the landscape's absolute elevation change – the change in height from its lowest to highest points. The second component is land-cover complexity, which is the total number of patches of different types of land cover, the degree of 'naturalness' of the land cover (on a continuum from native, untouched land cover to built-up areas), and the land cover's variety of different heights. Each element of landform and land-cover complexity was evaluated for a ten-acre parcel. Next the evaluations were combined to create a scenic score for each parcel.

A primary way people experience a landscape's scenic value is while driving. Thus another step in the process was to evaluate parcel scores within 250 meters of either side of any federal, state, or county state aid highway. This process helped determine the potential for any roadway section to be a scenic corridor. Finally, all these factors were combined to rate the areas of highest and lowest amenity value in the township.

## DEVELOPMENT SUITABILITY

The landscape features that make an area suitable for development fall into three categories: the soil's ability to support development, the landform's stability, and nearness to existing infrastructure. Soil suitability was determined by analyzing the soil's slope, its capacity to support septic systems, its susceptibility to frost heaving, and the water table depth. Landform stability was measured as a function of its slope. Areas with slopes <6% were deemed most suitable, slopes of 6–18% were considered less suitable, and slopes over 18% were identified as unsuitable for development. Next, the infrastructure considered important to be near to included roadways, urban and industrial areas, and areas zoned for commercial and industrial development. Combining all these factors produced a map of the township's areas suitable for development.

The maps created by the CRD's analysis were presented to over seventy-five township residents at a workshop in mid-September 2003. Workshop participants were recruited by flyers distributed around the township and by members of the Advisory Committee. The participants were divided into four groups (again, one for each area of analysis: water resources, biological diversity, commodity and amenity resources, and areas suitable for development). Each group was facilitated by an Advisory Committee member, and participants were asked to first write individual answers to the following questions:

- How important is this aspect to maintaining current quality of life in the township? Make a note of areas you consider that have high value through this single lens you're using.
- How important is this aspect to future quality of life in the township? Make a note of where losing this aspect would detract from quality of life.
- Where in the township does this aspect have the greatest potential to be realized? Locate and circle on the map, adding any new information on other locations you think need to be identified.

The participants subsequently exchanged and read each other's responses, then as a group discussed and categorized their responses and labeled the maps and/or photos to show them. Afterwards, the participants recommended three values for the CRD to keep in mind as it continued its work and prepared to revise the draft comprehensive plan. Next, all the groups reconvened and presented their findings to the whole workshop. Finally, in a common process fondly called 'dotmocracy', all the participants were given three dot-shaped labels to place next to the statements from any of the groups that represented the priority or value they considered most important.

## Phase II

Phase II presented a challenge for the CRD. As originally planned, the CRD would take the responses from the community workshop, the photography inventory, and input from the Advisory Committee to identify the community's priorities. These priorities would be used to generate design principles to be employed in creating alternative development scenarios of the township. The community could then choose from these scenarios their preferred direction for the township's development. However, the high priority placed by the workshop participants on protecting and improving water quality conflicted with their strong preference for low-density housing. (Research studies have shown that low-density development, e.g. of one dwelling unit per 5–20 acres for a particular area, more negatively affects water quality than development that is clustered at higher densities and leaves the rest of the area undeveloped.) Likewise, large-lot residential development presented problems for preserving the scenic views to open space and natural habitat that was also expressed as a priority during the workshop. Finally, the workshop participants expressed a desire to minimize, or outright prevent, commercial development along Highway 8, which ran counter to the desires of some landowners along the highway and Town Board members. Synthesizing these conflicting desires would require creativity and diplomacy.

## Phase III

During Phase III the following spring, the CRD created three alternative development scenarios and worked with the Advisory Committee to establish a set of guiding principles for land-use planning for the township. These principles would be used to aid the selection of a preferred development scenario. The CRD presented the alternative scenarios (Figures 6.6, 6.7, and 6.8) at another community workshop in April 2004 held at a local church hall. The CRD also discussed the guiding principles and gave a brief primer on some of the design tools, such as cluster development, easements, transfer of development rights, and highway development at commercial nodes which the scenarios employed, to balance the community's stated priorities.

The seventy workshop participants divided into small groups to discuss the three scenarios and score them, using a scorecard developed by the CRD. Advisory Committee members who facilitated the small group sessions reported back to the full assembly on points of consensus, controversial aspects, and group insights.

6.6
Alternative Scenario A
prepared for the Wyoming
Township workshop.

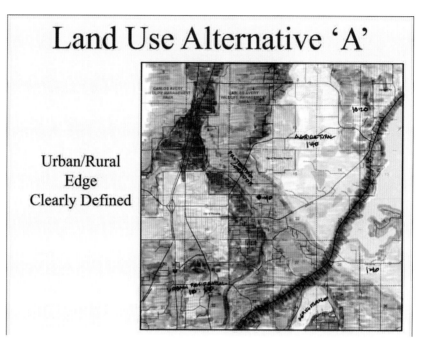

6.6
Alternative Scenario A
prepared for the Wyoming
Township workshop.

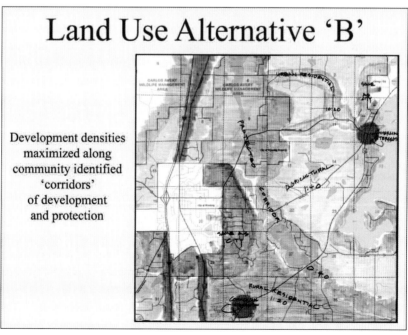

6.7
Alternative Scenario B
prepared for the Wyoming
Township workshop.

Land Use Alternative 'C'

Residential development dispersed across township outside city transition areas to become primary land use

6.8
Alternative Scenario C prepared for the Wyoming Township workshop.

There was agreement on the importance of preserving open space across the township. There was also consensus on protecting the Sunrise River corridor, but disagreement on how to achieve it. Some advocated for careful development within the corridor, but others wanted an outright prohibition on development. There was no clear consensus on the future of agriculture. Participants had concerns about the potential loss of control that individuals might face in deciding what to do with their property, but this was partially mitigated by the groups' interest in alternative patterns of commercial and residential design.

The surprising lesson for the CRD that arose from discussions with citizens while developing the alternative scenarios and from the workshop results were the differing definitions of 'rural'. For some, including those at the CRD, rural inherently included some agriculture. However, for many of the township residents, 'rural' meant open space, regardless of use. In effect, for them rural meant a lack of buildings and paved road infrastructure, and its meaning was not tied to any specific land use.

The CRD used the results of the workshop's discussion and the scorecards in Phase III to develop a preferred scenario that was a hybrid of those presented, and it was used to create a revised comprehensive plan for the township (Figure 6.9). Subsequent to the workshop, the fate of development along Highway 8 became a contentious topic between the Advisory Committee and the Township Board. The Advisory Committee favored a no-development policy along the highway, whereas the Township Board wanted to allow some development. The CRD ultimately presented the Township Board with two scenarios, one reflecting

Rural design strategies

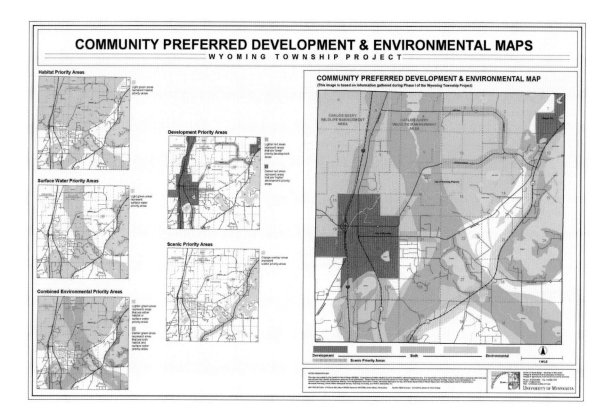

**COMMUNITY PREFERRED DEVELOPMENT & ENVIRONMENTAL MAPS**
WYOMING TOWNSHIP PROJECT

**6.9**
The final revised Comprehensive Plan for Wyoming Township that emerged from the planning process and was approved by the Township Board.

the Advisory Committee's vision and one preferred by the Township Board (and ultimately used in the updated comprehensive plan).

The updated comprehensive plan was prepared by the CRD in collaboration with a professional planning consultant, and presented to the Township Board. It was through the CRD's work that consensus was ultimately achieved around the updated comprehensive plan and the uproar of the township's first effort was not repeated.

## Lessons learned

For the CRD, the project demonstrated the value of the visioning process using the GIS method pioneered by David Pitt. It became clear to the CRD that the visioning process ultimately is an educational process by which rural designers and planners can educate community members about their landscape and its assets – creating hope and optimism for the future. Also, the visioning process can demonstrate to all a community's desires and vision. A Chisago County Commissioner who attended the final workshop confided to the CRD's director he wished all the county's townships could go through a similar process, for it would be invaluable information for the county in its comprehensive planning process and help foster good county/township relationships.

Another lesson that became clear to the CRD was the power of how ideas are represented on maps and the diversity in how they can be interpreted. The original proposed comprehensive plan showed large red areas labeled for dense and commercial development along Highway 8. The original creators of the map, however, meant those areas only to indicate that that type of development could occur somewhere within the red-shaded areas. The township's citizens on the other hand interpreted the red areas as being entirely filled with dense and commercial development, which helped precipitate the original controversy. The CRD's proposed map and concept sketches for the comprehensive plan update showed smaller, more limited areas for commercial development along the highway, concentrated at major intersections, which made the citizens feel more comfortable with the proposed plan update. The creators of the original map may have imagined very similar development taking place along the highway – but their intent was never fully communicated during the planning process

## Strategies learned

- Definitions of 'rural' can vary. Don't assume that yours is the same as others'.
- A community-visioning process is crucial to understanding a community's desires for their future.
- Be aware of the different interpretations people can have of maps and the potential for misunderstanding. Illustrative sketches showing the kinds of development anticipated will help people understand the intention and minimize miscommunication.

## Epilogue

Almost in the middle of the CRD's work with Wyoming Township, the nearby city of Chisago City announced plans to attempt to annex over 11,000 acres of the township, more than half its area and nearly 75% of its households (*Forest Lake Times*, http://www.forestlaketimes.com/2003/november/261126CCannexwyot. html, posted 11/26/03, accessed 7/11/08). Chisago is another fast-growing community feeling expansion pressures from population growth in the Twin Cities, and Wyoming Township was the only available open space for growth. Much citizen sentiment in Wyoming Township was against the annexation, for they feared denser development and losing the values and qualities they were trying to preserve with the CRD's help.

In 2005, Chisago City prevailed in annexing 5,000 acres of the Township. To protect itself from future threats, the township agreed to a 'friendly' annexation of the rest of its area by the city of Wyoming, but this sparked a battle from Chisago City and the town of Stacy who both wanted to annex additional portions of the township (*Forest Lake Times*, http://www.forestlaketimes.com/2007/january/ 31WyoAnnex1317.html, posted 1/31/07, accessed 10/21/08). Although, the particulars are still unsettled, the ultimate result will be the erasure of Wyoming

Township. This is a good example of the power imbalances between townships and cities, the disenfranchisement of rural communities, and the lack of concern for their values when sudden change occurs. This incident argues that a more regional perspective, nurturing collaboration and cooperation should have been taken. The project would have achieved more and the citizens' values been protected if there had been a better dialogue among Wyoming Township, the cities of Chisago City and Wyoming, and Chisago County to identify shared issues for mutual benefit. On the other hand, the project dealt with the issue as it was perceived and maybe as a result of the project it opened the door for achieving a result that crossed boundaries.

*Design team: CRD staff included Dewey Thorbeck, Thora Cartlidge, Steve Roos, Wesley Hellevik, and planning consultant Ken Nimmer. (Note: CRD staff Stephen Streng prepared this case study as the format for the following CRD case studies.)*

## Rural community scale: City of Roseau, Minnesota – aftermath of the 2002 flood (2002–2003)

On June 8, 2002, fourteen inches of rain fell on the City of Roseau in northwestern Minnesota. When a dike running along the Roseau River broke on June 10, the river flowed into the downtown and adjacent residential areas, and finally crested 7.5 feet above flood stage on June 12. The effect of fourteen inches of rain was much like dumping a glass of water on a table top – the water flowed rapidly everywhere.

The Roseau River bisects the City of Roseau which, with 3,000 residents, is the county seat and largest city in Roseau County. Located in the northwestern corner of Minnesota, ten miles south of the US border with Canada, the city sits at the southern end of the large, flat geographical area formed by glacial Lake Agassiz, which 11,000 years ago covered northwestern Minnesota, eastern North Dakota, and a large area of southern Manitoba, Canada.

The city is home to Polaris Industries, Inc., a major snowmobile and all-terrain vehicles manufacturing company employing over 2,000 people, and with the excellent lake bottom soils for growing commodities, the region provides a solid economic base for the community. Roseau County has 16,000 residents and is expected to grow to 19,000 by 2030. Sitting on the beautiful flat prairie, the Roseau community has a high quality of life with a strong agricultural and industrial economic base.

For over a hundred years the city had shared a physically intimate, if not always loving, relationship with the Roseau River. During the nineteenth and early twentieth centuries the river provided the major transportation route in the area, linking the fur traders, followed by the loggers, settlers, and farmers. Based on its location along the transportation route, the City of Roseau quickly grew into a major service center for the expanding agricultural community. Over the years, levees along the river had been constructed as temporary flood-control structures, but there had been levee failures and there was no long-range plan to effectively deal with severe flooding.

The flood damage from the June 12 deluge was enormous, resulting in significant damage to downtown businesses and private residences. Ninety percent of the 150 commercial buildings and most of the public buildings, along with public utilities, suffered major damage. Over fifty homes needed to be demolished and replaced – many owned by low-income families. The Roseau County Museum/ Interpretive Center, City Hall, and Library suffered great damage and needed to be demolished and reconstructed in a new location. Figure 6.10, a photo taken during the flood, indicates the extent of water damage throughout the community.

During early community discussions and planning for reconstruction following the flood, the City of Roseau took note of a paper presented at the 2002 meeting of the American Political Science Association. It reviewed the different approaches that Grand Forks, North Dakota and East Grand Forks, Minnesota took to recover from the Red River flood of April 1997. The study indicated that East Grand Forks, which instituted extensive citizen participation, had more political stability and less social dissatisfaction with reconstruction, and it was this approach that the Roseau leadership wanted to follow.

6.10
Aerial view of the flood of June 2002 in Roseau, Minnesota, which devastated the city and surrounding area.

Rural design strategies

The CRD is a strong proponent of community-based planning and design, and it was for this reason that civic leaders (including Robert Bergland, former United States Congressman, Secretary of the US Department of Agriculture, and Regent of the University of Minnesota) and the City of Roseau asked the CRD to assist them in creating a vision plan for a community-based recovery effort.

In October 2002, the director of the CRD, Dewey Thorbeck, travelled to Roseau and met with a group of approximately fifteen civic leaders. At that meeting it was decided to move forward with the community visioning process. CRD had used this process in Wyoming Township and, based on that experience, understood what was needed to provide a communication role between federal and state agencies, the city, and citizens about flood mitigation, design strategies, and resulting policy decisions.

The Northwest Minnesota Initiative Foundation and the city provided funds for the CRD to become involved in the visioning project which included a weekend 'design charrette' to engage citizens in the process. The Minnesota Design Team (MDT) – a longstanding organization of professional architects, landscape architects, and planners who volunteer to review and suggest ideas for community revitalization throughout the state – was asked to assist in the charrette process. The design charrette process utilized by MDT is an intensive two-day community-involved effort, with the first day dedicated to the community outlining what they think is important, and the second day devoted to teams of volunteer designers working to come up with design ideas looking at the city as a whole. Later in the evening the ideas are presented to the general public at an open meeting. It is a process that generates community excitement and has been very successful in assisting small rural cities by bringing design thinking into their communities.

The federal government and State of Minnesota were helping with financial assistance to restore infrastructure and repair damage caused by the flood, with the US Army Corps of Engineers planning to construct bypass drainage channels and a wider and higher earth levee or floodwall for the Roseau River, to protect the city in the future. At the same time, the Roseau River Watershed District was preparing a joint development plan between the city, Roseau County, and the watershed district to restore Old Roseau Lake, which had been allowed to go dry. While plans had not been completed, preliminary hydrological and engineering work was underway and that information was available for the visioning project.

For some time, citizens had been discussing the need for beautification and improvements to the downtown business district in order to entice more tourists traveling on Highway 11 – a scenic byway with many Canadian travelers – to stop and visit. A beautification committee had been organized to help in this effort. Likewise, a bike trail along the Roseau River had been in the planning stage. The city, along with the cities of Warroad, Baudette, and Thief River Falls, had worked with the University of Minnesota Tourism Center to develop a strategy to promote tourism to the region, and that strategy was integrated into flood-mitigation planning, along with the economic recovery and development efforts already underway.

The City of Roseau is ideally located in the middle of Roseau County, and with a new community plan for mitigating the flood, it hoped to become a catalyst in nurturing a shared community vision that included nearby townships following the flood. It was hoped that the vision would help make connections with other towns and citizens in the region that were sustainable, linked economic development with social and environmental issues, improved quality of life, and oriented to compete globally.

The community-based planning process started with the weekend design charrette, which took place in February 2003, in an elementary school that was not damaged by the flood. The volunteer team worked with the CRD during the weekend workshop with over 120 citizens, to sketch out broad-brush potentials for the vision plan. In that workshop, residents were asked to answer questions such as 'Is the Roseau River an asset or an enemy?' and 'What are the priorities for mitigation based on the options available?' Over the two-day period, design professionals from the CRD, the MDT, and community members worked together to create initial visual ideas and plans and flood control alternatives for the future of Roseau.

Following the weekend design charrette, the CRD worked closely for several months with the steering committee to identify ideas that seemed most pertinent, develop them for presentation and implementation, and assemble the final plan into a final report. The recommendations in the final plan were defined by the steering committee and outlined to the community at a public presentation.

Finally, after eight months of hard work, the steering committee and citizens felt that they had a handle on the recovery effort and were directing the work of all of the parties rather than being subject to decisions by others. Since the flood, a new city hall/library/community center has been constructed, along with a number of other city improvements, and the Roseau River is now thought of as a connector linking the two parts of the city rather than as a separator.

The final report of the planning effort, *Roseau: A Vision for Future,* was the result of a partnership between the CRD and the Roseau Community Vision for the Future Committee, a broad-based steering committee consisting of community leaders representing the City of Roseau, Roseau County, and Roseau Township, with the goal to create a community-based design vision and master plan for the city and surrounding area – and that goal was accomplished (Figure 6.11).

### Lessons learned

This project clearly demonstrated the power of a community-based design process where citizens become involved and participate in identifying assets, values, and opportunities for their community. With citizen involvement and a clear vision, city leadership had the confidence to make tough decisions regarding mitigation of flood damage with the Corps of Engineers and State officials, including planning for the future with a diversion channel that would provide storage capacity and an alternative for water to move by the city without overflowing banks along the Roseau River. The intensive weekend design charrette, with professionals

The Conceptual Vision Plan, which used the Roseau River, after flood mitigation, to connect neighborhoods with the downtown core and school complex.

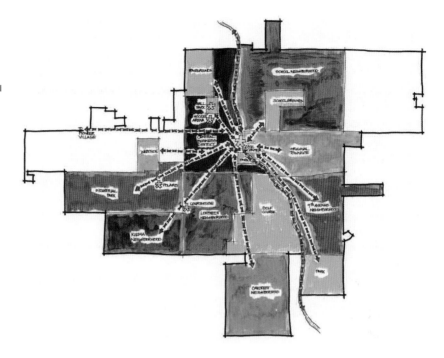

from the MDT and the CRD working with and involving citizens, was particularly effective in nurturing support for the final vision plan.

## Strategies learned

The utilization of GIS mapping with information from the Department of Natural Resources, as used for the Wyoming Township project, is not as effective when a small rural city is involved. The maps that were mostly utilized were based on the city's comprehensive plan and engineering drawings and aerial photographs. The detailed land information had to be assembled from many different parts and this took some time; however, they were still successful in providing adequate information to citizens and the design team during the charrette. The architectural and landscape implications of the plan were illustrated in the report, but without details as to how it would be accomplished and the associated costs. That would have to come later, as decisions were made and design professionals became involved.

The power of community-based planning and citizen participation in identifying values and making choices as stakeholders in the planning process proved again to be very successful. The community-based planning process utilized by the CRD stood the test when decision makers were challenged by individuals who wanted something different. It provided the city decision makers with the confidence to move forward for the betterment of the larger community rather than special interests. Special interests could have very easily deflected the recovery efforts, yet the decision makers stood strong because they knew they had broad community support.

The CRD believes that it is only through a community-based design and planning process that rural citizens will accept and embrace the results and the vision it presents. The spirit of individual freedom and property rights is very strong in rural regions of North America, and with consensus building through the community-based planning process, community trust is nurtured, with broad citizen confidence in the values expressed in the planning document.

## Epilogue

Eight years after the flood, in July 2010, Todd Peterson, Community Development Director for the City of Roseau described in a letter what had happened in the community since that fateful time in 2002:

> It has been a while since you were in town. I will say that things in Roseau are a little different now. It has been a lot of work but I think we have put Roseau back together again. I guess I don't know how much you know about what we did since the flood so I will summarize the best I can what all took place in the years after the flood.
>
> As you are aware the community had substantial damages to both public and private structures and infrastructure so we implemented a 6-year infrastructure repair and replacement schedule to completely rebuild the streets, sidewalks, water, sewer systems and the majority of the city's public facilities. One of the overriding themes that the City took in our reconstruction was rebuilding what was important to the community and changing what needed to be changed. The vision sessions that the Center for Rural Design organized helped focus these themes into certain areas such as rebuilding the heart of Roseau and the downtown district and embracing the river and the greenway concept.
>
> The City started with the concept of recreating a traditional 'Civic Center' at the heart of the community by constructing a new City Center building which houses our City Hall/Council Chambers, Public Library, County Museum, Police Department, Northland Community College Satellite, and a large community center auditorium all in one building. The City also worked with downtown business owners to rebuild and reha-bilitate Main Street. The City built a new building, along with purchasing and rehabilitating a flood-damaged building in the downtown area. These buildings and the upgrades to other buildings downtown along with various streetscape improvements have revitalized the downtown district. Unfortunately the current economic conditions have created more vacant storefronts than we would like to see, but the downtown district is still a meaningful and viable place in Roseau. Hopefully more business ventures will take advantage of this area once economic conditions improve.
>
> The City has continued to improve and expand the greenways, trails and parks along the Roseau River after the flood, including redeveloping the site across the river from the City Center with a recently completed park

gazebo and public service memorial. Trails have also been expanded in and around the City Center, connecting to other trails and sidewalks to the various local neighborhoods. We have also integrated a number of recreational and park features into some of our flood-protection projects. In one area where we constructed a large storm retention basin and pump station just south of the City Center we have incorporated park features, trail, and sledding hill. The City of Roseau recently broke ground on a Corps of Engineers flood-protection project that will take the entire city of Roseau out of the 100-year flood plain. This project, in addition to providing permanent flood protection also incorporated various recreational components, including 4.5 miles of multi-purpose recreational trail and ATV trail opportunities. All of these trails will link across the community and provide opportunity for residents to move about the community by bicycle, rollerblades, and walking.

Nearly all of these projects were guided by the ideas that flowed from the Roseau Vision for Future Planning effort which used as a basis much of the previous planning efforts of the City prior to the 2002 flood. The advantage these planning efforts provided in the post-flood reconstruction was a clear goal for what kind of community we were building. Having this planning document and public planning session did not stop controversy and contention over all of the elements being proposed and constructed, but it did help to guide our decision makers in following through on the final 'vision' for where we wanted the community to go. It also provided credibility to decisions by the City Council that were supported by public input, when individual interests began to sway development proposals. The plan was also vital for securing Federal and State financing for our project when we could show how we intended to spend funds and how we arrived at the projects we were proposing. It is my personal opinion that the City of Roseau could not have achieved the success in reconstructing the community as it did (particularly as fast as we did) after the flood without the planning that had been done in advance of the flood and without having the public buy-in of the reconstruction plans (articulated through the Center for Rural Design and Minnesota Design Team and the resulting Vision for the Future). The City did about 100 years' worth of building in 6 years, and I don't think there is much that we would have done differently, given the chance, and I believe it is because we were ready with a plan on what we would do if we could, and we just followed through with it.

Figures 6.12 and 6.13 illustrate the new Civic Center complex and other improvements which exemplify the remarkable recovery that the City has accomplished.

*Design team: CRD staff included Dewey Thorbeck, Thora Cartlidge, Steve Roos, Wesley Hellevik, and the non-profit volunteer MDT, organized and managed by the Minnesota AIA.*

6.12 (opposite top)
New Roseau Community
Center building, which was
constructed after the flood,
adjacent to a new levee park
along the Roseau River. It
includes the City Hall, Library,
History Museum and Ice Arena
(ice hockey is big in
Minnesota).

6.13 (opposite bottom)
Entrance to the new Roseau
Community Center.

## Rural farmstead scale: Community Dairy Partnership – protecting farming and the environment (1998–1999)

This project was started and funded by the CRD, and focused on a six-county area centered on the city of Litchfield, Minnesota and the First District Association Milk Processing Plant located there. The University of Minnesota's Department of Applied Economics had determined that the economic impact of adding 30,000 cows into the six counties would add about $18 million per year into the region's economy. They also determined that if a dairy family were earning its living only by selling milk, it would require the milk from 294 cows to produce the 1997 median Minnesota family income of approximately $45,000.

A series of meetings with a local group which supports the dairy industry in the region was organized to outline the study and illustrate how GIS could be used to develop environmental protection guidelines for the six counties. The effort in the six counties related to expanding or developing dairy farming, and culminated in a case study of an existing typical small dairy farm in Stearns County near St Cloud. The case study was intended to illustrate how design can create options for expanding a small family-owned dairy farm with diversity and multiple functions for economic benefit while protecting the environment and the ecosystem within which the farm is located.

The Jennissen Farm is a 60-cow family operation, with husband and wife (who both work outside the farm) and three daughters in high school and college. The 60-acre dairy farm has a small lake and is located near a creek. The development scenario recommended including a short- and long-range plan that the family could use for decision-making to improve and expand their dairy operation while protecting the environment. To properly plan for their future, an assessment was made of the environmental conditions surrounding and impacting their farm. GIS diagrams were prepared to indicate the types of information that were assembled, ending with a schematic design recommendation that was utilized to develop the long-range plan.

The 5-year plan represents a close approximation of what the Jennissen family is currently planning to do, but with improvements to land-cover management, including naturalized areas along with perennial and annual crop fields to eliminate runoff into the creek. The 10-year plan (Figure 6.14) outlined several options they are interested in, including eco-tourism, and, depending on decisions by one or more of the daughters to enter the family business, the plan illustrated how they could expand from 60 cows to 500. The study illustrated how rural design can create viable options for expanding a small family-owned dairy farm while protecting nearby neighbors and the environment from adverse impacts.

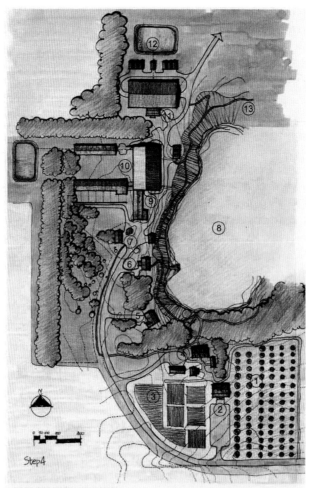

**6.14**
Strategic Master Plan
proposed for the Jennissen
Dairy Farm in Stearns County,
providing options for
expanding the dairy from 60
cows to 500, with related
value-adding features.

**Step4**

## JENNISSEN FARM
**1.** APPLE ORCHARD  **2.** MARKET  **3.** COMMUNITY SUPPORTED
AGRICULTURE FIELDS  **4.** NEW HOUSE FOR PARENTS  **5.** POTENTIAL
HOUSE FOR DAUGHTER  **6.** POTENTIAL HOUSE FOR DAUGHTER
**7.** EXISTING HOUSE AS OFFICE  **8.** EXISTING LAKE  **9.** EXISTING 60
COW BARN  **10.** STEP ONE: INCREASE TO 250 COWS  **11.** STEP TWO:
INCREASE TO 500 COWS  **12.** METHANE DIGESTER  **13.** TRAIL FOR
ECO-TOURISM

## *Lessons learned*

The most interesting aspect was to discover that the study, since it was being
funded by the CRD, was not taken seriously by the people involved. They were
very interested in participating and finding out what the CRD had to say, but when
it came to the next step to follow up on suggestions, most backed away. The lesson
learned is that people must have a financial investment in a rural design project
in order to become stakeholders and buy in to the product from the study. The
project did have a good outcome anyway, because it opened the door to several

other CRD research projects with the Minnesota Milk Producers Association as components of their Environmental Quality Assurance Program.

## Strategies learned

Rural design can be very effective at a wide range of scales, as long as the data are available to analyze and digitally represent in maps. Each state has its own methodology to collect and represent data and often the systems do not cross state boundaries. There should be a data standard that all states or provinces in North America should comply with in order to accomplish cross-jurisdictional planning when environmental and other issues cross state lines or national boundaries. For example: looking at both sides of the Mississippi River when it is the boundary between states, to study local food supply; or issues impacting fresh water quality in the Great Lakes involving multiple watersheds, a number of individual states, and internationally with Canada.

## Epilogue

The CRD has learned that the Jennissen family did move forward with an expansion of their farm, but not quite as it had been recommended by the study, and have had some problems with manure handling. They have started some of the other recommendations for agritourism and community-supported agriculture by planting an apple orchard, and are continuing to function as a growing dairy farm even in difficult economic times.

*Design team: CRD staff included Dewey Thorbeck, Thora Cartlidge, Steve Roos, and Wesley Hellevik, and as collaborators the Department of Applied Economics, Department of Biosystems and Agricultural Engineering, and the Minnesota Department of Agriculture.*

## Rural conflict: Visualizing Offset – identifying and analyzing the spatial relationships between feedlot odor and residential dwellings (2006)

Rural Minnesota has undergone continual change since its beginnings, with the immigration of mostly European settlers seeking to recreate the agricultural landscape of their homelands. Even though generally dominated by agricultural land uses, farms, and small towns servicing agriculture, the changes were stimulated by technology-enhanced farming practices which increased productivity while decreasing labor. As technology developed further, productivity became tied to the large-scale application of those technologies, fostering consolidation of individual farms into large operations that could take advantage of the economies of scale and reduction in the diversity of operation types and products.

During the last few decades, advances in technology have also fostered other land-use changes in the rural landscape. For example, improvements in transportation and communication technologies have made it increasingly feasible to work from home. This change, combined with other factors – like an aging population with retirees wanting to live in rural areas – has led to an increasing number of non-farm rural residents without strong cultural or knowledge connection to agricultural industries. These new residents often hold different cultural expectation about what rural life should be as compared to traditional farm families. The difference in cultural expectations increases the potential for conflict between neighbors (Figure 6.15).

Some complaints from new residents focus on farming practices, such as environmental concerns over fertilizer and pesticide applications or manure handling. Others focus on the externalities of farming, such as farm equipment on roadways, noise from livestock and machinery, or odor from feedlots or manure application to fields. While these aspects of farming are fundamental to its nature as a business (and often not significantly hazardous to the environment or human health) they do form the basis for the majority of conflicts in the rural landscape. In this project the focus was on odor and its impact on urban areas, as well as nearby non-farm residential development in a rural area.

6.15
Image from the Offset study, illustrating the spatial relationship between animal agriculture and residential dwellings and the potential conflict over odor when the farmer wants to expand the number of animals on his farm.

Figure 6.16 illustrates the potential for feedlot odor to impact residential dwellings at various distances, expressed as concentric rings (Roos *et al.*, 2007). The data used for this project were based on an 'Offset' model (Odor from Feedlot Setback Estimation Tool) developed by the Department of Biosystems and Agricultural Engineering at the University of Minnesota (Jacobson *et al.*, 2001). It was an outgrowth of their earlier work on air quality emissions to improve the siting of feedlots in Minnesota (Jacobson *et al.*, 1998). When a non-farm residential dwelling had an odor-annoyance-free rating of 99% it was very unlikely to complain, however if it was at 95% or 91% the frequency of complaints would increase. As such, the Offset model only provides a mechanism to help livestock farmers determine the conflicts they might have with their neighbors due to odor from feedlots.

Rural design can provide an understanding of the nature and extent of current land-use change and predict its future course. And, to a great extent, it can act as a mediator in conflicts between rural residents with different values. However, the best application of rural design is in guiding land-use change through the development and implementation of land-use plans that accommodate varying perspectives of divergent resident groups.

**6.16**
Offset diagram assessing impacts on urban areas, illustrating feedlots and buffer zones ranging from 91% to 99% odor-annoyance-free in relationship to small town and residential dwellings.

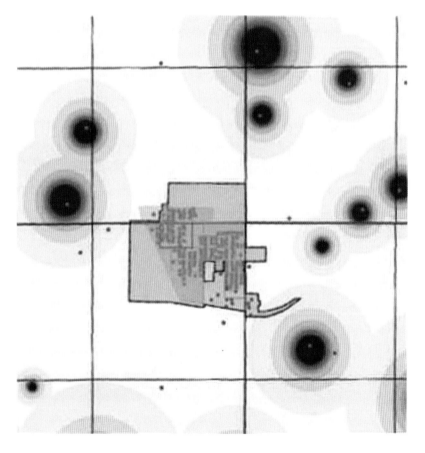

In order to achieve this, rural designers require tools that will allow them to analyze the potential for, predict the extent of, and come to some resolution over issues – and avoid, or at least mitigate, potential conflict. 'Offset' is such a tool and was created to estimate average odor impacts from a variety of animal facilities and manure storages. The model identifies suitable buffer distances from sources of manure odor, based on a variety of conditions and is intended to suit desired levels of odor-annoyance avoidance.

The project was organized into four tasks:

1.  Generating buffers based on Offset distances for different levels of odor-annoyance-free frequency. The setback (buffer) distances for each feedlot based on current conditions (animal numbers, facility size and type, climate data) and the expected degree of odor impact stated in terms of percentage of odor-annoyance-free days, ranging from 91% to 99%. These conditions are joined, using GIS mapping technology, to illustrate the odor-annoyance-free setbacks for the various percentages.

2.  Selecting an appropriate residential dwelling dataset, to examine the spatial relationships between the odor impact of feedlots and the places where people live in a township or county. This involved collecting data from township and county surveys to locate land-cover types that include urban and industrial areas, farmsteads and rural residences, rural residential development complexes, and other rural developments. The Offset program digitizes the information and illustrates buffer distances ranging from 91% to 99% odor-annoyance-free from each residential unit in the township or county.

3.  Identifying residences with the Offset buffers. The program uses GIS software packages and ArcMap to provide an overview of the residential selection process.

4.  Interpreting the analysis and answering questions specific to the community. Historically, land-use planning has been the process to avoid the impact of externalities from one land use on another land use. In this case the use of zoning to control the spatial relationship does not work when conflicting land uses are adjacent to each other. Offset, combined with GIS software, provides rural designers and policymakers with a set of tools to deal with the perplexing issue of odor in rural areas.

## Lessons learned

Integrating the Offset model into GIS technology is a methodology to explore the spatial relationships between rural residential locations and livestock farms. It can be a useful tool for rural land-use planners to assess the relationships and support the creation of appropriate policy and ordinances. The spatial relationships between animal agriculture and residential dwellings can now be analyzed, and conflicts avoided.

### Strategies learned

Research projects that are meant to inform rural citizens are not as effective if the citizens are not involved. Moving the Offset model into a digital visual format could be very helpful to livestock farmers who are considering expanding or constructing new animal facilities, but they have to have the technology and skills to utilize it. GIS is a very effective tool, but it requires computer programs, skills, and experience to use it, and research is required to develop the software so that farmers can use it. GeoDesign is a new research program which the developers of GIS software are launching, and it might be the first step toward making this technology work for farmers.

### Epilogue

Since GIS technology is not generally utilized by farmers, they continue to use an earlier Offset version developed by the University of Minnesota that has a table, based on estimates of average odor impacts from a variety of animal facilities and manure storages, providing a quick and simple calculation of setback distances required from farms at different odor-annoyance-free requirements. It is an example of the technology gap that exists, and even though farmers utilize the computer, the mapping systems are not yet common.

*Design team: CRD staff included Steve Roos and Tracey Kinney, and staff from the Department of Biosystems and Agricultural Engineering, Larry Jacobson, David Schmidt, and Susan Wood.*

## Rural environmental protection: Environmental practices on dairy farms – protecting the environment while protecting the dairy industry (2003)

The 'Environmental practices on dairy farms' project is the product of an initiative by the Minnesota Milk Producers Association to coalesce and build upon previous work done at the CRD related to the definition and spatial modeling of the Resource Protection Framework for agriculture (Cartlidge *et al.*, 1999) and earlier work on the Odor from Feedlot Setback Estimation Tool: Offset (Jacobson *et al.*, 2001). These two efforts resulted in a broader Environmental Quality Assurance Program which provided technical support and financial assistance to dairy producers that exceeds the level necessary to comply with environmental quality regulations. This effort was an outgrowth of a series of prior projects by the CRD and the Department of Landscape Architecture that sought to define and spatially model a Resource Protection Framework for the agricultural landscape using GIS technology. That work focused on spatially modeling: (a) habitat quality and diversity; (b) susceptibility of surface and ground water to contamination; and (c) the distribution of rural non-farm land uses.

That work also began examining the feasibility and constraints of applying the assessment across scales – essentially, attempting to apply regional-scale assessment to farm-scale design. There were other related projects which had determined that the externalities of manure handling were the primary source of potential conflict with other rural land uses. Both the rate and spatial extent of land-use change had accelerated dramatically and with it a growing understanding of ecological function and a greater appreciation for environmental quality and the environmental impacts of human use of the land. As a result, new regulations by both the state and local governments were enacted with new feedlot rules governing the management of animal manure, including dairy farms. The regulation extended to the storage, transportation, disposal, and utilization of animal manure with the primary intent of protecting the environment.

## Conceptual framework

Recognizing the impact the regulations would have on the dairy industry, the Minnesota Milk Producers Association chose to take a proactive approach to assisting dairy producers respond to the new rules. This applied research study was centered in one region in the state (central Minnesota) and one county (Wright) as an example of how to keep animal agriculture as an economically viable, socially productive, and environmentally responsible component of the rural landscape. The study was structured around four priority areas: (1) surface water; (2) ground water; (3) habitat; and (4) social sensitivity. The intent of the project was to combine these into a fifth priority area: Environmental Quality Assurance, as illustrated by Figure 6.17.

It is important to recognize that givens were acknowledged and assumptions made in terms of the GIS data and methodology, and that all priority areas would be the same:

- All data had to be pre-existing;
- All data had to be publicly available;
- All data must exist across the state;
- All data must be uniform in structure;
- The methodology would be widely applicable and replicable;
- Printed reproductions would be at a scale no larger than approximately 1:60,000.

The purpose was to create a uniform and simplified methodology that could be

Methodology diagram
illustrating protection
zones, focusing on one farm
within the township, for
environmental practices on
Minnesota dairy farms.

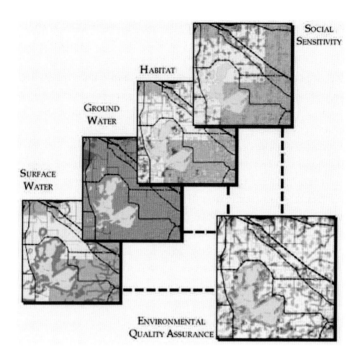

used throughout the state, and to provide usefully accurate results across varying regions and landscape conditions.

The five priority models using GIS were developed as follows:

- Surface water – with two subcomponents of Shoreland and Special protection.
- Ground water – with three subcomponents of Aquifers and wells, Depth to bedrock, and Overburden permeability.
- Habitat – with four subcomponents of Habitat size, Core forest, Coincidence, and Disturbance.
- Social sensitivity – focusing on a selected level of odor (94% annoyance-free) from livestock feedlots as defined by Offset at places of human habitation – primarily areas of residential development and recreation.
- The Environmental Quality Assurance model sums up the ratings of the other four areas into a combined model.

## Technical framework

This part of the project involved an inventory of both physical and cultural features and the various spatial relationships that exist between them. GIS was used as a tool to collect, store, analyze, manipulate, and display geographic data. This allowed the conceptual model to be converted into a digital model, which could be replicated and partially automated for multiple study areas throughout the state.

This process has three primary sections: (1) data selection and collection to choose appropriate datasets that met or exceeded project criteria, and preparing them for processing, involving geological, hydrologic, political, land-cover, topographic, and transportation issues; (2) data analysis and manipulation, involving converting the conceptual model in a series of macro programs that could manipulate and analyze the initial datasets using the four priority areas identified in the conceptual model; and (3) information display and dissemination within both a traditional paper-based cartographic layout and a web-based interactive environment, with sets of maps covering land use/land cover, each of the four priority components, and a combined priority map at both farm scale and county scale.

The overall goal of the technical process was to replicate the conceptual model of the 'Environmental practices on dairy farms' project as closely as possible and display its results in a visual format that could be used and understood by a variety of users.

## Atlas

An Atlas was prepared to provide a representation of the paper-based cartographic production associated with the project. Wright County was chosen for this purpose, with maps at both county scale and farm scale. The county-scale maps showed:

* Standard geographic features;
* Special protection areas;
* Surface water priority;
* Depth to bedrock;
* Ground water priority;
* Core forest;
* Presettlement/current land cover coincidence;
* Social sensitivity priority;
* Environmental Quality Assurance priority (Figure 6.18);
* Refined land use/land cover;
* Shoreland protection zone;
* Relative overburden permeability;
* Aquifers and wells;
* Habitat areas, classed by size;
* Human disturbance regime;
* Habitat priority.

**6.18**
Diagram of the Environmental
Quality Assurance Pri- for a
single dairy farm ('Pri-' refers
to environmental priority area
classification) as an example of
how the program can work.

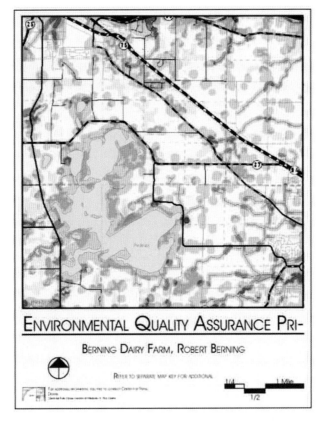

ENVIRONMENTAL QUALITY ASSURANCE PRI-

BERNING DAIRY FARM, ROBERT BERNING

REFER TO SEPARATE MAP KEY FOR ADDITIONAL

1/4          1 Mile

1/2

### Lessons learned

Rural design is a process for transitioning rural-oriented scientific research to
society. It can translate research data through computer visualization to make
complex issues understandable to citizens as well as farmers and regulatory
agencies.

*Design team: CRD staff included Steve Roos and Wesley Hellevik, David Pitt from the
Department of Landscape Architecture, Chris Hanson Design Solutions, and the
Department of Biosystems and Agricultural Engineering.*

## Designing for wellness: Isanti County Parks and
## Recreation Plan (2007–2008)

Isanti County is one of many counties that sit outside, but adjacent to, the
metropolitan area of Minneapolis and St Paul. It is a county that experienced
rapid growth throughout the 1990s, with a number of new housing developments on farm lands. A parks plan had been prepared in 1970, and then updated

in 1995 to define a framework for the identification and process of parkland acquisition.

In 2006, the CRD worked on a trails project with Isanti County Active Living, a citizen group that is part of Active Living by Design, a national advocacy group for the enhancement of built environments which seeks to integrate healthy living choices. The trails study was part of a larger wellness analysis for the county that was funded by the Robert Woods Johnson Foundation, and the CRD worked with a citizen steering committee to identify a major north-south trail that would connect with new and existing development on the eastern side of the county, which was experiencing the largest influx of new homes and businesses.

The trail plan included public workshops, questionnaires and web-based community engagement into the planning process, and focused on connections between the cities of Isanti, Cambridge, and Braham, and park properties. The intent of the plan was to promote utilization of outdoor environments for recreation and exercise as a way to improve wellness and public health. It identified the following goals for integrating physical activity into daily life:

- Develop and maintain partnerships to promote physical activity;
- Increase community awareness of the health and other benefits of active living;
- Increase access to and availability of diverse opportunities for physical activity;
- Enhance policy and organizational supports for physical activity;
- Improve manmade and natural environments to support active living.

A natural outgrowth of the trails planning project was the formation of a joint partnership between the Isanti County Parks and Recreation Commission and Isanti County Active Living group to develop a community and administrative vision for a parks and recreation plan for the entire county. This joint effort recognized the similar interests in recreation and public space, with the intent to integrate trails and parklands into a comprehensive and connected parks and recreation system for Isanti County. This planning work, again with the CRD providing design assistance, commenced in 2007 with the Isanti County Community Steering Committee leading the project.

Preservation of Isanti County's significant rural landscape areas is critical to providing clean air and water for future generations. The county is among the first ring of counties that surround the seven-county metropolitan area (Figure 6.19), and at the time of the study was experiencing higher than average rates of development, especially in its southern parts, nearest the metropolitan area. Isanti County's population and social economic data were an important aspect of the planning process. Census projections suggested that the county would experience a 35% population growth by 2030. Also, as in other regions, the population is getting older.

6.19
Location map of Isanti County
in relationship to the Twin
Cities metropolitan area. Isanti
County is adjacent to, but
outside the seven-county area.

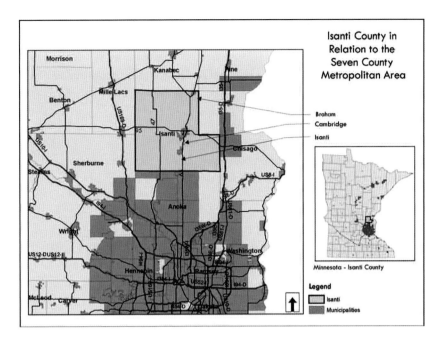

Typically, rural areas urbanize at lower densities and consume large areas of land in contrast to urban areas that develop more compactly, utilize less land, and are generally tied to available metropolitan water and sewer infrastructure. In rural areas the developments can be quite sporadic and are often not connected to sewer or water systems. This kind of development was threatening the county's significant rural landscape which was so critical to providing clean air and water for future generations. As such, rural development has a greater impact on the rural landscape and the early parks plan identified strategies for land acquisition and development to preserve and protect the Rum River, natural areas, and farmland.

The geography of the county also impacted planning decisions. It is located within the Anoka Sand Plain, which is the result of outwash from glacier melt steams that left sediment and sand in their wakes, providing well-drained soil conditions and, in some cases, sand dunes. The county resides within two biomes: the Laurentian Mixed Forest and the Eastern Broad Leaf Forest. The biomes provide a glimpse into the pre-settlement vegetation communities of well-drained and wet forest to oak savanna plant communities. The county's rolling topography is due to the major watersheds of the Upper Mississippi River and the St Croix River Basin.

Isanti County's parkland holdings total approximately 835 acres and provide a range of low-impact activities, from public water access to hiking and biking. The parkland is dispersed, allowing accessibility to residents in all four quadrants of the county. The question of how much parkland would be needed for the growing population was important and there is little research in the field of rural parkland needs. Several factors had to be considered including:

- Will current patterns for acquisition of parkland continue into the future?
- If not, how can the County determine the amount of parkland needed for the future population and preservation efforts?

The Metropolitan Council's guideline for parkland is 25 acres per 1,000 people, and to preserve natural areas and rural image it became the guiding principle for the project. In 2000 the county had 18 acres per 1,000 people, but with the growing population it was predicted to drop to 13 acres per 1,000 by the year 2030, if no new land was added. This issue determined that approximately 700 additional acres need to be added to the park system.

Public engagement was important to the development of the master plan for parks and recreation, and public workshops were being utilized in the Active Living by Design trails study and continued here for the county parks project. The Active Living by Design study had looked at recreation opportunities and facilities from a specific point of view: 'to support healthy lifestyles through physical activity, both recreational activity and normal daily activity.' Therefore it was proposed that both planning efforts should be conducted in tandem, to facilitate a cohesive vision for the parks plan and trail system, with the following goals:

1. Develop and maintain an effective partnership to promote physical activity;
2. Increase community awareness of the health and other benefits of active living;
3. Increase access to and availability of diverse opportunities for physical activity;
4. Enhance policy and organizational supports for physical activity;
5. Improve manmade and natural environments to support active living.

The public engagement process began with the formation of the steering committee, which organized the work into three phases: a research phase, a documentation phase, and an analysis phase (Figure 6.20). The Steering Committee included a diverse group of community members of the Parks and Recreation Commission, County Commissioners, Township boards, local organizations, and citizens at large. The role of the Steering Committee was to provide insight and guidance to the CRD for the Parks and Recreation Plan.

The research phase included four Steering Committee meetings, an inventory of the natural and rural character of the county, and a public workshop. The documentation phase included information gathered from the first phase, meetings with the Steering Committee, administrative questionnaires, and a second public workshop. The analysis phase assimilated information from the first two phases into a draft master plan which was presented to the Parks and Recreation Commission and County Commissioners for review and approval.

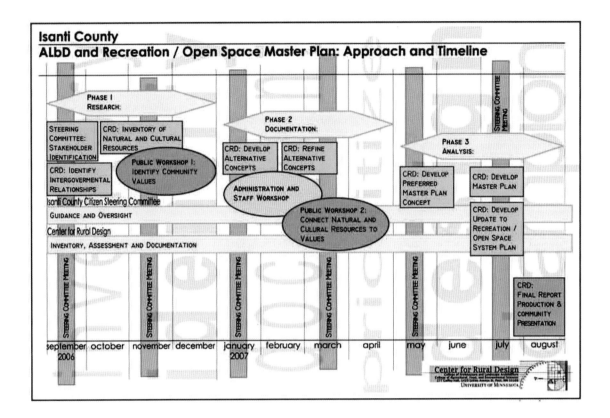

## Isanti County
## ALbD and Recreation / Open Space Master Plan: Approach and Timeline

PHASE 1
RESEARCH:

PHASE 2
DOCUMENTATION:

PHASE 3
ANALYSIS:

| STEERING COMMITTEE: STAKEHOLDER IDENTIFICATION | CRD: INVENTORY OF NATURAL AND CULTURAL RESOURCES |

PUBLIC WORKSHOP I: IDENTIFY COMMUNITY VALUES

CRD: IDENTIFY INTERGOVERMENTAL RELATIONSHIPS

CRD: DEVELOP ALTERNATIVE CONCEPTS

CRD: REFINE ALTERNATIVE CONCEPTS

ADMINISTRATION AND STAFF WORKSHOP

CRD: DEVELOP PREFERRED MASTER PLAN CONCEPT

CRD: DEVELOP MASTER PLAN

CRD: DEVELOP UPDATE TO RECREATION / OPEN SPACE SYSTEM PLAN

Isanti County Citizen Steering Committee

GUIDANCE AND OVERSIGHT

Center for Rural Design

INVENTORY, ASSESSMENT AND DOCUMENTATION

PUBLIC WORKSHOP 2: CONNECT NATURAL AND CULURAL RESOURCES TO VALUES

CRD: FINAL REPORT PRODUCTION & COMMUNITY PRESENTATION

STEERING COMMITTEE MEETING

| september october 2006 | november december | january 2007 | february | march | april | may | june | july | august |

Center for Rural Design
University of Minnesota

6.20
The process diagram that illustrated to the Community Steering Committee how the project was going to flow and interconnect with community workshops along the way.

It was determined that the mission of Isanti County in the Parks and Recreation Plan is to maintain, acquire, and/or expand parks that preserve natural areas, provide passive recreation opportunities, strive to maintain the rural character of the county, and promote the health, wellbeing, and quality of life for residents.

The Parks and Recreation Plan defined the wide range of providers: national, state, regional, county, local (school districts, townships, and cities), and private. All of these providers currently function in Isanti County and each has separate, loosely defined roles to perform:

* The US Fish and Wildlife Service, works with landowners to restore prairies and waterways with long-term commitments.
* The Minnesota Department of Natural Resources provides wildlife management areas, water access sites, and state game refuges. In addition, it provides campgrounds and state parks, but currently none exists in Isanti County.
* Isanti County currently has nine park sites and is in the process of making improvements for expanded use.

- Locally, the three cities in Isanti County provide most of the park facilities, with approximately twenty park facilities available for citizen use. The schools also offer recreation for students, but adult and summer recreation programs also utilize schools.
- Private entities most often provide for special needs like golf, tennis, and marinas.

Isanti County contains a substantial number of park and recreation opportunities, including water access sites and snowmobile trails. Some of the properties had plans for public improvements, but collectively they had never been pulled together into an integrated plan. The process included a great deal of public engagement through the steering committee and several public workshops.

The workshops engaged citizens to identify the importance of natural areas that have significant value to support environmental quality and health. These natural areas do not represent pristine wilderness, but rather areas that provide an ecological function somewhat less impacted by human activity, and which need careful consideration in planning for the future.

Citizens also identified areas that have significant scenic value related to the natural areas and farming practices that fundamentally defined the rural landscape. While the perception of rural character can vary between individuals, in general it was defined by the presence of both natural features and agriculture blending into a complex and interesting visual pattern.

The final Isanti County Parks and Bike Path Master Plan (Figure 6.21) represents the blending of the two projects of connecting bike routes with county parkland, based on citizen landscape preferences. As such, the plan reflects the partnership between Isanti County and Isanti County Active Living by Design. The partnership not only provides a representation of the plan and foundation for advancing the planning and implementation of the physical system of designated bikeways and dedicated trails, but also the foundation for a bicycle training and education program that will foster the use of the facilities by residents of the county.

### Lessons learned

The experience in Isanti County clearly illustrates the synergy that is possible when connections are made between parallel efforts to meet a goal. By combining the two projects, the County was able to more fully engage the public into the planning process, and as a result received broad citizen support for land acquisition and trail connections for recreational purposes for the broad demographics of the county.

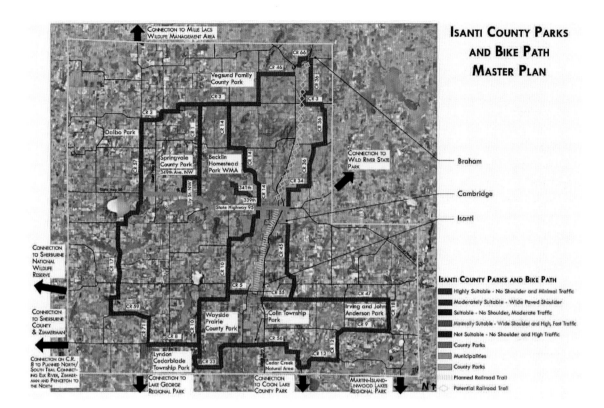

ISANTI COUNTY PARKS AND BIKE PATH

| | |
|---|---|
| ▓ | Highly Suitable - No Shoulder and Minimal Traffic |
| ▓ | Moderately Suitable - Wide Paved Shoulder |
| ▓ | Suitable - No Shoulder, Moderate Traffic |
| ▓ | Minimally Suitable - Wide Shoulder and High, Fast Traffic |
| ▓ | Not Suitable - No Shoulder and High Traffic |
| ▓ | County Parks |
| ▓ | Municipalities |
| ▓ | County Parks |
| | Planned Railroad Trail |
| | Potential Railroad Trail |

**6.21**

The recommended vision plan for the Isanti County Parks and bike paths.

## *Strategies learned*

GIS mapping is critical to the public engagement process for its ability to help citizens understand landscape characteristics and the potentials and opportunities that the natural and agricultural landscapes provide for recreation and active living. As a nation, health is paramount and the promotion of wellness through active outdoor recreation may become an important aspect of quality of life.

*Design team: CRD staff included Steve Roos, Tracey Kinney, and the Steering Committee co-chaired by Bill Carlson and Joe Crocker, with Secretary Maureen Johnson and thirteen citizen members.*

## Rural character: Scott County – defining the rural character of the Detailed Area Plan (2009)

Scott County is one of the seven counties that comprise Minnesota's Twin Cities metropolitan area, and is located on the southern edge, between the central city of Minneapolis and more rural areas to the south (Figure 6.22). Over 2.5 million people live and work in the metropolitan area. Each county and city within the

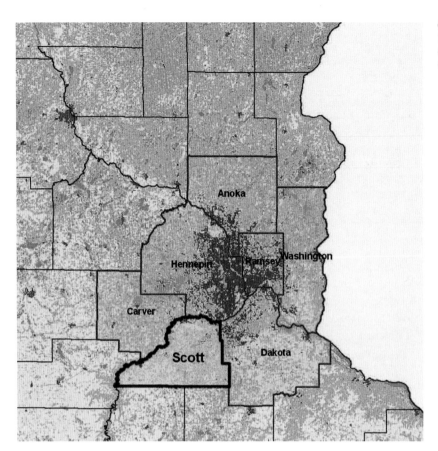

6.22
Location map of Scott County,
one of the seven in the Twin
Cities metropolitan area.

seven counties needs to prepare their own Comprehensive Plan for review and approval of the regional planning body: the Metropolitan Council.

The Detailed Area Plan (DAP) had been designated as 'permanently rural' through a joint study by Scott County and the Metropolitan Council which sought to identify the ultimate service area for projected new regional waste water treatment facilities for residential development in the area in the future. 'Permanently rural' is a land-use designation that allows for residential development such as one house on 10 acres. Depending on how that is done agriculture can be eliminated in the future, but if done a different way it will allow residential development and maintain agricultural production. The DAP was outside the metropolitan service area, but experiencing heavy pressure for new housing developments.

Early in 2008 Scott County received a grant from the McKnight Foundation for a series of projects designed to implement portions of the County's 2030 Comprehensive Plan Update. A significant component of the grant was directed toward initiating the development of a detailed plan for the four townships identified (about one quarter of the Scott Count land base totalling 67 square miles of land). The plan for the DAP was intended to accomplish three basic goals and be accomplished in three phases:

- Phase 1: Identify the rural character of the DAP by gaining broad public support to preserve and protect the environmental/cultural functions of the area, based on the perceptions that residents of the area have of those functions.
- Phase 2: Translate the rural character into an appropriate pattern of development and development types across the DAP with a set of design guidelines and a design pattern book that would guide development toward the most sensitive environmental outcomes while maintaining a character that is attractive to current and future residents.
- Phase 3: Validate the Design Guidelines and Design Pattern Book with the citizens of the DAP through community workshops to solicit input.

In September 2008, the CRD and the Management Team began a collaborative effort to accomplish the goals. The first phase of the project to determine rural character has been completed, but funding is needed to complete the project.

The process for defining rural character had three phases and a schedule that was utilized by the Management Team and the CRD. Phase 1 focused efforts on touring the DAP and organizing detailed spatial data into an inventory of the land, using GIS. Phase 2 included an in-house pre-community workshop meeting, and the public workshop. The pre-workshop meeting was a 'dry run' for the public workshop and included a presentation by the CRD on rural character units, along with two image-preference surveys with residents that lived in the DAP, and a summary of available literature on the potential for innovation for review. The intent of the Rural Character Units Map delineated the DAP into areas with the potential to have different rural character. The result of the mapping was to gain a common understanding of the spatial character of the DAP and begin a conversation about the commonalities and differences.

The image-preference surveys were intended to define citizen perceptions of what is rural and what it is not, and what good rural development is. This phase included the public workshop that was intended to educate the public about the significant design considerations in rural planning that have implications for defining the desired rural character and to gauge the public interest in the significance of rural character in the DAP and gain insight into the kind of guidance necessary to shape that rural character.

Phase 3 of the study entailed the documentation of the public workshop results and production of a report on defining rural character for the DAP. To stimulate discussion, the CRD developed a list of 'Principles of Rural Design' (Figure 6.23) which provided a framework for public discourse about important landscape characteristics and their preservation.

Landscape character is the uniqueness of place that determines the range and nature of the physical elements expressed. These physical elements are the basis for defining the rural character of that place and are referred to as 'character units'. For the Scott County project, GIS maps were prepared and presented, covering land use and land cover, parcel data, and landform.

## Principles of Rural Design

Broader Arrangement of Land Uses in the Rural Landscape
- ❑ Clustered Development with surrounding open space (agriculture, natural resource management and / or natural restoration)
- ❑ Hopscotch v. cohesive patterns of open space
- ❑ Hamlets (public gathering space) providing other types of land uses vs. individual development (private gathering space)

View from the Road
- ❑ Screening new development along roadways (vegetation, berming)
- ❑ Single access points into development v. keyboard plats
- ❑ Deeper setbacks for homes/lots accessed from township roads
- ❑ Parallel trails/shared bike lanes
- ❑ Urban section (curb & gutter) v. rural cross section (ditches)
- ❑ Planning roads along natural area corridors
- ❑ Local street widths and design (linear v. curve)
- ❑ Ridge top and hilltop home and outbuilding development
- ❑ Placement of utilities and towers

Site Landscape Character
- ❑ Smaller arrangment of development communities and open spaces
  - • Small lots – privately owned, communal open space
  - • Large lots – privately owned open space
- ❑ Storm water design (LID)
- ❑ Developing near shore land areas
- ❑ Excessive grading for desired floor plans
- ❑ Screening vs. not screening of utilities and neighbor's houses
- ❑ Manicured v. more natural looking vegetation (use of natives, etc.)

Site Architectural Character
- ❑ Architectural typology (Community Center, farm stead, hamlet, and other 'theme' oriented developments)
- ❑ Architectural style (farm house, ranch house, tudor, rustic, prairie, etc.)
- ❑ Matching outbuildings to principal buildings (color, scale, size, exterior materials)
- ❑ Preservation and reuse of existing farm buildings (barns, silos, coops, etc.)
- ❑ Residential fence types (barb wire, picket, wood)

The integration of all of the information available and responses from participants in the public workshop resulted in a map that defined local rural character for the four townships as expressed by citizens (Figure 6.24). The local rural landscape character types are:

- • Mixed Land Cover in areas designated as rural residential, defining areas that contain a diverse mix of land cover on relatively smaller parcels, indicating a higher level of residential development.
- • Natural Land Cover in areas designated as rural residential, defining areas that are predominately natural in character (woodlands and wetlands) on relatively smaller parcels, indicating a higher level of residential development.

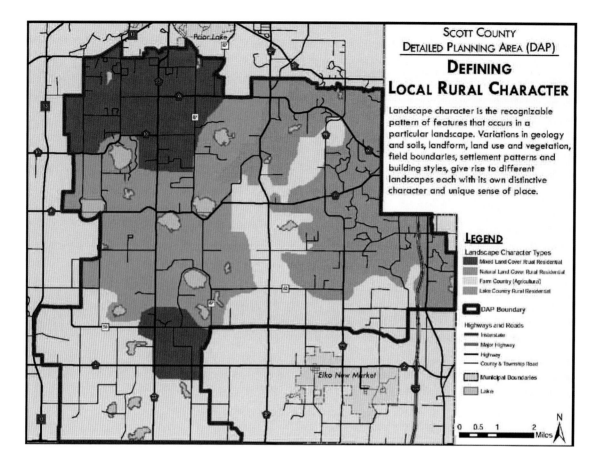

SCOTT COUNTY
DETAILED PLANNING AREA (DAP)

## DEFINING
## LOCAL RURAL CHARACTER

Landscape character is the recognizable pattern of features that occurs in a particular landscape. Variations in geology and soils, landform, land use and vegetation, field boundaries, settlement patterns and building styles, give rise to different landscapes each with its own distinctive character and unique sense of place.

**LEGEND**

Landscape Character Types
- Mixed Land Cover Rural Residential
- Natural Land Cover Rural Residential
- Farm Country (Agricultural)
- Lake Country Rural Residential

DAP Boundary

Highways and Roads
- Interstate
- Major Highway
- Highway
- County & Township Road
- Municipal Boundaries
- Lake

0   0.5   1        2
                    Miles

N

6.24
Integrated rural character map for the four township planning area, defining local perceptions of landscape characteristics.

- Farm Country (agricultural) defining areas that are predominantly agriculture on somewhat larger parcels.
- Lake Country in areas designated as rural residential, defining areas distinguished by the presence of several significant lakes, along with a somewhat high level of residential development.

An important aspect of the first stage of the project was an image-preference survey, where participants were asked to review a number of images and identify their preferences in three exercises:

Exercise 1.   What is rural? Identifying characteristics of the land and its housing and other development to clarify what, in the participants' opinion, is 'rural'.

Exercise 2.   What is rural in each character unit? Within the DAP, identifying what are the most important aspects of each character unit.

Exercise 3.   Which principles of rural design are already evident in the detailed planning area and which need more attention to make them evident?

(This exercise also identified ways that planning and design guide-lines could be useful in directing future development in the detailed planning area.)

As indicated previously, funding was only available for Phase 1, leaving the four townships dangling as to their future. Phase 2 would result in a set of design guidelines and a design pattern book that would serve to steer development toward the most sensitive environmental outcomes, while maintaining a character that is attractive to current and future residents; and Phase 3 would validate the Design Guidelines and Design Pattern Book with the citizens of the DAP through an open house to solicit input.

## Lessons learned

Although obvious that all phases of a project need to be completed before a con-clusion and work product can be prepared, the outcome of the first phase provided public education about the issues of rural character and how it is defined. Public participation is essential to have a planning product that truly reflects citizen values. Some of the things learned include:

- The process for public participation needs to be more refined and improved. Asking value-based questions is critical to guide decision making, and the type of questions is critical to acquiring meaningful answers. Balancing public education and public input is an important consideration and it is only through the process that balance can be achieved.
- More dialogue is necessary to develop a reasonable consensus on the definition of rural character and the citizen values it embodies. A wider cross-section of residents and representatives from affected jurisdictions and the development sector is needed to define the key character issues that need to be preserved.
- The design guidelines need to reflect citizen values to provide the confidence needed to make decisions that impact land planning, land management, and design that support rural character. These can be devel-oped as alternative development scenarios that meet the goals of the guidelines while providing flexibility to meet changing future conditions and economies.

Ultimately, the community's own definition of rural character is the single and most important part of its preservation. Each community must decide what its rural character is and, subsequently, what should be preserved and how devel-opment should take place. Rural design is a community-based planning process that works well in addressing cross-border land-use issues.

*Epilogue*

In 2010, the CRD and Scott County submitted a new proposal to the McKnight Foundation to complete the project, and to do it in a way such that it is a model for other townships on the fringes of the built-up metropolitan area that want to preserve their rural character. Unfortunately, funding was not provided and other sources are being sought.

*Design team: CRD staff included Dewey Thorbeck, Steve Roos, and Tracey Kinney, working with staff of Scott County planning, parks and natural resources, transportation, and environmental health; and supervisors representing the four townships of Spring Lake, Cedar Lake, New Market, and Credit River.*

## Rural town scale: Community of the City of Morris – creating a vision and reuse plan for the elementary school site (2006)

In the fall of 2005 a new elementary school facility was opened on a different site in Morris, bringing to a close the long history of education at the historic Morris Elementary School complex. The old property included a 17.7 acre site that would be the single largest redevelopment project within the historic portion of the original Morris town site. Today Morris is a community of nearly 5,000 people, including the students and faculty connected with the University of Minnesota campus which is located there. In 2004, the University of Minnesota Morris, led by the Center for Small Towns and in partnership with the City of Morris, initiated a broad-reaching project called 'Adapting to Change: Managing Urbanization in Rural America', funded by a grant from the Community Outreach Partnership Centers program of the US Department of Housing and Urban Development. Exploring the future of the elementary school site (Figure 6.25) was one component of that project, and the CRD was selected to assist in that component.

The historic school (Figure 6.26) was constructed in 1914 in a Craftsman-style building to house public elementary and high school classes. In 2001 the building and several additions in 1934 and 1949 were determined to be eligible for the National Register of Historic Places, and the school was listed as one of the most endangered historic preservation sites in Minnesota.

The MDT had provided a weekend design charrette in October 2005 (similar to the one they did with the CRD and the City of Roseau), and it served the purpose of identifying the social, cultural, and physical character of the city, defining the opportunities and challenges the city was facing, and a broad look at ways to address the issues. A particularly significant outcome of the three-day visit and charrette was the creation of a Citizen Action Team specifically to focus on reuse of the elementary school site, and this team became the steering committee that the CRD worked closely with.

6.25
Aerial map of the City of
Morris, showing the historic
elementary school site and
its relationship to the rest of
the city. The map shows the
shifted street pattern of the city
from typical north-south
layouts.

The elementary school site is located in the heart of the city, with strong connections to the community on all sides. The opportunity to reuse the site could significantly improve the character of a large portion of the city and have a positive impact on the daily lives of the residents living in the surrounding neighborhoods. The steering committee developed a list of criteria that should be explored in the development of alternative scenarios and the selection of the preferred plan. These included:

•   Preserve and reuse the historic 1914 school building and the 1934 audi-
    torium. Redevelopment of the buildings should be dedicated to a mix of

uses, including residential, business incubator, public offices, social services, and non-profit organizations.

- Preserve and enhance public open space to include uses most compatible with uses on the rest of the site and the surrounding neighborhood. A public pool could be a compatible use with careful site location and adequate landscape buffering; and provide pedestrian linkages to other parks, University of Minnesota, and downtown business area.
- Develop lifecycle housing that would fill the needs of cross-generational, small-scale, affordable, and quality-housing niche markets, that employs sustainable design and building practices, and architecturally blends with the surrounding neighborhoods.
- Reserve open space for cemetery expansion, which will reinforce the sense of history and social institution within the neighborhood, while providing additional quiet open space on the site.
- Direct the conceptual design of the entire site toward becoming a demonstration site for the application of sustainable design practices in rural communities.

The project started with a community workshop to respond to alternative scenarios. The results of the workshop were then organized into most important issues, moderately important, and least important. These were further defined as opportunities for economic development (such as housing and a business incubator) and opportunities for public/private/academic partnerships (such as public agencies using space and promoting private sector utilization of the site to attract outside investment while maintaining the rural town character and values of the community). These were diagrammed as site givens, illustrating: (a) pedestrian connections between downtown and the university campus; (b) intersecting grids of the Morris street grid; (c) preserving land for the cemetery; and (d) preserving the historic buildings. All design work by the CRD that followed was developed around those givens.

As the planning proceeded, three scenarios were developed and reviewed with the steering committee. Each responded to the criteria outlined above and to diagrams prepared by the steering committee, but placed different emphasis on different elements. For example open space was indicated with more or less active functions (including the swimming pool); different housing types ranging from single-family to rental apartments; and different reuses of the historic buildings. The preferred site organization, selected by the steering committee, was an outcome of the public workshop and defined the four precincts for development: Historic Building Complex Precinct, Multi-Generational Housing Precinct, City Park/Open Space Precinct, and Cemetery Precinct.

The resulting Vision and Reuse Plan for the Morris Area Elementary School Site (Figure 6.27) illustrates the precinct idea and the preferred scenario selected by the steering committee and validated by the public workshop. The major focus of the planning effort was to create synergistic relationships between the City of Morris, University of Minnesota, and Stevens County to enhance aesthetics, economic development, environmental health, quality of life, and tourism for the City of Morris and the larger region.

The project approach sought to integrate community input and the planning process with the explicit goal to produce a Vision and Reuse Plan for the Morris Area Elementary School Site. The CRD functioned both as facilitator during workshop sessions and as planner. The steering committee was created to ensure that public engagement was adequately handled, to provide guidance to the CRD and to become the Reuse Action Team to function as a champion for the project after the visioning process.

The project approach consisted of an integral planning and community participation process meaning that the relationship of planning and participation was inseparable and synergistic. The final plan report included Sustainable Design Guidelines for the development that: (a) was affordable; (b) maintained rural community quality of life; (c) protected the environment; (d) protected the surrounding agricultural landscape as the defining feature of the rural community; and (e) made financial sense. The report also included more detailed plans for each of the precincts, to demonstrate the potential of each for redevelopment meeting the criteria established by the steering committee and the community.

### Lessons learned

The project illustrates how a rural community can focus on one of its assets to try and enhance the region's economic development, environmental health, quality

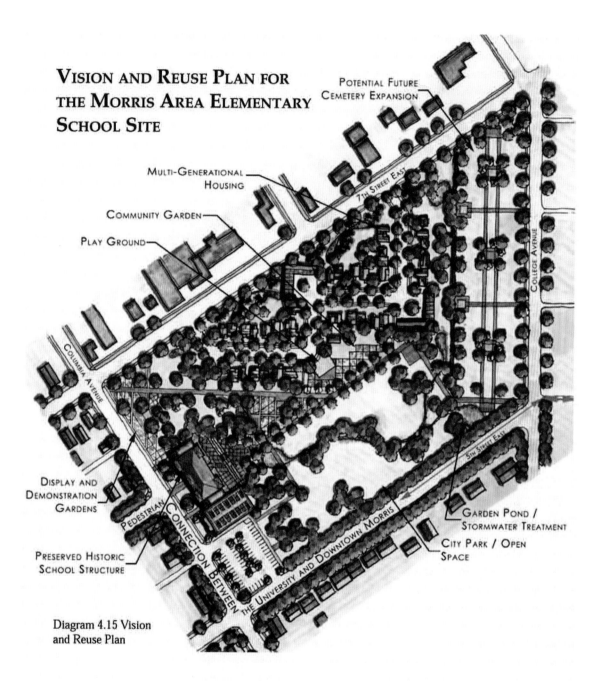

## VISION AND REUSE PLAN FOR THE MORRIS AREA ELEMENTARY SCHOOL SITE

POTENTIAL FUTURE CEMETERY EXPANSION

MULTI-GENERATIONAL HOUSING

COMMUNITY GARDEN

PLAY GROUND

7TH STREET EAST

COLLEGE AVENUE

COLUMBIA AVENUE

5TH STREET EAST

DISPLAY AND DEMONSTRATION GARDENS

PEDESTRIAN CONNECTION BETWEEN THE UNIVERSITY AND DOWNTOWN MORRIS

PRESERVED HISTORIC SCHOOL STRUCTURE

GARDEN POND / STORMWATER TREATMENT

CITY PARK / OPEN SPACE

Diagram 4.15 Vision and Reuse Plan

6.27

The Vision and Reuse Plan for the elementary school site, developed with a citizen steering committee.

of life, tourism, and social and cultural values. The community-based planning process worked very well to create linkages between the University of Minnesota Morris, City of Morris, and Stevens County, and the vision plan played a central role as the City continued to seek out opportunities for reuse of the elementary school site. The project helped identify the region as a welcoming integrated community and location for research and business development, based on agriculture and renewable energy. Even though there was very strong community support for reuse of the historic property, economic circumstances can change, forcing different scenarios to be investigated. The lesson learned is that community determination and persistence in realizing the vision is critical to long-term success. If the vision was prepared with the community, and has strong support, the vision can guide the development process. If intention is achieved – even if the manifestation is different – it will be a successful community endeavor.

## *Epilogue*

Following completion of the vision and reuse plan for the site, the community moved forward with a number of development opportunities. These efforts included relocating the city hall to the historic school; community efforts for a new swimming pool; looking at demonstration affordable and sustainable housing on the entire site if the historic buildings were removed; and seeking out a rule change by the US Department of Agriculture to allow for an entrepreneurial initiative on the site that could be a model for rural areas. None of these efforts has yet become successful, however, and with the current economic recession the Reuse Action Team has not met since the spring of 2009. In an update on what has happened, one of the members of the steering committee, David Fluegel, recently stated:

> Many scenarios for the future of the school property are possible, with the two most likely (from my view) being: First, Morris does have a history of entrepreneur development. The City will eventually get enough money to plan the property and will figure out how to move forward with their plan to complete the initial development and sell the remaining lots to a developer, with eco-friendly planning and zoning covenants in place. The second scenario is that the City will not have money to invest in this project and will grow weary of the maintenance and insurance costs and eventually be pressured to view the property as an unwanted liability, selling it to the highest bidder. My nervous hopes are with the first scenario.

Time will tell. The linkages between the university, city, and county that have been created through this project may be the most important impact of the project.

*Design team: CRD staff included Dewey Thorbeck, Steve Roos, and Tracey Kinney, along with graduate assistants Nathan Burt and Andy Schilling; Center for Small Towns included David Fluegel and Joseph Basel; and the Reuse Action Team was chaired by Sue Dieter and included fifteen Morris citizens.*

## Empowering rural communities: Digital Town – helping rural communities get on the map (2010–2011)

Google Earth has brought mapping and way-finding to a new level that is powerful for identifying and understanding community assets in the built and natural environment. It provides an opportunity for online community visibility, community asset identification, and planning, including economic development and tourism. The Digital Town project, currently underway, is a joint effort of the CRD, School of Architecture, and Extension Educators who are experienced in rural community engagement. It seeks to build social capital by exposing community leaders to social, cultural, environmental, and online tools. Also, it will strengthen the community's institutional capacity by providing an online presence. The project has several goals:

- Enable participants to identify, model, and map community social, cultural, and environmental assets.
- Build social capital within the community across all age groups, with special emphasis on young adults.
- Educate participants and community members in the value of community identity and online exposure.
- Foster historic and cultural preservation of places and institutions.
- Empower the community to seek opportunities for economic development, including increased tourism.
- Develop a cohesive and tested training program that can be replicated with future communities.

The Digital Town project involves three rural Minnesota partnership communities which will be selected through a competitive application process intended to identify broad community buy-in and readiness to engage in the process. Each community will have a four-session training program developed, piloted, refined, and re-piloted over a two-year timeframe. In the first year the design team will engage with one community to develop and pilot the initial training curricula, incorporating feedback from reviews by Extension staff. The curricula will then be re-piloted with the other two communities in succession, to allow for additional refinement between each training session.

The project will result in a documented and replicable curriculum for the training program and be published in a final report which could provide the basis for peer-reviewed publication. It is expected that the short-term success of Digital Town is how it impacts community actions, including skills, behavior, practices, policies, and decision making. This will be measured by qualitative before-and-after surveys, interviews, and feedback from project participants.

Participants will develop skills in creating three-dimensional models (Figure 6.28) using Google SketchUp, and place their three-dimensional models into Google Earth, with the goal that this will assist their communities economically, environmentally, socially, and civically.

### Lessons learned

The design process is rapidly becoming more and more understood as providing a very valid and cohesive approach to integrating issues. For rural regions it can bring a whole range of skills to bear on the resolution of an issue, but also in the process it can provide training to rural people to develop skills by which they can analyze their community and create three-dimensional images of potential changes to guide development.

*Design team: CRD staff included Dewey Thorbeck, Steve Roos, and Tracey Kinney, working with Lee Anderson, Associate Professor of Architecture with extensive experience in graphics software; and Extension Educators, Neil Linscheid and Adeel Ahmed.*

### Urban/rural edge: Concept master plan for Vermillion Highlands (2008–2009)

Vermillion Highlands – a 2,840-acre parcel located on the southern side of UMore Park – was established in 2006 by the Minnesota Legislature. UMore Park (UMore

6.28
An example of the kind of three-dimensional imagery expected to be an outcome of the Digital Town project that can be used by rural communities.

stands for University of Minnesota Outreach, Research, and Education) is a project to design and build a new sustainable community of 30,000 people based on the academic mission (education, research, and public engagement) of a land-grant university. The Vermillion Highlands land was sold by the University of Minnesota to the State Department of Natural Resources (DNR) for partial funding of a new football stadium on the Minneapolis Campus. The site is designated as a research, recreation, and modified wildlife management area (Figure 6.29) which balances three elements: university research, education, and public engagement; public access for diverse, high-quality recreation; and wildlife management and hunting.

The legislative report outlined a relationship between the University and DNR along with Dakota County and its effort to establish a regional park. Later, Empire Township was invited to become a member of the steering committee. In October 2007 the steering committee selected the CRD to develop a concept master plan for the property and adjacent proposed park. The plan was intended to reflect the unified sustainability goals of the three participants and their individual interests. It established a contemporary vision for how Vermillion Highlands will be managed, used, and improved, along with an implementation strategy to achieve the vision. It covered year-round issues related to:

6.29

Map illustrating Vermillion Highlands and its regional context with regional trails and greenway corridor connections.

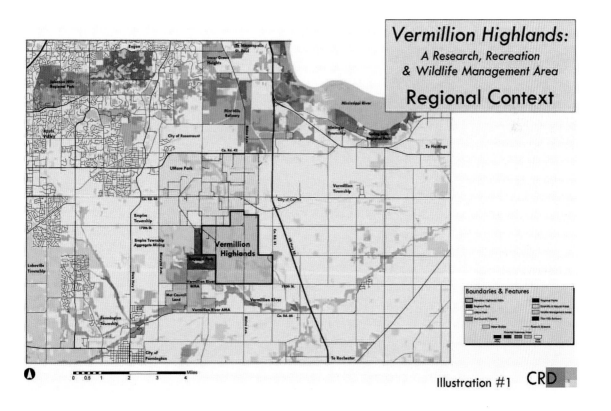

- The University of Minnesota's research, recreation, and wildlife management activities on the entire site, including 1,000 acres of agricultural research. Research opportunities are open to faculty from across the University system.
- Environmental preservation and protection, wildlife management and educational opportunities related to the DNR's interest in providing high-quality hunting.
- Natural-resource-based recreation, open space preservation, greenway connectivity, and environmental education related to Dakota County Parks and Open Space Department public service provisions.

Minnesota has a deep-seated heritage in, and appreciation for, its rural landscapes, and Vermillion Highlands is a unique site within the Twin Cities metropolitan area. The property offers a rare opportunity to celebrate rural heritage with the rapidly expanding metropolitan area, and it should be maintained in a manner that preserves its existing rural character. The CRD created five alternative scenarios, outlining different land uses and management options. The preferred scenario is defined by intensity of use, providing: environmental connections to the north through UMore Park to the Mississippi River corridor; recreational connections including bicycle and hiking trails; and flexibility in

6.30
The concept master plan drawing for Vermillion Highlands, illustrating relationships to UMore Park Sustainable Community, Regional Park, and Wildlife Management areas of the DNR.

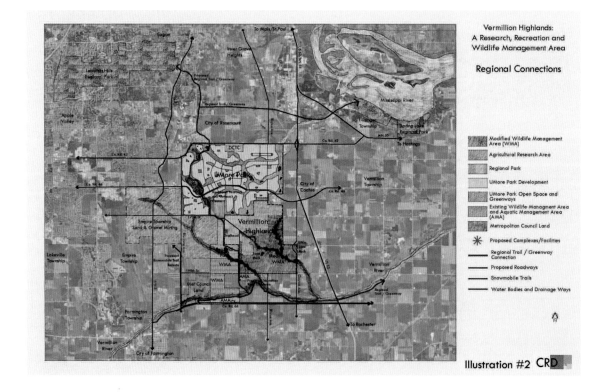

land-use management, research, and education related to the three land holdings.

The preferred scenario for the concept master plan (Figure 6.30) is manifested in a series of illustrations. The key illustrations are:

- Zone descriptions map #4 (Figure 6.31) with a description of the land-cover features and land-use objectives in each zone: Wildlife Management Zone, Agricultural Research Zone, Wildlife and Aquatic Management Area, and Regional Park.
- Research opportunities map #5 (Figure 6.32) illustrating zones for: Environmental and Natural Resource Research, Agricultural Research, and Recreation Research.
- Recreation opportunities map #6 (Figure 6.33) showing zones for: Limited Recreation, Managed Recreation, and Natural Resource Recreation.
- Hunting and trapping opportunities map #7 (Figure 6.34) showing zones for: Open Hunting and Trapping, Managed Hunting and Trapping, and Limited Hunting.
- Intensity of use map #8 (Figure 6.35) showing the three intensity of use zones.
- Management zones map #9 (Figure 6.36) outlining the two primary zones and relationships to the Regional Park and UMore Park.

6.31
Zones plan for Vermillion Highlands.

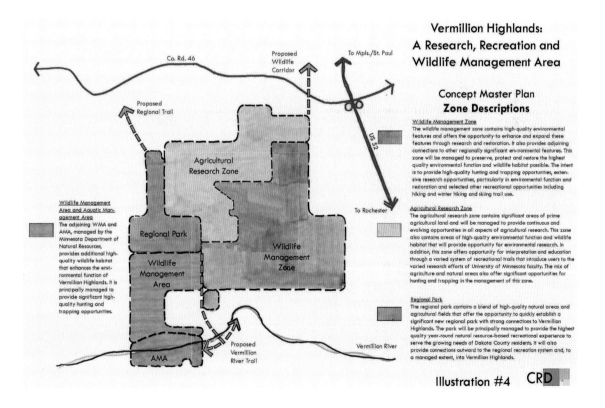

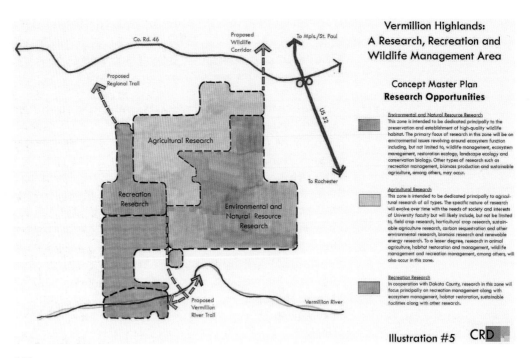

**6.32**
Research zones for Vermillion Highlands.

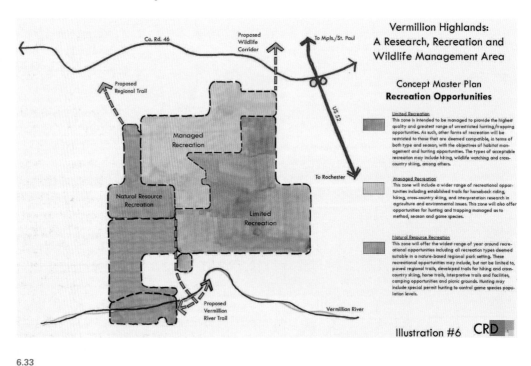

**6.33**
Recreation zones for multiple use (bicycling, hiking, skiing and snowshoeing, and horse riding and other recreational uses) in Vermillion Highlands.

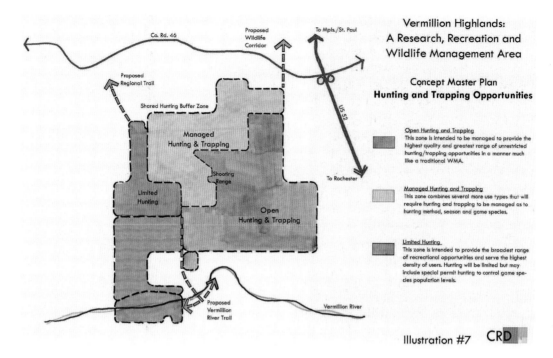

6.34
Hunting and Trapping definitions for the Vermillion Highlands wildlife management areas.

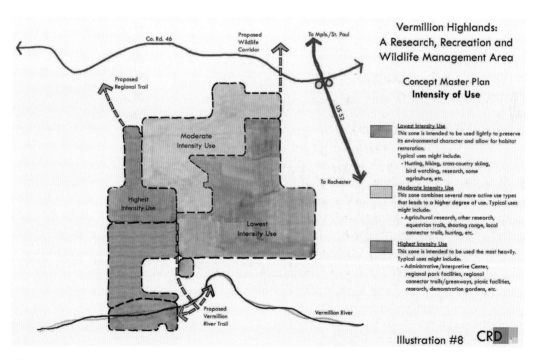

6.35
Intensity of use map to delineate different levels and intensity of land use related to zones.

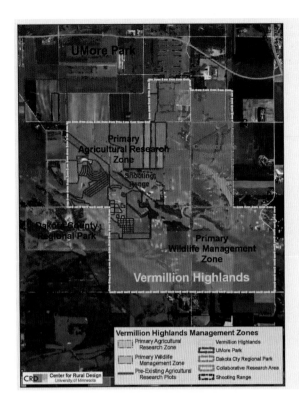

**Vermillion Highlands:
A Research, Recreation and
Wildlife Management Area**

**Concept Master Plan
Management Zones**

Vermillion Highlands Management Zones - this map identifies
two primary zones within Vermillion Highlands, each with its
own management priorities.

**Primary Agricultural Research Zone:**
This zone will be managed to maximize the
opportunity for continued University
agricultural research.

**Primary Wildlife Management Zone:**
This zone will be managed to maximize the
character and quality of wildlife habitat to
provide opportunity for high quality hunting
and trapping. Within this zone are areas
designated for the existing shooting range
and collaborative research combined with
specialty hunting opportunities for youth and
disabled hunters.

Activities in both of these zones will include University research,
hunting and trapping opportunities, and recreational trail
opportunities. The nature and character of these opportunities
will vary between zones to best meet their individual primary
management goal.

Illustration #9

The intention of the concept master plan is to provide management flexibility to allow changes to take place, within the guidelines established by the Minnesota Legislature, to maximize the site for a range of university research, recreational, and environmental activities, and as a modified Wildlife Management Area in perpetuity.

6.36
Management zones for
land-use management among
the multi-party partnership,
which includes the University
of Minnesota, the DNR, Dakota
County, and Empire Township.

## Lessons learned

Since the land that Vermillion Highlands covers was always being considered by the University as a location for conservation, research, and recreation, the sale of the land to the State for funding for the new University football stadium turned out to be a very good opportunity. This joint effort of the University of Minnesota, the DNR, Dakota County, and Empire Township illustrates how disparate institutions can collaborate and cooperate for mutual benefit within a cross-jurisdictional management structure; and that when rural landscapes are involved, rural design provides a planning process that can shape a land-use resolution to the benefit of all.

*Design team: CRD staff included Dewey Thorbeck, Steve Roos, Tracey Kinney, and Stephen Streng, and graduate assistants Zach Jorgensen and Peter Dahlberg. They worked closely along with the staff level Operations Committee and the administrative level Steering Committee that represented the University of Minnesota, the DNR, Dakota County, and Empire Township.*

# Chapter 7

# Interdisciplinary connections

Rural design is by nature a multidisciplinary process, opening up many opportunities for interdisciplinary design thinking to effectively address rural issues – particularly those issues that promote social equity, innovation, and entrepreneurship. Rural design may be the most effective process to connect and take full advantage of regional assets by linking science, policy, and practice in new and creative ways. Rural design strives to be a strong connection between research knowledge and society, and can be a very effective way to bring rural people, institutions, and science together to actively seek better ways to accomplish economic development and create job opportunities.

The intent of rural design and design thinking is to find interdisciplinary and social opportunities for economic development while protecting the environment and improving quality of life. Opportunities are emerging as rural areas cope with global climate and economic changes that require an entrepreneurial way of thinking and acting to take advantage of change. In addition, rural regions must find and promote the natural amenities they have, to retain and attract people to live there. People like to visit a region for the same reason people like to live there, and the amenities and natural assets of a region will be crucial in attracting people, enhancing quality of life, creating job opportunities, and promoting economic development.

A recent study about demographic changes in the United States indicated that the low quality of natural amenities and the large farm scale of agriculture being practiced were major causes for rural population decline. Another impact was distance. The further a rural region is from services found in a larger rural city, the greater the population decline. Those regions that maintained or increased their population often had Hispanics working in agriculture, or Native American populations building and operating casinos. The report indicated that low-amenity regions must either deal with industrial agriculture or experience continued population loss (McGranahan and Beale, 2002).

A report by the Task Force on National Energy Policy and Midwestern Regional Competiveness suggests that the Midwest region of the United States needs to unite around a set of defined actions and principles to help forge a national consensus in the development of renewable energy and carbon sequestration. The interdisciplinary opportunities it outlined for the Midwest regions include:

* Maximizing the energy efficiency of its buildings, industries, and transportation systems;
* Modernizing outdated infrastructure;
* Developing the new energy technologies needed to cope with future carbon constraints;
* Engaging Midwest universities in leading-edge energy research and innovation;
* Addressing critical workforce issues;
* Improving regional coordination and cross-jurisdictional decision-making processes for interstate transmission, and carbon capture and storage infrastructure.

The task force report goes on to state that the investments required for these activities must come through public–private partnerships, but primarily from the private sector. The report declares that the Midwest, with its strong industrial and manufacturing base and technical expertise has an opportunity to lead the nation in developing new energy markets – primarily through vehicle technology and wind, nuclear, coal, gas, and bioenergy technologies (Livingston *et al.*, 2009).

Climate change, renewable energy, and food and fiber production, along with social and environmental enhancement, are great challenges that rural design as an interdisciplinary process can focus on to outline opportunities for research as well as translating that research into practice to resolve societal problems. Rural design as a design-thinking process provides interdisciplinary and systemic connections, linking academia with society to create a sustainable, healthy, and vibrant rural quality of life.

## Rural design and design thinking

Rural design and design thinking are inexorably connected and, as a new design discipline, rural design is not hindered by old definitions. It is free to pursue the problem-solving process that design thinking provides to deal with a broad range of rural issues. As I have tried to argue in this book, rural design is not just about the spatial arrangement of rural landscapes. It is fundamentally a problem-solving process and to be effective it must function through an evidence-based design approach. Rural design offers flexibility to interpret rural issues to find the most innovative and transformative path to resolve the issues, regardless of what they are. Design thinking is a process and rural design brings it forward as a way to deal with rural problems.

In his book *Change by Design*, Tim Brown (2009) argues for design thinking as a way to transform organizations as well as inspire innovation. He writes:

> What we need is an approach to innovation that is powerful, effective, and broadly accessible, that can be integrated into all aspects of business and society, and that individuals and teams can use to generate breakthrough ideas that are implemented and that therefore have an impact. Design thinking offers such an approach.
>
> (Brown, 2009)

Rural design is a vehicle to bring design thinking and the problem-solving process of design to resolve rural environmental, social, and economic issues. For the 40% of the earth's land surface that is agricultural and rural-oriented it is a focus for bringing community-based and evidence-driven rural design together with science to inspire creative innovation and entrepreneurship in rural regions worldwide.

In North America there are a number of challenges that rural design and design thinking can address. These are similar to issues that are impacting rural regions worldwide:

* *Design for climate change:* Recent predictions for the Midwest describe warmer and drier summers and warmer and wetter winters and springs and these conditions will: impact energy demands; provide opportunities for new viruses for humans, animals, and plants; increase the stress on water supplies; and affect ecosystem compositions for flora and fauna through climate stress on native species and invasion from species previously prevented by the colder original climate. If the predicted changes occur, rural landscapes, communities, and ecosystems will be significantly affected, impacting economic and social systems. These changes will require new landscape patterns, infrastructure, economies, and community identities, and the planning for these potential changes should begin immediately. Communities must have the tools and information, particularly the problem-solving process of rural design, to effectively adapt to and manage change. As the world's population approaches a doubling by 2050, food will become an issue of greater and greater concern since the land available for producing food is finite and where and how it is distributed may become a cause for conflict. Rural design can help find interdisciplinary ways to reduce the negative impacts of climate change while improving rural quality of life.
* *Design for ecosystem health:* The concept of ecosystem health was originally developed in the environmental and natural resources fields, but starting in the 1980s a more diverse and interdisciplinary approach began and more

recently, as previously discussed, it has evolved into the 'One Health' idea of integrating human, animal, and environmental health. Research is needed to explore how this paradigm can describe interventions and what knowledge/data is needed to apply the idea in rural design. This will require conceptualization of different sub-ecosystems such as economic, social, political, and agricultural, and how they interact and relate to each other as an integrated ecosystem. Other ideas such as resiliency need to be considered as to whether they are health components to be used alone or in conjunction with others, like sustainable agriculture, multifunctional landscapes, and bioclimate and biomimetic building design. To effectively deal with these and other global issues, a research integration of ecosystem health with land use and agriculture could become a new global focus for interdisciplinary research. Design thinking and the rural design process can be very helpful in creating innovative and breakthrough ideas in this new research effort to find ways to improve human, animal, and environmental health.

- *Design for community vitality:* It has been said that rural residents in North America suffer higher mortality, disability, obesity, and chronic disease rates than urban people. The CRD has been involved in one project (Isanti County) to create outdoor trails and locate them so that people have easy access to them and are encouraged to use them for exercise and wellness through experiencing nature. However, no research has yet been done to prove that what was proposed will perform as expected. Also, many strategies for achieving ecosystem health (human, animal, and environmental) can become ways to invigorate communities through new landscape patterns and farming practices. They may provide rural communities with more economic development by supplying a diversity of products and material for new local business, carbon storage to gain economic benefit, and lower costs for producers by decreasing reliance on imported fertilizers and pesticides. A more independent local economy has a higher potential to strengthen social ties and build social capital. Rural design can create community vitality.

- *Design for rural character:* What are the aesthetic issues that rural design needs to consider? From research projects at the CRD we know that rural character perception influences how rural residents see themselves and how others see rural areas. This dichotomy is one source of urban/rural tension and potential for conflict between new rural residents and those that have lived in a rural place for a long time. Aesthetics is a cultural dimension and if new landscape patterns designed to improve ecosystem health are not perceived by rural residents as beautiful or if they cannot identify with its character it might fail. More research into how rural character is analyzed and perceived is required, including rural architecture and its connections to place and climate. The more rural people understand the architectural and landscape heritage of a rural region, the more likely they are to want a contemporary interpretation if it demonstrates a conceptual linkage to the geological and cultural heritage of place. Rural design can be very effective in helping people understand and embrace the unique qualities of where they live and can assist in finding innovative ways to improve quality of life.

- *Design with rural indigenous people:* Rural indigenous communities have at best been underserved by the design and planning professions and at worst disserved. Why this is so is unclear. How can rural indigenous communities be encouraged to embrace rural design and contribute to defining a curriculum that trains designers to work with them? What are the core values of indigenous people that designers need? How can we as a nation encourage more indigenous youth to enter into the design professions? How can rural design support indigenous communities to better control their land assets and the benefits derived from them? Most importantly, what can rural design learn from indigenous people's design traditions and how can they be employed for the benefit of all societies without losing their own unique intrinsic character and importance? These are a few of the questions that need to be discussed with rural indigenous communities. Similarly, they are questions that need to be part of a dialogue with other ethnic and immigrant communities who are living and working in rural regions. Rural design recognizes the experience of indigenous people in the sustainable way they designed their lives to be in harmony with and supportive of their environments, providing a paradigm for decision making today.

- *Regional definitions:* Most of the challenges facing rural regions today do not respect political or jurisdictional boundaries and neither can any solutions put forth to deal with them. Nevertheless, longstanding traditions of political boundaries for cities, townships, counties, and states must continue to be recognized and respected, even as solutions that cross borders are put forth. Defining a region is difficult, but best understood when people living within it recognize and identify with the region's unique landscape character, culture, and geography. Research into this political and social issue is very important if regional collaboration and cooperation for economic advantage is going to work and be effective. Rural design does not advocate for reworking political boundaries, rather it argues for multi-jurisdictional planning and design thinking for mutual benefit through regional cooperation and collaboration.

- *Transferring design skills to rural communities:* Design is unique in the educational system in the United States in that it is the only learning activity that is only taught to students who are enrolled in design. However, everyone uses design skills in some way in their daily life and people learn about it on their own. Design fundamentals and design thinking are being introduced as electives in some business schools to equip their students with the problem-solving skills that design thinking and the design process can bring. At the same time, the design schools rarely introduce design students to teambuilding and group management dynamics, yet that is how designers function in practice, and intern designers must quickly learn these skills. Research is needed as to how to empower rural residents and communities with design knowledge and skills to understand and solve new problems and challenges with visions for their communities. In rural regions this might be provided through legislatively funded university design assistance programs for those communities that cannot afford to hire rural design consultants. Other community efforts might take the form of workshops, online learning, and community outreach on using design thinking as a problem-solving process. One of the major goals of rural design is to bring design tools into the hands of rural people who may not think of themselves as rural designers, so that they can incorporate design thinking into their daily lives.

- *Educating policymakers:* Elected officials and agency representatives need the knowledge that science suggests to create and manage rural policies, but often the issues are looked at independently. Rural design is a methodology to integrate and plan holistically, and policymakers need design thinking to understand data and interpret the impacts of alternative scenarios. Design thinking can help affected businesses and citizen groups understand the connections and impacts of optional choices and resulting regulations. One size does not 'fit all', and the unique differences that regional landscapes have must be a part of the policy and regulatory system. If rural people in one region perceive the broad policy as unfair to their region it will not be an effective policy. Rural design is a methodology to bring fairness into rural planning and decision making.

Rural design may be the most effective way that rural people can shape their environments to deal with the big global issues impacting rural regions worldwide. By linking rural issues with urban issues, rural design can assist rural decision making by becoming the catalyst for the opportunity that Tim Brown outlines at the end of his book, *Change by Design*:

> Today we have an opportunity . . . to unleash the power of design thinking as a means of exploring new possibilities, creating new choices, and bringing new solutions to the world. In the process we may find that we have made our societies healthier, our businesses more profitable, and our own lives richer, more impactful, and meaningful.
>
> (Brown, 2009)

Rural design is an exciting, innovative and creative means to engage urban issues and rural problems and rural people at the scale on which they occur, using all of the knowledge, tools, and management skills that design thinking can bring, without confinement to disciplinary or political boundaries.

## Urban/rural synergy

Understanding the differences, relationships, and characteristics of what is urban and what is rural is essential to creating a healthy and economic future for both urban and rural regions. Rural design and urban design have many similarities, in that both embrace quality of life. Rural design, however, seeks to understand and embody the unique characteristics of open landscapes and systems where buildings and towns are components of the landscape, rather than defining infrastructure and public space, as in urban design.

This fundamental difference is the basis for understanding how rural design as a problem-solving methodology can contribute to quality of rural life. Rural design can help define region and shape rural agricultural and natural landscapes, create better architecture for agriculture, enhance sustainable principles and improve rural economics and livability, with a strong sense of unique place and climate.

Since the 1950s, the character of the rural landscape has changed dramatically due to shifts from a rural to an urban economy, more efficient and economic farming methods, and global competition. The small, diversified farm with its cluster of unique farm buildings, like the central Minnesota farm shown in Figure 7.1, has mostly disappeared. This was a self-contained family farm, constructed by Norwegian immigrants (the Eidem family) in 1894, with a broad diversity of animals and crops. Growing potatoes was its cash crop, providing food for the nearby city of Minneapolis. The farmstead is functioning today as an 1890s Living

7.1
Entrance road to the Brooklyn Park Historic Farm, near the city of Minneapolis, Minnesota.

History Interpretive Farm, providing visitors with a glimpse of what rural farm life was once like.

The small diversified farm has been mostly replaced by larger specialized farms focusing on one animal, with industrial-type metal-skinned buildings, like the hog-growing farmstead in southwestern Minnesota shown in Figure 7.2. The farm is family owned and the farmhouse is still the central building, but now the storage bins and the mill providing feed for swine operations are the largest and most prominent structures. The pigs are housed in a number of identical pole-barn buildings on this and several other detached farms. Each barn is carefully engineered and constructed for a specific aspect of raising hogs, but with an architecture that gives the impression of an impersonal industrialized process. The pre-engineered pole-barn construction system, with metal roof and wall panels, that is commonly used for new specialized animal facilities is not inherently bad architecture, as Figure 7.3 (showing an example of a pole barn for beef and sheep) illustrates. When form follows function, climate, and place, the result can be good architecture.

7.2
Entrance road to a specialized swine farm in southwestern Minnesota, with historic house and old barn adjacent to a new large feed storage and mixing complex, providing feed for a number of pre-engineered industrial swine buildings in the background. The feed complex serves hog facilities on this and several other separate farms.

7.3
The popular pole-barn construction system has been transformed into architecture for this beef and sheep barn in northern Minnesota, through the use of sensitive proportions and details, and the selection and arrangement of material and color – with form following function, climate, and place.

Many old barns and farmhouses have been demolished, blown down, or now stand empty and deteriorating. These empty structures signify the end of the immigrants' dream to come to America and own and live on a farm. The concept of living in the rural landscape continues today, however, with new housing being constructed in rural areas by people who want a rural lifestyle, but do not want to be farmers. This situation often creates conflicts between existing farmers and new non-farming residents over farming operations, primarily odor from animals, fear of groundwater contamination, and field dust from farm equipment. This conflict often arises as a public issue when a livestock farmer wants to significantly expand, and needs to go through the permit process.

People who live in rural regions that have animal agriculture need to understand the character of the landscape, so that rational choices can be made to reconcile the social, economic, and environmental issues that influence how land is used and the quality of life that landscape character implies. The look and character of rural landscapes and the buildings constructed within them need to be emphasized and promoted in the context of unique regional character. By designing and shaping rural buildings and landscapes around regional assets and sense of rural place and climate, rural communities are more likely to be in harmony and support economic competitiveness in the international marketplace.

Traditional views of agriculture and the rural landscape are not consistent with the realities of farming today, yet farming is still an inherent part of America's culture, economy, and heritage. Today nearly 80% of the growing US population lives and works in urban areas, with only minimal knowledge of where their food and fiber come from. The global nature of agriculture and its impacts on local economics and farming practices, and the public demand for cheap food are having major impacts on land-use choices and the types of buildings constructed to support farming operations in North America.

The specialized nature of contemporary farming and its impact on rural communities is a societal issue which needs both urban and rural citizen support for policies that ensure rural future. For America it is important to define the social and environmental value of the landscapes and the kinds of agriculture within each rural region and how they are to be preserved and enhanced. National and state policies are needed that: recognize regional differences; provide incentives for regional cooperation, collaboration, and entrepreneurial action; and promote public confidence in the future of rural America and quality of life for both urban and rural people.

## Land use and the urban/rural edge

The urban/rural edge and urban sprawl is an area of particular land-use concern worldwide, especially in regions where many people live in squalid settlements at the fringes. Some have lamented that rural change is the urbanization of the agricultural environment by creating an urban economic culture that diminishes traditional rural values. I think that the best rural future will be found in rural regions' abilities to identify with their urban neighbors and to enhance the agricultural and natural landscape assets they jointly value the most.

The future of urban areas and their relationship with the rural landscape is an emerging research issue. In a recent paper, Stephan Graham (2002) argues that contemporary cities are becoming socio-technical constructs, receiving materials and sending out products and by-products; and that their infrastructure is rapidly changing in response to globalization by exploiting differences between places. The impact of these changes is being reflected in communication technologies, airport and goods-handling locations, and warehousing and manufacturing facilities. Large cities have responded by becoming more interconnected with other large cities, but more divorced from the rural region where much of their materials come from. This situation will require new thinking about how cities and people in them work, live, and play in the twenty-first century, and their relationships with the regional rural landscape and its economic and social character (Graham, 2002).

Rural people need to work together with urban people to clarify what is urban, what is rural, and what is agriculture. Visual paradigms to help illustrate what the rural environment can be like and how the urban/rural edge should be defined are needed to help rural farming and non-farming communities – as well as urban communities – make intelligent choices. It is important to think and act holistically when making choices about using the land and constructing buildings in the rural landscape. What is the impact on the visual appearance of the rural landscape? What are the issues that need to be considered?

An integrated holistic approach to agricultural systems, land uses, and construction will facilitate decision making in the context of a rapidly changing rural economic environment. Consumers of food and fiber need to understand the fundamental relationship between the cost of growing food and fiber, and the cost of production. This requires interdisciplinary research to provide the data on which design solutions are based. Rural design as a problem-solving process brings architecture, planning, and landscape architecture together to provide design thinking, but the research base for rural design will come from a variety of other engineering, agricultural, and social disciplines involved in rural issues.

## Problems with animal agriculture

The economic and technological changes taking place in animal agriculture have had a dramatic effect on the shape and character of contemporary farm buildings and the appearance of the rural landscape. In the past, barns were constructed to reflect the small, diversified nature of a family farm and the economic forces prevalent at the time, even though they changed very slowly. Today, economic realities – such as the national desire for cheap, processed food and government policies favoring large farms to assure food supply – have led to the construction of large, specialized structures for livestock and large grain storage containers for feed and grains, as well as a more mechanized, specialized farming system. These phenomena, supported by government subsidies, along with the movement of rural people to urban areas, have resulted in fewer farmers and larger farms.

As a result, new farm buildings are generally designed to accommodate larger numbers of animals than traditional buildings and employ pre-engineered structures to meet specialized requirements. With these structures, the only visible connection to the land is to bulldoze it flat and construct buildings that all look the same, regardless of their location. The new metal-skinned buildings, reflecting an industrial aesthetic, have little visual appeal. Although these buildings incorporate animal science research, with animal care being the highest priority, the impression is that they all look the same, without any noticeable connection to the character of the landscape within which they are located. This perception influences negative public opinion about livestock farming and is partially the reason for strong public outcry against 'factory'-type farms and industrial agriculture.

Before the 1960s any trip to the countryside by town people was enhanced by seeing animals in the landscape. Today, farmers use standardized confinement-type buildings because they are the most economical method for livestock farming, resulting in far fewer numbers of animals outside on the land, and creating the impression that the animals suffer because they are confined indoors throughout their lives. Yet, animal care is the highest priority on the farm – because healthy and more productive animals bring more income to the farmer.

Environmental protection regulations are based on the number of animal units. As the unit count goes up in confinement- or feed-lot-type facilities, the regulations become more stringent, yet the public is suspicious that environmental concerns are not being properly addressed. This concern, along with the public's uneasiness with their perceptions of 'factory farming' creates a conflict between farmers and non-farmers over the future of animal agriculture. Also, the regulations generally are state-wide and do not adequately address the unique land characteristics of regions within the state, which may have a variety of geological differences.

Interdisciplinary research is needed to develop integrated performance metrics for sustainable commercial animal buildings based on production, energy, environmental, economic, animal welfare, workplace environmental health, and social criteria that will bring large-scale animal facilities to the same level as commercial/industrial building design and construction. These metrics will be effective when they optimize animal productivity, reduce energy consumption of fossil fuels and animal feed, and maintain cost competiveness over building life. The metrics will encourage use of more environmentally friendly building components, better working conditions and worker health, improve animal health by maintaining biosecurity, and provide for increased food safety and security (Jacobson et al., 2009).

An example of a future commercial facility that recognizes this challenge is a design proposal for a sustainable 2,500-cow dairy barn (Figure 7.4) developed

7.4 (opposite)
A 2,500-cow dairy barn, with fabric roof supported by aluminium trusses for a new complex, following guidelines in an Environmental Quality Protection Program for dairy farmers in Minnesota. It illustrates the potential of new structural technology adapted to a building for animal agriculture.

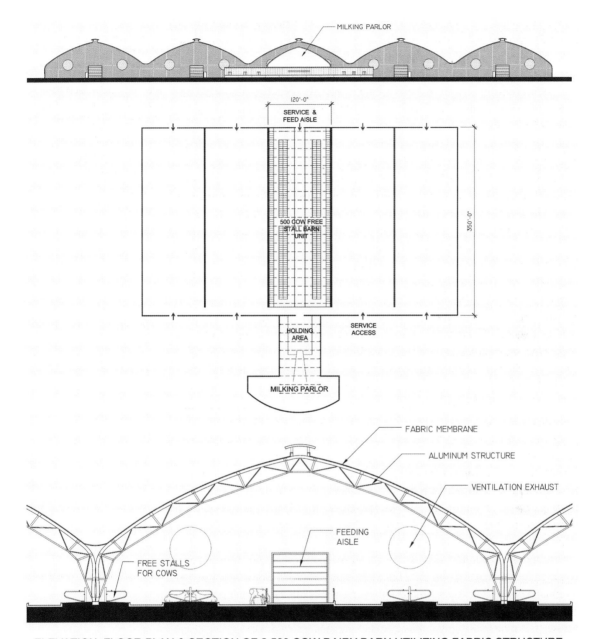

MILKING PARLOR

120'-0"

SERVICE &
FEED AISLE

350'-0"

500 COW FREE
STALL BARN
UNIT

HOLDING
AREA

SERVICE
ACCESS

MILKING PARLOR

FABRIC MEMBRANE

ALUMINUM STRUCTURE

VENTILATION EXHAUST

FEEDING
AISLE

FREE STALLS
FOR COWS

**ELEVATION, FLOOR PLAN & SECTION OF 2,500 COW DAIRY BARN UTILIZING FABRIC STRUCTURE**

by the CRD, which uses fabric as the roof material in a series of adjacent and connected animal spaces. It functions with a single rotary milking parlor for fifty cows which operates 24 hours a day. Manure is processed through an anaerobic digester, to create methane gas to generate electricity for farm operations and supply extra power into the electric grid. Solid waste is separated in the process, and recycled as bedding, while liquid waste is spread on fields as fertilizer.

This design proposal was developed to provide an example of how a new dairy barn could respond to an earlier CRD study which outlined improvements to environmental practices on dairy farms. Financed by the state legislature, it was a study for the dairy industry in Minnesota that: (1) developed an environmental inventory of landscape features and resources, including human features impacting the dairy industry; (2) assessed the priority of importance of the features of the inventory; and (3) analyzed methods to accommodate and integrate the features through the planning and design process. The study linked four high-priority environmental models for dairy farms – surface water, ground water, habitat, and community relations – and then combined them to create a fifth model that became the Minnesota Environmental Quality Assurance Program for existing and new dairy farms (Roos *et al.*, 2003).

The industrialization of the swine industry is causing considerable stress on rural communities concerning the odor, environmental, social, and economic consequences of large-scale hog operations. With high concentrations of animals, manure handling is a large odor and environmental issue, through ventilation exhaust from the barns and storing waste in open lagoons. Since pigs are inside year round, the public cannot see them, creating concern for animal welfare. Poultry farming is similar, in that specialized industrial-type buildings are also used for housing birds for egg and meat production, with similar odor and manure-handling issues and environmental and social concerns.

There are some promising new efforts to produce bioenergy from animal and agricultural processing waste, and research needs to continue to explore ways that this can economically happen. A new bioenergy facility in Minnesota (owned by an association of eleven rural cities which also have a number of operating wind turbines) is being planned that will utilize the anaerobic process to convert corn silage and feedstock from poultry farms and agricultural processing plants to produce biogas and solid fuel pellets for burning to generate electricity for the cities involved. It is a way that regional collaboration and cooperation can create synergy for economic, social, and environmental gain.

The major issue for large-scale industrial-type animal agriculture is balancing an individual farm's profits with the economic and social impact it has on rural communities. Sustainable agriculture, proponents argue, is an emerging small-scale alternative that endeavors to enhance rural economies while preserving the environment. It may be that the design direction for livestock farming in the future (and its architecture) will be found in understanding the social, economic, political, and environmental impacts as a cultural, societal, and health issue affecting both urban and rural people (Thu and Durrenberger, 1998).

## Multifunctional agriculture and land use

US agricultural policies have for a long time subsidized agricultural commodities, including corn, wheat, soybeans, cotton, and rice. The result of this subsidized support is that US agriculture perennially produces surpluses, yet the potential environmental consequences of large quantities of land area in single crops is ignored. This support over the long term has contributed to fewer farms and larger producers, often resulting in loss of rural population, depressed rural economies, and small towns struggling to exist. The changes that are taking place on many farmsteads through subsidies is illustrated by a southern Minnesota farm (Figure 7.5) with its cluster of new large grain-storage bins constructed in contrast to the historic farmhouse with its traditional barn and silo. The image illustrates the scale change over time due to concentration on growing and harvesting one crop – corn for feed and fuel.

In Europe many countries heavily subsidize rural farmers to maintain the cultural landscape, based on a national desire to preserve traditional agriculture and the historic landscape to attract tourists and ensure a higher standard of living. Maintaining the countryside for its agrarian beauty is a policy strongly supportive of tourism and the economy that it brings. Norway is notable for its investment in roads and bridges connecting many small islands with the mainland all along the very long western seacoast from Stavanger on the southern end to the far north city of Kirkenes near the Norwegian-Russian border. Italy has also been very effective in preserving the unique qualities of its rural landscape for agricultural production, but also for scenic value and tourism. Each region of Italy celebrates its own unique food and agricultural heritage, making it one of the most interesting and exciting countries to visit and explore.

More recognition of the value of the culturally based regional landscape in North America will be increasingly important as it adjusts to the need to provide food, fiber, and fuel for a growing world population. If done well in a sustainable way it can help improve the economic and community vitality of rural regions,

7.5
Entrance road to a farmstead in southern Minnesota, illustrating changes in farming operations and buildings over time – from a small diversified farm in the 1950s to large single-crop corn production and storage bins today.

while enhancing quality of life. Rural design can help create alternative land-use scenarios to help citizens make the decisions that support their community values.

This phenomenon of recognizing the value of rural landscapes – and spending to preserve and enhance it – is elaborated upon in an interesting and beautifully illustrated book called *The Values of the Agrarian Landscapes Across Europe and North America* (Terwan *et al.*, 2004). It outlines the importance that these rural landscapes and their architecture have for bridging cultural heritage and social connections within local and national economies. The book outlines many kinds of geography and forms of agriculture from around the world, and the wide range of social, cultural, scenic, and natural values and benefits they bring to national identity. It discusses working landscapes, the cultural and heritage value and the unique regional products they have, and the challenges they face (Terwan *et al.*, 2004).

How agricultural polices impact the rural landscape was discussed in a recent study published in *BioScience* (Boody *et al.*, 2005) which described community-driven sustainable scenarios that would allow participants in the study a series of production activities from which they could choose. The benefits of each scenario depended on changes to current agricultural policies. Environmental benefits included better water quality, healthier fish in lakes and streams, increased carbon sequestration, and decreased greenhouse gas emissions. Economic benefits included social capital formation and greater farm profitability.

The study indicated that diversifying agriculture on actively farmed land could provide greater environmental, social, and economic benefits, and if present land-use trends continued the problems related to these issues would worsen. The study concluded that the nonmarket environmental and economic benefits of diversifying agriculture merit greater inclusion in current US farm policy. It went on to suggest that a larger number of moderate-sized farms would increase rural population and make for healthier small towns and the businesses that go with them. Agricultural policies need to enhance multifunctional agriculture to develop a future agriculture that produces food and fiber while protecting the ecosystems within which they function. This is a model that could have great impact on the human, cultivated, natural, and agrarian landscapes around the world, as farmers and rural citizens fight to preserve and protect the values and benefits that those landscapes bring to their region's economy and quality of life (Boody *et al.*, 2005).

Globalization and diversity are rapidly impacting and driving change in societies and its institutions. In a book about the higher education system in America, *Driving Change Through Diversity and Globalization,* Anderson (2008) argues that the best opportunity for successfully integrating diversity rests in an institution's ability to engage in cross-sectional activities. This works best when critical issues, processes, and personal outcomes are intertwined in a synergistic relationship. Diversity from a biological and human perspective is critical to achieving long-term rural economic development and enhanced rural quality of life. Each inhabitant of an ecosystem is interdependent to some extent with all of the others, and every inhabitant and industry must think about and enhance the connections to the cultural and natural landscapes around them (McDonough and Braungart, 2002).

## Designing for food supply, food security, and health

The question of food supply for a growing world population is a major social and cultural global issue. According to the United Nations Population Fund, the world population is expected to increase from 6.5 billion in 2010, to 8.2 billion by 2030, proceeding to 9 billion by 2050. Since there is only so much land on the planet for growing food, how and where food is grown and how it is distributed may become the most important global issue the world must address.

In America, many believe that it is important to quickly establish environmental and land-use concepts that preserve and protect high-quality agricultural lands still available for farming, so that future generations can be provided with adequate and safe food, and with a landscape character that all can enjoy. Norman Borlaug – the Nobel winner who was responsible for the green revolution in third world nations by helping farmers incorporate fertilizers into their farming practice to grow more food – has argued that the next revolution must come from bioengineering (Borlaug, 2008).

Today, a growing number of organic farms are often considered by economists to be more sustainable and contribute more to the local economy than large-scale agriculture. These farms are often found in and near large metropolitan regions, and provide food for farmers' markets, restaurants, and people who appreciate fresh and local food. This movement is closely connected with local food initiatives working to encourage more wholesome food choices, while supporting local farmers.

This issue of local food creates an opportunity for an urban agriculture that can be integrated into existing built-up urban areas. With urban sprawl, vegetable farmers are being pushed further and further away from where people live and shop. Transportation costs are increasing the cost of food in farmers' markets and new concepts, like high-rise hydroponic greenhouses for growing fruits and vegetables, have been proposed.

New concepts for community gardens, community-supported agriculture, and utilization of greenhouses for growing fruits and vegetables will continue to be part of the fabric of urban regions. How these ideas are incorporated into the urban landscape, and still provide high-quality foods at competitive costs, is not yet fully resolved. Nor are the relationships between the cost of food and its impact on health fully understood. It will certainly be part of ongoing public policies regarding the supply and security of food. If sustainability landscapes and the benefits of those landscapes become a high priority, then policies must be designed to maintain natural, scenic, and cultural values.

This argument suggests that fair prices are fundamental to keeping farmers on the land. The landscapes and the people who live and work on the land need innovation, with new equipment for managing the land, new methods for pest control, and new arrangements between farmers and citizens to meet and share common interests. This suggests that public policies move away from subsidizing a narrowly focused agricultural efficiency toward a more multi-purpose and integrated relationship, supporting ecosystem health while providing food security and a high quality of rural life (Terwan *et al.*, 2004).

Rural regions and communities in America face a host of challenges related to the built environment and the larger rural landscape. These include: a lack of economic opportunity; conflicts between established and new residents, especially along the urban/rural boundary; environmental degradation from changing land use and agricultural practices; and a natural resource base changing in response to new temperature and rainfall patterns.

It is critical that rural design utilizes a bottom-up approach even as it deals with broad regulatory and political issues. Studies have pointed out that rural residents have greater health issues than urban residents, and multidisciplinary research is needed to find the links between rural lifestyle, economic opportunity, and land use. Can rural communities find the dots which they can connect to create economic development while improving human, animal, and environmental health? The rural design process can accomplish that, but rural communities need to have the skills and technologies to identify and quantify choices, even if they cannot afford it.

## Design economy

How land is used is a dominant issue around the world as established and developing nations ponder how to use the available land to feed a rapidly increasing world population. Globalization is impacting everything we do, and rural design thinking is a methodology to manage change and create innovative and effective models for redefining rural economies. Bruce Tonn (2007) argues, in a paper published by the World Future Society, that people must learn to live as if our futures matter. He believes this can be accomplished through: (1) universal responsibility to do the right thing; (2) universal belongingness linking past, present, and future; (3) socio-diversity through communication and cooperation; (4) universal involvement and the noosphere (group thinking) to enhance quality of life for everyone; and (5) extending human lifespans to help build more and stronger relationships between people (Tonn, 2007).

In another essay, Joe Costello (2010) argues that new understandings about the natural world and new communication technologies are creating and transforming the industrial society and reshaping it to produce the next economy, just as technology moved us beyond the agrarian society. He calls it the design economy, as a way to deal with issues arising from climate change, health, and environmental problems. As the world moves into the design economy, he asks, what are the roles, identities, institutions, and processes of design? Design has always been part of human history, with the designing of hunting tools, farming implements, and industrial technologies; and as institutions evolve they must understand that design is the primary value, creating opportunities for participation, efficiency, elegance, and quality. Costello argues that it is the process of design that society needs to value, and that the design process must involve citizens and give value to their participation (Costello, 2010).

Rural design is a manifestation of the design economy and a model of how rural regions can gain control over technology, so that the production of goods and services through regional cooperation and collaboration contributes to rural economic development, environmental improvements, and quality of life. The design economy is a concept that nurtures the democratic ideal and free flow of information. It can create a social and business environment where innovation and entrepreneurship will flourish.

Richard Florida (2002) calls people who like to function this way the 'creative class'. In an essay, he states that more and more businesses understand the importance that diversity has in hiring and retaining creative employees, yet most civic leaders fail to understand the same relationship. Places that succeed in attracting and retaining creative people are more likely to prosper. Those places generally have greater diversity of people and higher levels of environmental quality – places that accept newcomers and immigrants quickly into all sorts of social and economic situations. Florida goes on to argue that creative people value diversity in all of its manifestations, enjoy a mix of influences, with different kinds of music, and try different kinds of food. They want to meet and socialize with a wide range of people. Also, creative people value outdoor recreation very highly and are drawn to places and communities where many outdoor activities are available. Openness to migration is particularly important for smaller cities and rural regions. To attract and welcome creative people they have to develop the kind of social opportunities creative people value (Florida, 2002).

The importance of social capital should not be underestimated. It is often described as two types: external bridging, which connects people from different groups; and internal bonding within a homogenous group. It is essential that both types of social capital be involved in developing the kind of community so crucial to the problem-solving process of rural design thinking in addressing and resolving rural needs. When human diversity and academic knowledge are joined through the rural design process great things can happen.

# Chapter 8

# Rural futures

In the introduction to this book I began an argument for a new rural design discipline that could apply design thinking and design practice to rural issues, using a community-centered and evidence-based design approach. It is an approach that can have a positive impact on rural regions by providing community leaders and public officials with information and ideas, as they work to improve quality of life. Rural communities must deal with and adapt to a wide variety of rapidly changing issues and challenges that are both *internal*, like demographic and economic changes, and *external*, like global climate change and the global economy. The most important assistance that rural design can provide to rural regions, and the communities within them, is helping them connect the dots to find opportunities to become entrepreneurial and compete in the global economy.

The Community Development Society is an international organization dedicated to improving the economic, environmental, and social health of communities. Headquartered in Columbus, Ohio, they encourage creative approaches to capitalizing on local assets and opportunities, to bring about needed changes within communities. Recognizing that universities, non-profit organizations, and design professions are becoming increasingly involved in working with communities to help identify and implement creative approaches to manage change, they hope to become a clearing house to share innovative ideas. The Society has outlined (CDS, 2010) five principles of good public engagement practice:

- Promote active and representative participation toward enabling all community members to meaningfully influence the decisions that affect their lives.
- Engage community members in learning about and understanding community issues, and the economic, social, environmental, political, psychological, and other impacts associated with alternative courses of action.
- Incorporate the diverse interests and cultures of the community in the community development process; and disengage from support of any effort that is likely to adversely affect the disadvantaged members of a community.

- Work actively to enhance the leadership capacity of community members, leaders, and groups within the community.
- Be open to using the full range of action strategies to work toward the long-term sustainability and wellbeing of the community.

Community leaders and public officials in rural regions struggle daily with a wide range of rapidly changing challenges and issues and they need design thinking to foster strategies for their communities. One of the key components of rural design is that its problem-solving and evidence-based design process must function as a two-way link between science and society to be effective and transformative. As outlined in the ten case studies in Chapter 6, the CRD now has a great deal of experience of working with rural communities, at a wide range of scales and issues. The fundamental question that emerged from the work is: How can rural design help communities cope with and manage change to preserve what they value the most, while promoting economic development and improving quality of life?

Rural development has often been seen as an 'external' phenomenon, whereby rural regions engage experts to suggest changes and provide guidance to a specific program. For example, if a rural city wants to establish an industrial park to promote new businesses and jobs, it often hires planners and consultants who have designed other industrial parks to develop a plan. Even when the community is involved in the planning process, the recommended plan often reflects the thinking and skills of the consultants rather than the unique land assets of the region and the values citizens place on it. Externally driven plans may have good ideas, but often lack the community support necessary to become successful.

On the other hand, rural development that is 'internally' driven is much more likely to gain community support and achieve consensus on a strategy, but may not be so successful in implementation. For example, if a regional industrial park is a goal for economic development, a rural region might form a non-profit entity or government authority to coordinate and manage efforts to entice a company to locate and construct a building in the park. Often this role becomes part of the local Chamber of Commerce, and while the intention is good, and may have strong local support, the real opportunities and innovative options for entrepreneurship and business expansion may have been overlooked.

Sustainable rural development can be best achieved when it embraces and fosters systemic and holistic thinking. In the example of a regional industrial park for economic development, the community-based rural design approach would first survey and determine regional land assets, find connections between economic development, education, financing, tourism, and quality of life; and then, through community workshops, define the values the community places on them. By using the community-based process of rural design, consultants can work with citizens to outline options, provide alternatives and create a vision for the regional industrial park as an integral part of the social, economic, environmental, political, and cultural fabric of the community. As a result of a vision based on regional assets the name 'industrial park' might be reconsidered by the community and become branded as a 'center for innovation' and embrace entrepreneurship, market technological creativity, and promote human diversity as a way to use its assets to effectively compete in the global economy.

This planning process might utilize geo-spatial data and computer visualization, with three-dimensional images to illustrate the resulting character and impacts of alternative visions and choices which might enhance economic prosperity to participants. Figure 8.1 shows an image from a CRD project to visualize what old mining pits might look like when filled with water, and their potential for community enhancement. This kind of visual process enhances citizen understanding of the problem and helps in the selection of a preferred alternative with a strong vision. The community becomes a stakeholder and feels empowered to shape public policy and government action to implement economic strategy and support entrepreneurial activity.

This economic strategy would create an advantage by innovatively utilizing the ecological, cultural, historical, and social resources and assets of the landscape and the surrounding region. It is a strategy that synergistically integrates and enhances quality of life, diversity of work force, affordable housing, educational and recreational amenities, economic development, and job opportunities as a holistic and integrated region-based economic system.

Systemic analysis and planning for rural economic development is a complex process. Jean Richardson (2000), in her book based on her experience over a number of years in Vermont with the Environmental Partnerships in Communities, has outlined key principles for attaining sustainable rural com-

8.1
A three-dimensional image prepared by the CRD to illustrate one of the various land-use scenarios for new development and landscaping of abandoned mines, after they fill with water, in the Iron Range region of northeastern Minnesota.

munity development. These principles parallel the experience of the CRD and are paraphrased here:

- *Empower community members:* Utilize a community-based planning process that engages citizens.
- *Strengthen democracy:* Incorporate citizens so that any recommendation is strengthened by the involvement of community leaders.
- *Encourage women to be key leaders:* Women are very successful at understanding the complexity of community-based planning and design and participating in making ideas work.
- *Involve youth:* Future sustainability is dependent on developing future leaders, and engaging youth is critical to the rural design process.
- *Encourage systems thinking:* Rural issues are complex and, if not looked at systemically and holistically, the opportunities for rural development and community vitality could easily be missed.
- *Encourage innovation:* Foster innovation at all levels to find creative institutional structures that are transformative. Connect the dots to enhance knowledge, encourage entrepreneurship, and maximize impact.
- *Foster rural and urban linkages:* Rural and urban societies are inextricably connected and interwoven, and the linkages must be identified and enhanced for mutual benefit.

Rural planning takes place one way or another in response to issues, whether proactively designed (internally) to manage change, or reactively designed as a result of external forces. The principles of rural design are meant to be a guiding framework, so that the process of rural design can, over time, become much more effective in resolving rural issues and benefiting society. Since rural design is a problem-solving process and a way of systemic design thinking, oriented toward place and climate, the principles of rural design can function and be effective anywhere.

## Connecting the dots

More than anything else, rural design is an interdisciplinary process and a methodology for integrating issues. Its practice of 'connecting the dots' (Figure 8.2) increases the opportunity for innovation and synergy among the disciplines and people involved. Design as a problem-solving process can be learned and practiced in different ways; however, the most effective results will emerge from community-based collaboration and integration of interdisciplinary knowledge, design, and planning skills.

Many disciplines involved in rural research issues are fundamentally and traditionally organized as separate silos to study rural cultures, landscapes, and environments, but not oriented to cross boundaries and find ways that the silos

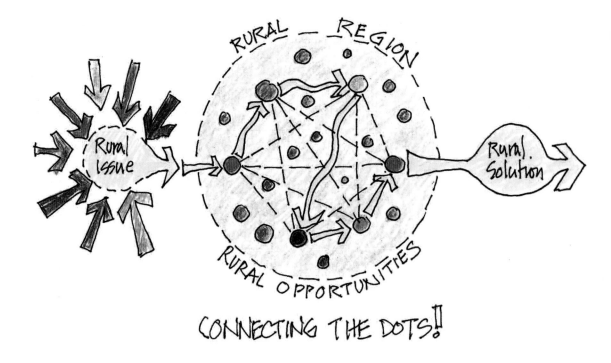

RURAL — REGION

Rural
Issue

Rural
Solution

RURAL OPPORTUNITIES

CONNECTING THE DOTS!

can communicate and work together to improve quality of rural life. For example, geographers may look at a contemporary rural landscape as a product of the continuing impact of humans on nature. To them the rural landscape is something you need to live in, look at, talk about, and study to find out why it is the way it is. Agronomists might look at the plants, soils, and climate of a particular place to determine why some things grow there, why some don't, and why those that do are unique to that place. To them it is an issue of the functionality of the landscape and how it can be nurtured and cultivated for the future. Economists might study the increase in economic growth, based on certain trends, and from the data identify reasons why the economic change took place. Architects may study rural people and the buildings they construct and the materials they use to determine the functions and purposes of vernacular structures. What were the dreams of those who paid for it, and how did they connect with place? Planners may study the policies and organization of rural land uses and regulations to protect the landscape. To them it is how the uses are separated and controlled, but often they look at it from an urban perspective. Engineers seek to service the rural population by designing rural utility systems – water, power, waste, communications – to make them available for human endeavors. Landscape architects love the land and the flora and fauna it contains, and like to imagine outdoor spaces, utilizing landforms and plants to define edges and create shapes and patterns in the landscape.

Rural design as a process can be learned and practiced by any one of the above disciplines (and others) to define and resolve a rural issue; and for the

8.2
A diagram prepared by the CRD to illustrate the synergistic impact of connecting the dots to create solutions that cross boundaries, using the natural assets of a rural region while encouraging strategic partnerships for cooperation and collaboration within their regional framework.

science disciplines it is a way to move beyond their silos. By understanding the principles of the rural design process, they will seek out ways to connect with other disciplines and merge different ways of looking at and thinking about the human, natural, and cultivated landscapes. By holistically connecting the dots they will find the activities working within it and begin to understand it as an integrated system. With the process of rural design they can determine the data and information needed to bring new interdisciplinary insights to the design and planning effort, and through the process develop innovative and creative design solutions that can be transformative.

For the rural design process to be effective and meaningful to rural society the most critical element is community engagement. In a time when the issues impacting rural areas are changing so rapidly, citizens must be involved in shaping a landscape vision for their future that reflects their values. Rural design is a community-based design process for dealing with real problems, and without community involvement in its practice it would remain an academic exercise.

Rural design is an effective link between rural science and rural society. Since change is inevitable and ongoing, and rural land issues are so complex and varied, rural design is a methodology to manage the dynamics to assist rural communities in determining long-term sustainability – economic, social, and health (human, animal, and environmental).

To effectively deal with rural change, it is essential that rural design becomes a strong stand-alone discipline within the design professions, focusing on rural regions and rural problems and issues – just as urban design and planning have evolved to deal with urban issues. Rural design is more than the opposite side of the coin. It deals with entirely different issues within a rural landscape that is complex – with human, animal, and environmental systems which are organized around cultural and natural characteristics that are quite different from an urban context and its infrastructure.

To understand the rural landscape and its integrated complexity the rural designer needs to analyze it from a variety of integrated angles:

- The landforms and the features of the regional land surface and their geological history that make it unique and function as an ecosystem, including the systems of land division and how they are publicly recorded and perceived by the people who live there;
- The vegetation and plants that cover the surface, and the systems that are connected to provide for the economy and services of the region and how they integrate with soils, water, and climate;
- The structures that humans have constructed over time, including domestic, business, and industrial buildings and the construction systems integral to the villages, towns, and cities serving the regional economy;
- The arts, culture, and diversity of the region that bring extraordinary vitality to rural quality of life and economic development.

It is, of course, one thing to analyze and define the rural landscape in terms of its historic development, but another thing to speculate on its future. That is where the interdisciplinary knowledge base becomes so important. To understand the landscape – economically, environmentally, and socially – the rural designer must have data regarding the character of the landscape involved. To speculate on the future, the community must be involved in the speculation process and in the development of any plans for the future which might emerge out of the process.

## New design technologies

'Spatial science' is a fast growing field that studies spatial aspects of people, places, and systems, using and developing information technologies. It has been identified by the White House as one of the three most important industries in the twenty-first century (nanotechnology and biotechnology being the other two), and as a technology that has great potential for assisting rural communities to understand the implications of various alternatives that could impact their future. The CRD has been providing geo-spatial analysis and documentation on its land-based projects and is working to find new ways to assist rural communities to visualize their past, present, and future.

For example, Google Earth is powerful for identifying and understanding community assets in the built and natural environment – worldwide. It provides a vehicle to assist in online community visibility, asset identification and planning, and economic development – particularly in visualizing how places change over time. SketchUp advances typical two-dimensional drawing by providing the power to create three-dimensional environments. By pairing Google Earth and SketchUp, users can geographically locate buildings and landscapes, shape them to illustrate community assets, and translate that visibility into opportunities for local economic development. While most large rural cities have planners and a high level of coverage on Google Earth, smaller towns and rural communities lack institutional capacity and social capital to accomplish three-dimensional planning.

To fill this gap, the CRD is working with faculty in the School of Architecture and Extension Educators to develop a new program. 'Digital Town' (discussed in Chapter 6) is a program to teach multi-generational community members about Google Earth and SketchUp, to visualize the unique qualities of their town and build and locate three-dimensional models of those places, transpose those models to Google Earth, and present the product to the larger community and local officials. The program seeks to build social capital by exposing community members to social, cultural, environmental, and online tools to strengthen the community's institutional capacity by:

- Enabling participants to identify, model, and map community social, cultural, and environmental assets.

- Building social capital with the community across all age groups, with special emphasis on youth and young adults.
- Educating participants and community members in the value of community identity and online exposure.
- Fostering historic, artistic, and cultural preservation of places and institutions.
- Empowering the community to seek opportunities for economic development, including strengthened business retention and enhanced business recruitment.
- Developing a cohesive and tested training program that can be replicated over time with future communities.

The project is an active partnership between the project team and community citizens. The project team provides experience that increases community capacity for recognizing and valuing community assets, building inter-generational social capital, and identifying economic development opportunities (Roos *et al.*, 2010).

## Rural design education

Rural design is all about connections between humans and landscapes in a rural setting and has great potential to become an effective catalyst in assisting rural people to envision their future while preserving those aspects of where they live that they value the most. In 2002, the CRD initiated a feasibility study for a graduate program in rural design through the College of Continuing Education at the University of Minnesota. This effort accomplished preliminary explorations into marketing (student and professional interest surveys), curriculum development and competitive programs within the University of Minnesota and other institutions, nationally and internationally. Significantly, no other program dedicated to rural design as a problem-solving process in the rural landscape was identified, anywhere.

One of the original reasons for founding the CRD was to begin to fill the need for an academic multidisciplinary curriculum program in rural design. A program that recognized the unique relationships between the professions of architecture, landscape architecture, engineering, and planning in the rural landscape, involving a broader exploration of scientific research and sustainable human activity in rural regions, including urban/rural edge issues. Other disciplines that have become involved in discussions and activities with the CRD on its research projects at the University of Minnesota include: agronomy, ecology, soils, geology, geography, public health, bio-system engineering, anthropology, sociology, veterinary medicine, applied economics, and forestry.

From the survey and its experience working with rural communities, the CRD believes that a graduate curriculum program in rural design must address the needs of the professional design community, rural citizens, and public officials, while meeting academic goals in the following ways:

- Providing students with the opportunity for an educational experience focused directly on design thinking and related rural natural, cultural, and human landscape issues at the local, state, national, and global levels and their connections.
- Including fundamental and applied research understanding and knowledge specifically directed at the under-explored rural landscape and the interaction of its heritage, cultures, economies, and environments, and how they have changed over time.
- Expanding opportunities for land-grant universities to better fulfill their mission of public engagement, providing outreach and support to community leaders and public officials by bringing design thinking into public engagement issues.
- Addressing new areas of knowledge and understanding of rural issues for the professional community, and aiding in expanding economic and employment opportunities for design professionals in under-served rural regions.
- Providing rural design programs that incorporate and do not duplicate existing programs within universities or other institutions nationally by seeking innovative and creative ways that design thinking can connect the dots to enhance the problem-solving process.
- Documenting significant interest in a program in rural design by both potential students and the professional community who may be working in remote rural areas by aggressively marketing the program, utilizing all means of communication including social networks and long-distance learning.

Clarifying rural issues and establishing the research foundation for effective rural design is a continuous and rigorous search for ecological, social, cultural, economic, political, and health meaning, connected to place and climate, while responding to global issues in a global economy. These issues require new approaches to resolving global problems resulting from climate change, food supply and security, renewable energy, water resources and quality, and health – human, animal, and environmental. Rural design offers a new approach that brings design thinking and the problem-solving process of design to these rural issues, and their resolution will fundamentally alter the economic and social foundations of rural areas and the relationships between urban and rural areas in the twenty-first century (Thorbeck, 2010).

## Rural Design Certificate program

As the first step toward a graduate program in rural design, the CRD has developed a non-credit, on demand, online Rural Design Certificate program, focusing on issues challenging rural areas and developing creative solutions to meet those challenges. This first ever rural design program, launched in 2011, provides students with the knowledge base and methodology of rural design to assist them in their work with rural communities to develop creative solutions for the issues challenging rural regions worldwide. Students gain knowledge about rural landscape character, the community-based process of rural design, and design strategies, allowing them to address rural problems comprehensively, scale appropriately, and, thus, effectively.

The Rural Design Certificate (RDC) enhances professional practice in a wide range of disciplines, including architecture, landscape architecture, planning, agronomy, civil engineering, natural resource management, rural sociology, and community economic development. By taking the courses and obtaining the certificate, professionals are better equipped to meet the challenges of rapidly changing global issues impacting rural regions while gaining continuing education credits for their professional registration.

The RDC program provides on-demand learning, with a body of classes designed to meet the goal of gaining an understanding of rural issues and the process of developing solutions. It comprises 40 hours of instruction: 20 hours of core courses and 20 hours of electives. Each course is a set of webcasts utilizing PowerPoint, with voiceovers, quizzes, and options to include video and weblinks.

Available globally online, the RDC is readily accessible and presented in enroll-anytime class modules. Each core area includes one required core class and multiple related electives. The core classes present an overview of the key issues and concepts in that core area. The electives highlight aspects of the core area in depth and breadth, provide knowledge on new technologies and research, and showcase exemplary scholars who are experts in specific areas. The four core areas of the RDC program are:

1. **Rural Landscapes:** Landscape patterns in the rural environment are easy to discern but hard to describe, due to multiple definitions and experiences based on geographic, climatic, and cultural differences around the world. Some questions this core area will explore are:

   - What is 'rural' and how is it different than 'urban'?
   - How do communities determine and preserve rural character?
   - What are the impacts of climate change?
   - What makes a place 'a place'?

   The core class in Rural Landscapes assists students to develop an understanding of the fundamental issues related to rural areas by presenting a body of key terms, an exploration of the many definitions of 'rural', and an exploration of rural character and place making.

2. **Rural Culture and Society:** Rural landscapes vary by region, geography, climate, population, and community history, among many other factors. The core class presents an historical analysis of rural culture and the rural human landscape, studies the implications of current and projected demographic changes, and examines political processes related to land use. This

core class provides students with an understanding of rural cultural and social issues. In addition, this class explores issues of multi-jurisdictional cooperation and collaboration for economic advantage and culturally appropriate design.

3.  **Rural Sustainability:** Sustainability is a framework for short- and long-term rural community success which embodies a synergistic relationship between the human and natural environments, society and culture, and the economy. The core class explores sustainability as a framework for developing sustainable solutions for rural issues and their impacts, including: climate change; renewable energy; sustainable resource use and production methods; community vitality and leadership; and human, animal, and environmental health.

4.  **Rural Design:** The new design discipline of rural design is an interdisciplinary process for defining rural issues, managing rural change, and creating solutions to resolve them. The core class explores design tools and processes to develop integrated and creative solutions to rural issues, with rural sustainability as a guiding framework. The class presents a body of knowledge that includes design thinking, planning and design processes, using cases studies as key examples. Rural design as a connecting link between scientific research and its use by society is integral to the class.

The target audience for the RDC is primarily professionals in architecture, landscape architecture, planning, civil engineering, natural resource management, and community economic development. In most countries, registered design, planning, and engineering professionals need to maintain their state or province licensure by taking accredited continuing education units. Graduate students in these professional areas and others, such as agronomy, water resources, sociology, forestry, soils, ecology, public health, and wildlife management, will also find the RDC valuable because they can learn about a new field of design and receive a certificate validating their efforts.

The RDC is, however, only the first step toward a graduate school curriculum program in rural design. For rural design to have the stature that rural communities deserve, it needs to be fully recognized in the academic and professional communities as a graduate-level program in rural design at research universities providing a graduate-level degree. Even though the RDC program is oriented primarily to design students in North America, the reason for outlining it here is to provide information for academic institutions worldwide to jump-start a rural design program in their countries.

## Rural sustainability

Issues of sustainability in the rural landscape are distinct from the urban landscape, although they overlap in many areas, such as energy, food supply and delivery, transportation, recreation, and communications. Definitions of sustainability are many, but the one that is most common is: 'Development that meets the needs of the present without compromising the ability of future generations to meet their own needs.' This definition was created in 1987 at the World Commission on Environment and Development (the Brundtland Commission).

When it comes to sustainable agriculture, the definition becomes more complex. According to the United States Department of Agriculture, 'sustainable agriculture' means:

> An integrated system of plant and animal production practices having a site-specific application that will, over the long term:
>
> - satisfy human food and fiber needs;
> - enhance environmental quality and the natural resource base upon which the agriculture economy depends;
> - make the most efficient use of non-renewable resources and on-farm resources and integrate, where appropriate, natural biological cycles and controls;
> - sustain the economic viability of farm operations;
> - enhance the quality of life for farmers and society as a whole.

'Sustainable rural development' has been described by Jean Richardson in a rather convoluted sentence, indicating that it is not a fixed state of harmony. She describes it as:

> A collaborative process that strives to reconcile the promotion of economic opportunities and livable communities with the conservation of ecological integrity and biodiversity, a process of change in which exploitation of resources, natural and human, direction of investments, orientation of technological development, and institutional trends are made consistent with future as well as present needs.
>
> (Richardson, 2000)

A definition by the CRD is more direct. The CRD describes 'sustainable rural development' simply as: 'The shaping of rural environments to provide an integrated system of human communities, plants and animal production that meets the needs of people, the economy, and the environment in the present without compromising for the future.'

## The International Organization for Rural Design

During the First International Symposium on Rural Design, which was held at the University of Minnesota in January 2010, participants discussed the creation of an 'international organization for rural design' dedicated to fostering the development of rural design as both an area of academic inquiry and as a professional discipline. The following are the key points for the proposed organization as expressed by participants:

- Need to ensure that members have a clear, compelling reason to belong;
- The organization must remain focused on how it can help rural communities;
- The participants should be all doers, and an orientation to action should be reflected in the organization;
- Collaborate to efficiently and effectively use scarce resources, but make sure there is an award for all participants;
- The organization should serve to coordinate our individual project outputs into meaningful outcomes;
- Organizational models include communities of practice, citizen-driven organizations such as regional partnerships, and joint public official/ practitioner organizations like the American Planning Association;
- The organization's agenda must be driven by those affected;
- Do not let funders dictate the agenda.

The symposium participants agreed that rural design might not be a need identified by rural citizens, but they will often identify the needs that can be met by design. As a 'quality of life' issue it helps explain why many young adults leave rural areas for better designed urban areas that are more culturally diverse. Yet, the promise of rural design is that it offers potential solutions which encourage diversity and a process that offers a better chance to make a difference and achieve a successful, tangible outcome (Streng, 2010).

The international organization moved forward in the spring of 2011, with an interactive website for global discussion and presentation. Currently there are approximately 500 academics, practitioners, and others worldwide who have expressed strong interest in the organization. Anyone can join by writing to the Center for Rural Design at the University of Minnesota, 277 Coffey Hall, 1420 Eckles Avenue, St Paul, MN 55108, USA, or by email: crdinfo@umn.edu.


## Global challenges

The challenges for rural futures are enormous because it is the rural environments around the world that provide the food and fiber necessary for life. If these environments are to be sustainable then their agricultural interconnections with social and economic forces, both urban and rural, and the impacts of climate change and rapid population increase need to be understood and balanced. One of the objectives of rural design as a new design discipline lies in valuing and explaining the long-term consequences and benefits of short-term decisions.

Based on the experiences of the CRD and what we have learned from other disciplines and the international symposium, the principles of rural design can help in understanding, analyzing, and creating solutions for sustainable rural environments worldwide. These rural design principles include:

- Social, cultural, artistic, and environmental diversity is rewarding for all people who live, work, and play in rural communities, and for their quality of life. The arts can become a vehicle for learning, social interaction, entertainment, and inspiration and an integral aspect of economic development.
- Empowering women to become community leaders is more likely to provide effective resolution of the complexity of rural issues.
- Making connections between human, animal, and environmental health is crucial to understanding wellness. Keeping people, animals, and environments healthy is economically preferable to taking care of them when they are sick.
- Sustainable rural development is directly connected to sustainable rural production. It is finding and enhancing the connections between them that will best impact social, economic, and environmental issues.
- Design of sustainable buildings and landscapes must reflect uniqueness of cultural and landscape character – form follows function, climate, and place.
- Food, including its supply, production, distribution, and security, is an interdisciplinary rural design problem. Rural food systems can be mapped and their interactions studied to develop strategic plans and farming practices that are unique to place, helping to ensure safe and adequate food supplies in the future.
- Economic and community viability is crucial for short-term as well as long-term rural design endeavors; however, long-term objectives must take precedence over short-term gain.
- Renewable energy from solar, wind, and biomass are interrelated, and can be considered as an integral aspect of rural agriculture – harvesting the sun and wind, including using agriculture for carbon sequestration and reduction of greenhouse gases.
- Improving rural quality of life is the primary goal of rural design.

If rural and urban communities are to preserve those qualities of the land integral to their landscape heritage that are admired and valued, then rural design provides a process for creating options and assisting in making decisions that can result in a positive impact on the visual, social, economic, and environmental character and values of the rural landscape and rural quality of life.

Rural design is an emerging new design discipline, bringing the problem-solving process of design to rural issues. It can assist rural communities in meeting the challenges for rural futures, by becoming:

- A process for linking rural science and rural society, and available globally;
- A methodology to resolve rural land-use issues, including the urban/rural edge, and environmental issues impacting both rural and urban people;
- A way to use three-dimensional geo-spatial systems and other communication methodologies to enhance citizen knowledge and public participation;
- A community-based design process to empower rural citizens in making informed decisions about land use;
- A way to create synergism through systemic linkages and connections within the artistic, cultural, and natural landscapes;
- A way to understand the relationships between quality of life and sense of place in the rural landscape;
- A way to connect sustainable rural economic, environmental, artistic, cultural, and social issues;
- A way to view, understand, and admire the diversity of the world.

I hope this book makes you as excited about rural environments and the potential of rural design to shape rural futures, as it does me. Years ago I had the opportunity to travel throughout rural Italy and I discovered the wonderful hill towns and their unique relationship with the countryside. As I reflect back, the realization that these beautiful rural landscapes and communities had been designed and shaped by humans, helped me later realize how powerful a new academic discipline of rural design could be as a way of bringing design thinking and problem solving to rural issues today.

Rural design is a way to shape rural environments and make beautiful spatial connections between the infrastructure of rural living and the landscape and ecosystems that we as humans on this planet depend on for food and sustenance. The world is changing very rapidly, with most people living in cities that are growing and adapting to global impacts. Likewise, rural regions are changing, with people who are passionate about rural life and their connections to the land.

Rural design is a discipline by which design professionals and others concerned for rural futures can work with rural communities, and bring design thinking and its problem-solving process to the wide range of issues and scales impacting rural areas worldwide. Never has the time been more opportune for rural design, nor is it more needed. As stated in the Foreword to this book, 'if we have designed our way into problems, we can also design our way out of them'.

# Chapter 9

# Epilogue

This book is intended to be an introduction to rural design, yet its future is still to be written. I hope that the Center for Rural Design at the University of Minnesota can be a model for other universities and agencies in working together, using design as a problem-solving process to seek solutions to rural issues.

Rural design is an emerging new design discipline, poised to address rural issues in a global economy and respond to the challenges and opportunities it brings. How the world's agricultural landscape is used and the kind of sustainable agriculture needed to provide safe food, fiber, and fuel for a rapidly growing world population, while preserving the environment, is a critical global land-use issue.

Writing about leadership in higher education, James Anderson (2008) indicates that the 'readiness of a college or university to confront its 21st century responsibilities is directly correlated with the degree to which it has embedded diversity and globalism concerns in the basic philosophy and infrastructure of the institution'. For rural design, diversity has a very broad meaning. It includes the relationships between urban and rural people and their mutual benefits and responsibilities. As a new design program, rural design can cross jurisdictional and academic disciplines to bring science and technology to the benefit of both rural and urban people. For it to be effective, it must function with an evidence-based community-planning process to arrive at sustainable recommendations that people will be excited about and support. For people with a passion for rural life, rural design can transform design thinking about, and living and working in, rural regions.

As the world's population nearly doubles by 2050, issues of climate change, renewable energy, fresh water resources, safe food, and wellness will dominate land-use decisions. If agriculture uses 40% of the available land on the planet, and land is a finite resource, then to feed a rapidly expanding world population with different densities and demographics in each region of the world, land is going to have to be shaped and utilized with new and innovative technologies and methods.

## Process of discovery

During my long career as an architect and teacher, designing a variety of buildings, working with rural communities, and learning about the changes taking place in rural regions in North America, I slowly came to realize the need for a new rural design discipline dedicated to the shaping of rural environments. For me it has been an exciting process of discovery.

I was born and raised near the source of the Mississippi River in the small rural town of Bagley in northern Minnesota. From an early age I was fascinated by visits to my immigrant Norwegian grandparents' farms and the discovery of how they lived on a farm, worked with animals, and tilled the land. Those early experiences created an innate passion and love of barns, farmsteads, small towns, and the people who live and work in the rural countryside.

After graduation from high school I left for the twin cities of Minneapolis and St Paul and enrolled in a small liberal arts college, where I discovered, through an enlightened engineering professor, the exciting world of architecture. Once I realized that there was an architectural profession and that as an architect I could think about, draw, and design buildings for people, I knew immediately that would be my life career. The next day I transferred into the School of Architecture at the University of Minnesota, where I began to learn about the design process and how buildings were constructed and worked. It was there that I received a Bachelor of Architecture degree while working part-time for architectural firms. For graduate school I enrolled in Yale University for a Master of Architecture and shortly after graduation I applied for, and was fortunate to be awarded, the prestigious Rome Prize Fellowship in Architecture to the American Academy in Rome.

The Rome Prize is awarded each year to a select group of artists and scholars to pursue their work in a collegial atmosphere of intellectual and artistic freedom, interdisciplinary discussion, and spirit of innovation. The Academy is located high on the Janiculum Hill overlooking Rome, and the Fellowship provided a large studio and a stipend that allowed two years of independent architectural study, with extensive travels throughout Italy and the rest of Europe. That experience changed my life.

My work at the Academy focused on the development of urban housing from Roman times to the present. This involved visiting a variety of Roman sites, including touring with Yale architectural historian and former fellow, William E. MacDonald, who had hired me to draw illustrations for his seminal book, *The Architecture of the Roman Empire* (1982). On one of those tours, MacDonald introduced me to the importance of Ostia, the ancient seaport for Rome. It was there that one can walk the stone pavements, tour buildings, and envision what living in Rome was like 2,000 years ago. I was intrigued by the sophistication of the multi-story apartment houses constructed with balconies, interior courtyards, indoor plumbing, and warm air heating systems. The apartment buildings in Ostia were similar to those constructed in Rome and reflected building code requirements controlling height, ventilation, heating, and construction for dense urban living.

**9.1**

Drawing of Casa Di Diana, an apartment building in Ostia Antica, the ancient seaport of Rome, illustrating a typical Roman apartment house with ground-floor shops and living quarters above. The apartment house was constructed with an interior central courtyard, indoor plumbing, and warm air heating system. This organization became a paradigm for urban living throughout the Roman world.

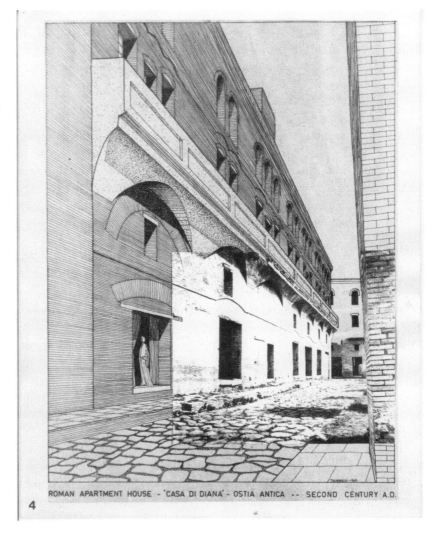

ROMAN APARTMENT HOUSE - 'CASA DI DIANA' - OSTIA ANTICA -- SECOND CENTURY A.D.

As part of my studies I created a reconstruction drawing of one of the apartment buildings in Ostia (Casa Di Diana from the second century), which illustrates the basic Roman organization of urban living along a street, with shops on the ground floor and living quarters above (Figure 9.1). This form of urban house and pattern of living was used extensively in towns, settlements, and cities throughout Europe during Roman times, and carried forward during the Middle Ages into the attached townhouse or apartment house in cities that we know today.

In his book, MacDonald (1982) talks about Roman architecture and its connections to ritual and culture. He points out that it is their architecture that most reflected Roman traditions, and it extended throughout the lands that the Romans occupied. For example, city markets were in the same cultural category as imperial baths, and the city market became an important social gathering place where rural people and urban people could meet and exchange ideas, goods, and services.

The Romans constructed most of their major public buildings in support of social harmony, so that their architecture was basically cultural in nature and contemporary in implementation, to serve and symbolize the state throughout the Roman Empire. MacDonald ends his book with this statement about the influence of Rome on Western Europe and the lands around the Mediterranean Sea:

> The principles of this architecture, for centuries an effective instrument of Roman culture, were not lost when the political framework of ancient society collapsed. They survived the transition to the early middle ages, and together with Roman literature and law have continued ever since to give inspiration and instruction. And Roman architecture has never ceased to be relevant to the study of the nature and meaning of architectural form, for it was an expressive and powerful art, defining a critically important experience of Mediterranean and Western man.
>
> (MacDonald, 1982)

The Romans organized the countryside and implemented agrarian systems to supply food and fiber to urban populations, and this organization was reflected in the military-like layout and organization of rural landscapes and farms. In some parts of northern Italy, northeast of Padua, one can still identify farm layouts surveyed by the military, with straight boundary lines as farm estates for retired legionnaires. From several books on rural life in the northern Roman frontier I sketched the plan (Figure 9.2) of a typical Roman villa and its organization within a walled compound, and the utilization of farm machinery for harvesting crops in Germania.

The books describe rural estates and farming practices that were very similar in rural regions throughout the Roman Empire. These traditions, particularly the building of roads and clearing of land for agriculture, have influenced farm layouts and rural landscapes throughout Western civilization (Schultz, 1985; Wightman, 1970). While travelling throughout Italy, I visited a number of hill towns and rural cities, and as I think back, those rural places and the visual connections between architecture and landscape were more interesting and had a greater impact on my careers than the important urban public buildings and public spaces.

My travels throughout Europe also provided the opportunity to discover the farming heritage that immigrants brought to North America. Their national and ethnic culture blended and melded with the culture of others, and it is the diversity of people, climate, and landscape that created the intrinsic character of farms, farmsteads, and small towns in rural America. The immigrants' desire was to create institutions and a built environment in the expanding American frontier that would last. The classical courthouses constructed in the late nineteenth and early twentieth centuries reflected this desire for permanence, and Roman architecture was a powerful paradigm for what these buildings should look like.

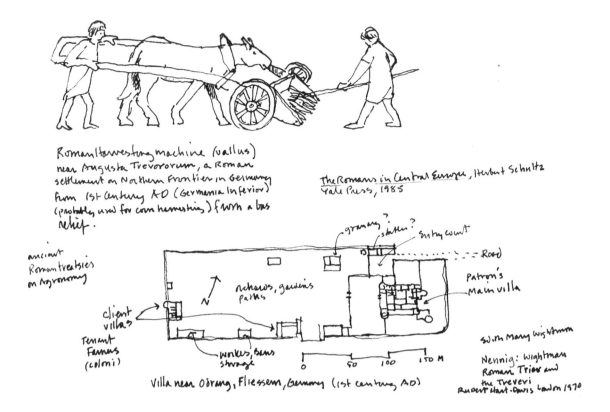

Roman Harvesting machine (vallus)
near Augusta Trevororum, a Roman
settlement on Northern Frontier in Germany
from 1st Century AD (Germania Inferior)
(probably used for corn harvesting) from a bas
relief.

The Romans in Central Europe, Herbert Schultz
Yale Press, 1985

ancient
Roman treatsies
on Agronomy

granary? shelter? Entry court
Road
Patron's
Main villa

orchards, gardens
parks

client
villas

Tenant
Farms
(colmi)

workers, barns
storage

N

0    50   100   150 M

s.with Mary Wightman

Nennig: Wightman
Roman Trier and
the Trevevi
Rupert Hart-Davis London 1970

Villa near Odrang, Fliessem, Germany (1st century AD)

## Integrating buildings and landscapes

9.2
A sketch from two books about first-century Roman villas in Germania, showing a plan of a farmstead and its organization of functional buildings around an open space, and a detail sketch of a bas-relief, showing a horse and machine for harvesting corn.

In both my professional and academic careers, I developed a special interest and focus on connecting buildings and landscapes. I was fortunate to have the opportunity to learn about and design a wide range of buildings for animals, agriculture, and environmental education and interpretation. They are projects where I tried to respect heritage, connect to landscape and respond to climate and place, expressing meaning, connection, and sustainability in the design of buildings and communities.

A beautiful building that is part of nature is poetic, and this philosophy guides my professional and academic work. In support of this idea, I often tell my students that if I was not an architect I would probably be a dairy farmer – I happen to like cows. This probably stems from those boyhood visits to my grandparents' farms where the barn, with its animals, smells, and ambience was the most exciting and fascinating place to explore, work, and play. It was on these visits that I first experienced a working farmstead and the harmonious relationships between humans, landscapes, and animals – rooted in a particular place and climate – that became a fundamental aspect of my professional and academic ethos.

My rural background and architectural education all came together when in 1970 I started an interdisciplinary design firm with another architect, a landscape architect, a graphic designer, and a computer specialist. This was a time shortly after American astronauts first walked on the moon and we saw images of Earth from outer space. Those images made us keenly aware of how all life was connected on the planet as it moved through space. It helped in formulating the kind of interdisciplinary firm we thought was important.

Less than a year old, the first major commission we received was winning the competition to design a new zoological garden in Minnesota (Figures 9.3 and 9.4). That exciting project, to create the first northern climate zoo in the world designed to remain open year-round – and its broad implications for evidence-based design and the integrated relationships between humans, animals, and their habitats – had a profound impact on my architectural and academic careers. The zoo received a number of design awards and established a strong desire for knowledge and understanding about the diverse relationships between humans, animals, and the environment.

The Minnesota Zoological Garden opened the door to other projects, which provided an opportunity to think about the architecture of agriculture and connections between cultural and natural landscapes. On all of those projects, and other

9.3
The Minnesota Zoological Garden after its completion, overlooking the central lake. The diamond-shaped building is the 1.5 acre Tropical Exhibit, and the earth-covered roof is over the educational component.

Interior of the Tropical Exhibit at the Minnesota Zoological Garden, housing a wide range of animals from Southeast Asia in their natural habitats. The exhibit was designed to create the illusion that the animals were free and the visitors confined.

cultural and public buildings projects I was working on, I struggled to understand and respond to function, climate and place, and to make connections by blurring the line between architecture and landscape.

## Drawing and rural design

During extensive travels over the years I recorded in drawings special places I visited where architecture and landscape meet, and have compiled a large collection of travel sketches which illustrate those connections. They include a sketch from Orvieto (Figure 9.5), one of the famous hill towns north of Rome (Siena, San Gimignano, Cortona, Montepulciano, Chiusi, Gubbio, and Urbino are some others), that shows a typical Italian hill town and its close urban architectural relationship on the hill top and the agricultural fields in the valley below.

The towns were organized on hills for defensive purposes during the Middle Ages. The farmers lived in compact urban houses, with shops and/or animals on the ground floor and living quarters above – similar to those I saw in Roman Ostia.

The houses, constructed with stone walls, stucco, and tile roofs, express unique architectural character and form as they step up and down along narrow streets with changing topography.

Every day, farmers would rise in the morning, load their donkeys or oxen and travel down into the valleys to tend to fields. When the day became darker they returned to the safety of the tightly knit community on top of the hill. This pattern of living in villages on a hill top worked well for defense, and preserved open space and prime agricultural land in the valleys for food production. Today there are fewer farmers and larger farms in Italy, just like in North America and other parts of Europe, but the pattern and organization or rural living still exists, providing the wonderful Italian landscape of Tuscany, Umbria, and other rural regions that tourists love to visit.

Other sketches illustrate similar cultural relationships and connections between landscape and architecture. Two sketches (Figures 9.6 and 9.7) from the Lofoten Islands in Norway, near the Arctic Circle, illustrate vernacular connections between water, landscape, and building, reflecting Norwegian culture and the importance of the fishing industry. This is near the region that my fisherman grandfather emigrated from in 1893, and these simple functional wood buildings perched at the water's edge represent vernacular architecture at its best. The rendition of fishing, water, and landscape, working together for mutual benefit, is clearly expressed in their function, design, material, and construction.

In Canada, a large three-story stone and wood barn and granary (Figure 9.8), constructed as part of Covenhaven Farm on Minister's Island near St

9.5
Orvieto is a typical Italian hill town, with housing on top of the hill and agriculture in the valley below. The Italian hill town and its relationship to the agricultural landscape are greatly admired by tourists.

**9.6**
A working harbor in Henningsvær, in the Lofoten Islands, shows a warehouse building that is a transition structure between the land and the sea. Functional need created these simple vernacular buildings for harvesting the sea.

Henningsvaer Harbor
(The Venice of Lofoten)
6/1/05
Dewey

**9.7**
A fish house and home on the Lofoten Islands expresses a powerful connection between sea, land, and architecture. The beautiful delicacy of the fish house, perched on the edge of the water, and its reflection in the harbor is the epitome of 'less is more'.

The Barn at Covenhaven
Minister's Island
St Andrews, NB, Canada
5/31/11 Dwyer

Andrews, New Brunswick, similarly illustrates how functional purpose and local materials can be used to create an indigenous architectural form. Here, stone from a quarry on the farm is used to shape and retain the land, providing a base for wood construction on top. Silos for storing feed and the basilica arrangement of the barn for animals and storage reflect their functional purposes – providing light, ventilation, and access for interior and exterior animal care and farm-work operations. The barn housed cattle at the lower level, horses and equipment on the second, and a large loft for hay storage on the third. The Covenhaven barn is a clear expression of vernacular architecture, with form following function, place, and climate.

Machu Picchu in Peru (Figure 9.9), located 8,000 feet above sea level, high on a mountain ridge above the Urubamba Valley, is the place that best exemplifies a sacred and poetic relationship between architecture and landscape. It is perhaps the most beautiful place on the planet for experiencing and reflecting on human efforts to construct a spiritual connection between buildings, animals, and landscape. Constructed in the fifteenth century as an estate for the Inca emperor, it was abandoned a hundred years later during the Spanish conquest. The site location (Figure 9.10), below the towering Huayna Picchu, was chosen because of its sacred landscape relationships with Incan astronomical events that were considered ritually important. There are other places that are equally awe-inspiring, like the Great Wall in China or the Taj Mahal in India, but nowhere is

9.8
This large stone and wood barn and granary was constructed on Minister's Island, St Andrews, New Brunswick. The barn dominates the island farm, but fits into the landscape with functional and aesthetic purpose. It was carefully constructed and detailed with materials found on the island.

9.9 (opposite)
Machu Picchu in Peru is one of the most beautiful places on earth for experiencing a sacred and human integration of architecture and place. This exciting mountain-top center uniquely illustrates the experiential power that architecture and landscape working together can have.

the integrated spiritual connection between humans, landscape, and buildings more strongly expressed and experienced than at Machu Picchu.

Not far from Machu Picchu, the Peruvian fortress of Sacsayhuaman is located 12,000 feet above sea level near Cusco, the capital of the Inca empire. It is unbelievable for its construction, using large and irregular stones, shaped and fitted into its rampart walls. The polished and dry set stones were cut from quarries, hauled long distances, and shaped to interlock and fit together so tightly that

Machu Picchu
Agricultural Sector
11/1/05
Dewey

9.10
Aerial photograph of Machu Picchu from the top of the mountain, illustrating the agricultural and building zones, and their relationship to each other and the surrounding landscape.

no mortar was required. Scholars have been unable to determine how they did this. Sacsayhuaman is a site illustrating the epitome of human ingenuity and perseverance, using local material to accomplish extraordinary construction (Figure 9.11). After the Spanish conquest, the Spaniards used many of the smaller stones to build colonial Cusco. Only the largest stones still remain and yet the site and its construction are still awe-inspiring.

Architects, landscape architects, or planners who draw and record their travels in sketches have a special way of seeing the world. It is a methodology where images are engraved in the mind rather than on film. The photograph shows you reality as seen through the camera lens, while the sketch records the emotion and character of place as seen through the eyes and hands of the artist.

In a time where digital cameras and computer renderings dominate the design professions, the tradition of hand drawing what one sees and experiences is a valuable means of learning to see, understand, and design. Drawing is a way to communicate inherent ideas about people and cultures and landscapes, and it can be used to promote human understanding and appreciation of the incredible and exciting diversity of the world we live in.

Sagsaywamen gateway
gray andesite stone

## Shaping rural futures

**9.11**
**9.11**
Sacsayhuaman was the fortress guarding Cusco, the capital of the Inca empire in Peru. It was constructed with mammoth stones that are fitted, polished, and locked together without mortar. It is a mystery as to how the work was accomplished, and certainly awe-inspiring as to the cultural and the technical capability of Inca people.

This book is a result of what I have discovered about the challenges that rural people, rural communities, and rural regions have in managing change and about addressing those challenges to compete in a global economy. I have tried to present a vision for a new rural design discipline that provides a way of thinking about rural landscapes throughout the world.

In Norway, scholars at the Barents Institute have been studying the reasons why people choose to live in rural areas in remote parts of northern Scandinavia and northern Russia. They call the phenomenon 'lust for rural living'. It is the passion that rural citizens have about their place, their landscape, climate, and quality of life that makes the discipline of rural design meaningful, challenging, and exciting as a design process to help shape rural futures. A large percentage of the useable land on the planet is agricultural, and rural regions and rural communities around the world deserve a rural design discipline that can help rural people address their needs – expressing their lust for rural living.

If design thinking can transform organizations and inspire innovation, as Tim Brown argues in his book about nurturing change through design (Brown, 2009), then rural design is a way to bring design thinking to rural issues to create ideas that can become transformative. The power of design thinking is enormous as a means to understand where we have been, where we are today, and to speculate on where we can be in the future.

Design is an exciting journey and process of discovery. It is a way to explore options, create new choices, and find new solutions. The global crisis in land use and agriculture makes it imperative to find solutions that can feed the rapidly growing world population. If the design process primarily focuses on urban people, issues, and businesses because that is where most of the people on the planet live, we endanger future quality of life.

The only effective way to deal with global rural issues is to look at them systemically and holistically, from both an urban and a rural perspective. Rural design offers a new way of design thinking about land use, agriculture, and rural living, and a methodology for finding creative and transformative concepts and innovations for a healthy and prosperous future for everyone – urban as well as rural – in North America and around the world.

# References

Adams, William Howard (1983) *Jefferson's Monticello* (New York: Abbeville Press).

Agnitsch, K., Flora, J., and Ryan, V. (2006) Bonding and bridging social capital: The interactive effects on community action, *Community Development, Journal of the Community Development Society*, 37(1).

Anderson, J. (2008) *Driving Change Through Diversity and Globalization: Transformative Leadership in the Academy* (Sterling, VA: Stylus).

Arendt, R. (1994) *Rural by Design: Maintaining Small Town Character* (Cambridge, MA: Lincoln Land Institute, American Planning Association).

Barrie, T. (2010) *The Sacred In-Between: The Mediating Roles of Architecture* (London: Routledge).

Bellona Foundation (2008) *The Bellona Scenario* (Oslo: Bellona Foundation).

Ben Abed, Äicha (ed.) (2006) *Stories in Stone: Conserving Mosaics of Roman Africa* (Los Angeles: Getty Publications).

Boody, G., Vondracek, B., Andow, D., Krinke, M., Westra, J., Zimmerman, J., and Welle, P. (2005) Multifunctional agriculture in the United States, *BioScience*, 55(1).

Borchert, J. (1987) *America's Northern Heartland* (Minneapolis: University of Minnesota Press).

Borlaug, N. (2008) Comment by Borlaug in a lecture at the University of Minnesota.

Brown, F.E. (1961) *Roman Architecture* (New York: George Braziller).

Brown, T. (2009) *Change by Design* (New York: HarperCollins).

Carmody, J., Goldberg, L., Strong, R., and MacDonagh, P. (2010) Performance-based research on housing and infrastructure development at UMore Park (unpublished report, University of Minnesota).

Cartlidge, T., Thorbeck, D., Hellevik, W., and Hanson, C. (1999) Making room for sustainable animal agriculture in the rural landscape: The Central Minnesota Community Dairy Partnership (unpublished report, University of Minnesota).

Center for Rural Policy and Development (CRPD) (2009) Understanding small business development and entrepreneurialism in Greater Minnesota (research paper).

Community Development Society (CDS) (2010) http://www.comm-dev.org/.

Costello, J. (2010) We just went through 200 years of radical economic upheaval – the next economy era offers us a chance to control it, Archein essay published by AlterNet, November 8, http://www.alternet.org/story/148215/.

Davidson-Hunt, I. (2003) Indigenous lands management, cultural landscapes and Anishinaabe people of Shoal Lake, Northwestern Ontario, Canada, *Environments*, 31(1).

De Belie, N., Richardson, M., Braam, C., Svennerstedt, J., Lenechan, J., and Sonck, B. (2000) Durability of building materials and components in the agricultural environment: Part 1, the agricultural environment and timber structures, *Journal of Agricultural Engineering Research*, 75(3).

Drabenstott, M. (2010) *Past Silos and Smokestacks* (Chicago: Chicago Council on Global Affairs).

Eaton, L. (1972) *American Architecture Comes of Age* (Cambridge, MA: MIT Press).

Espiritu, A. (2009) RE/EN acting masculinity: Constructing identity in the Northern Barents, *Northern Experiments: The Barents Urban Survey*, www.northernexperiments. net.

European Network for Rural Development (ENRD) (2010) www.enrd.ec.europa.eu/ and European Commission on Agriculture and Rural Development.

Florida, R. (2002) The rise of the creative class: Why cities without gays and rock bands are losing the economic development race, *Washington Monthly*, May http://www. washingtonmonthly.com/features/2001/0205/florida.html.

Foley, J. (2009) The other inconvenient truth: The crisis in global land use, *Yale Environment*, 360.

Fraser Hart, J. (1998) *The Rural Landscape* (Baltimore, MD: Johns Hopkins University Press).

Gabler, W.A. (1997) *Death of the Dream: Farmhouses in the Heartland* (Afton, MN: Afton Historical Society Press).

Gjerde, J. (1985) *From Peasants to Farmers: The Migration from Balestrand, Norway to the Upper Middle West* (Cambridge: Cambridge University Press).

Graham, S. (2002) FlowCity: Networked mobilities and the contemporary metropolis, *Journal of Urban Technology*, 9(1).

Hamilton, K. and Watkins, D. (2009) *Evidence-Based Design for Multiple Building Types* (Hoboken, NJ: Wiley).

Hamin, E. and Marcucci, D. (2008) Ad hoc rural regionalism, *Journal of Rural Studies*, 24.

Hoskins, W.G. (1955) *The Making of the English Landscape* (London: Hodder & Stoughton).

Hueston, W. (2009) Global initiative for food systems leadership, *One to One Newsletter*, 4.

Jacobs, J. (1961) *Death and Life of Great American Cities* (New York: Random House).

Jacobson, L., Schmidt, D., and Wood, S. (2001) *OFFSET: Odor From Feedlots Setback Estimation Tool* (Minneapolis: University of Minnesota Extension Service).

Jacobson, L., Schmidt, D., Nicolai, R., and Bicudo, J. (1998) *Odor Control for Animal Agriculture* (Minneapolis: University of Minnesota Extension Service).

Jacobson, L., Janni, K., Thorbeck, D., and Carmody, J. (2009) Integrated performance guidelines for sustainable commercial animal buildings (unpublished proposal to the National Science Foundation, Emerging Frontiers in Research and Innovation – Science in Engineering and Environmental Design).

Joenniemi, P. and Sergunin, A. (2008) The model of twin cities experiences from Northern Europe, *Barents Institute Reprint*, 2.

Kotkin, J. ( 2010) *The Next Hundred Million: America in 2050* (London: Penguin).

Livingston, J., Mason, S., and Rowe, J. (2009) *Embracing the Future: The Midwest and a New National Energy Policy* (Chicago: Chicago Council on Global Affairs).

Longworth, R. (2008) The Balkanized Midwest and what to do about it (paper prepared for Chicago Council on Global Affairs conference: Developing a Regional View of the Midwest Economy).

MacDonald, W. (1982) *The Architecture of the Roman Empire* (New Haven, CT: Yale University Press).

Mahon, J. (2008) Moving the middle forward, *The Region* (Federal Reserve Bank of Minneapolis), September.

McDonough, W. and Braungart, M. (2002) *Cradle to Grave* (San Francisco: North Point Press).

McGranahan, D. and Beale, C. (2002) Understanding rural population loss, *Rural America*, 17(4).

McNeeley, J. and Pitt, D. (eds) (1985) *Culture and Conservation: The Human Dimension in Environmental Planning* (London: Croom Helm).

Metropolitan Council (2010) The regional planning agency serving the seven-county metropolitan area of the Town Cities, Minnesota, www.metrocouncil.org.

Miller, C. (2009) Trapping greenhouse gases: A role for Minnesota agriculture in climate change policy, *Rural Minnesota Journal*, 4.

Millett, L. (1985) *The Curve of the Arch* (St Paul: Minnesota Historical Society Press).

Minnesota Pollution Control Agency (MPLA) (2007) *Global Climate Change* (Climate Change Publications: Reports and Fact Sheets) (Minneapolis: MPCA).

Nassauer, J. and Opdam, P. (2008) Design in science: Extending the landscape ecology paradigm, *Landscape Ecology*, 23(6).

Pitt, D., Snyder, D., and Smith, L. (1995) Evaluating the consequences of development on the scenic character of a national park: A case study integration of geographic information systems and digital visualization technology (unpublished paper from the proceedings of the 1995 National Recreational Resource Planning Conference).

Qualey, C. (1972) Diary of a Swedish immigrant horticulturist 1855–1898, *Minnesota History*, Summer.

Richardson, J. (2000) *Partnerships in Communities: Reweaving the Fabric of Rural America* (Washington, DC: Island Press).

Roe, K. (1988) *Corncribs: In History, Folklife, and Architecture* (Ames: Iowa State University Press).

Roos, S. and Kinney, T. (2009) Scott County: Defining the rural character for the Detailed Planning Area (unpublished CRD report).

Roos, S., Hellevik, W., and Pitt, D. (2003) Environmental practices on dairy farms (unpublished CRD report for the Minnesota Milk Producers Association as part of their Environmental Quality Assurance Program).

Roos, S., Jacobson, L., and Schmidt, D. (2007) Visualizing Offset: Identifying and analyzing the spatial relationships between feedlot odor and residential development (unpublished appendix to Minnesota Department of Agriculture report: *Air Quality Emission Improvements to Facilitate Feedlot Siting in Minnesota*).

Roos, S., Thorbeck, D., Anderson, L., Linscheid, N., and Ahmed, A. (2010) Digital Town: Helping rural communities get on the map (unpublished report from a CRD-funded project).

Rostovtzeff, M. (1957) *The Social and Economic History of the Roman Empire*, Second edition (Oxford: Clarendon).

Rudofsky, B. (1977) *The Prodigious Builders* (New York: Harcourt Brace Jovanovich).

Schultz, H. (1985) *The Romans in Central Europe* (New Haven, CT: Yale University Press).

Scully, V., Jr. (1960) *Frank Lloyd Wright* (New York: George Braziller).

Semmingsen, I. (1978) *Norway to America: A History of the Migration*, trans. Einar Haugen (Minneapolis: University of Minnesota Press).

Senge, P. (1990) *The Fifth Discipline: The Art and Practice of the Learning Organization* (New York: Doubleday).

Statistics Canada (2006) *The Population Pattern in Canada's Watersheds 1981–2001*, www.statcan.gc.ca.

Stinson, T. and Gillaspy, T. (2006) Spatially separated neighborhoods and ruralplexus, *Rural Minnesota Journal*, January.

Streng, S. (ed.) (2010) The First International Symposium on Rural Design: New approaches of inquiry and practice (unpublished CRD report).

Tassinari, P., Torreggianis, D., Paolinelli, G., and Benni, S. (2007) Rural buildings and their integration in landscape management, *Agricultural Engineering International: The CIGR EJournal*, IX.

Terwan, P., Ritchie, M., van der Weijden, W., Verschuur, G., and Joannides, J. (2004) Values of agrarian landscapes in Europe and North America (a project of the Center for Agriculture and Environment, Renewing the Countryside and the Institute for Agricultural and Trade Policy) (London: Reed Business Information).

Thorbeck, D. (2010) *Rural Design: Establishing the Research Foundation for a New Design Discipline* (Washington, DC: International ARCC/EAEE 2010 Conference).

Thorbeck, D. and Streng, S. (2009) *White Paper on Rural Design* (Minneapolis: Center for Rural Design).

Thu, K. and Durrenberger, E. (1998) *Pigs, Profits and Rural Communities* (Albany, NY: State University of New York Press).

Todeschini, F. (2010) *Placing Design Central to Urban Decision Making* (Cape Town: University of Cape Town).

Tonn, B. (2007) Living as if futures matter. In Timothy Mack (ed.) *Hopes and Visions for the 21st Century* (Bethesda, MD: World Future Society).

United States Department of Agriculture Economic Research Service (USDA ERS) (2008) National and State Indicator Tables, http://www.ers.usda.gov/Data/RuralDefinitions/Indicators.htm.

USLegal, Inc., http://definitions.uslegal.com/f/food-and-agricultural-sciences/.

Veleva, V., Hart, M., Greiner, T., and Crumbley, C. (2001) Indicators of sustainable production, *Journal of Cleaner Production*, 9.

Weatherhogg, J., Dixon, J., and d'Alwis, K. (2001) *Global Farming Systems Study: Challenges and Priorities to 2030* (Rome: Food and Agricultural Organization of the United Nations).

Wightman, E. (1970) *Roman Trier and the Treveri* (London: Rupert Hart-Davis).

World Health Organization (WHO) (2008) *Closing the Gap in a Generation: Health Equity through Action of the Social Determinants of Health* (Geneva: WHO).

Zalamans, D. (2009) Haparanda and Tornio: From marginalized towns to regional centre, www.northernexperiments.net (Barents Urban Survey).

Zhang, F., Zhao, H., Huang, D., Li, J., and Zhao, T. (2010) The spatial planning of agriculture in Beijing: Towards producing a more livable city (unpublished paper).

# Illustration credits

All the photographs and sketches in the book were taken or drawn by the author and/or prepared by the Center for Rural Design, unless otherwise noted.

| | |
|---|---|
| 1.1 | Minnesota Historic Society Press |
| 2.1 | Bardo Museum, Tunis from Ben Abed (2006) |
| 2.2, 2.3 | National Trust, Swindon |
| 2.4 | Frank Forsberg |
| 2.7 | FeaturePics |
| 2.10 | Otter Tail County Historical Society |
| 2.35 | Thomas Gillespie OSB, copyright Saint John's Abbey |
| 3.1, 3.3 | Minnesota Historical Society |
| 3.4, 3.5, 3.6 | University of Minnesota Metropolitan Design Center |
| 3.9 | David Hanson, University of Minnesota Experiment Station |
| 3.14, 3.15 | Bormida & Yanzow Architects |
| 3.18, 3.19 | Robert Pettu |
| 3.20, 3.21 | StudioKAP Architects |
| 3.22, 3.23, 9.3, 9.4 | Dennis Saari |
| 3.24, 3.25 | Loom Architects |
| 3.28, 3.29 | Burr and MacCallum Architects |
| 3.30, 3.31 | Chuck Choi |
| 3.32, 3.33 | SPF Architects |
| 4.1 | Jonathan Moore |
| 4.4, 4.5, 4.6 | Fengron Zhang |
| 4.7, 4.10 | Barents Institute, Norway |
| 4.8, 4.9 | en.wikipedia.org |
| 4.11, 4.12 | Clint Pecanka |
| 4.14 | Center for Rural Policy, from Stinson and Gillaspy (2006) |
| 5.3 | University of Minnesota Center for Sustainable Building Research |

Back cover image
(bottom), 6.1, 6.2, 6.3     Riverview Dairy, Minnesota
6.10                         Roseau School District
6.12, 6.13                   Ron Woolever
6.15                         University of Minnesota Metropolitan Design Center
9.10                         Steve Bennett (Wikimedia Commons)

Every effort has been made to contact and acknowledge copyright owners, but the author and publisher would be pleased to have any errors or omissions brought to their attention so that corrections may be published at a later printing.

# Index

Figures in **bold** refer to illustrations

Active Living by Design 164, 166
Ada (Minnesota) 33
Adams, William Howard 23
ad hoc rural regionalism 82
Aesthetic issues 58
Agriculture, Department of (Minnesota) 58, 155
Agricultural Management Center (Crookston, MN) 70
alternative scenarios 140, **141**, **142**
Amed, Adeel 182
*Amenity resources* 138
American Academy in Rome (Italy) 13, 224
American Planning Association 220
American Political Science Association 146
Amish farmstead **28**
Andean landscape 65
Andeluna winery 65
Anderson, Lee 182
Anderson, James 223
animal agriculture 125
Animal Education Center (Milton Hershey School, Hershey, PA) 72
Anoka sand plain 165
Applied Economics, Department of (U of MN) 153, 155
applied research 2
ArcMap 158
areas of public concern 134
Austrian farmstead **18**

Bagley (Minnesota) 224
Bardo Museum (Tunisia) 15
Barents Institute (Norway) 94, 235
Barrie, Thomas 40
Basel, Joseph 180
basilica form 15
Beijing, China 55
Bellona Foundation 115
*Bellona Scenario* 115
Berglund, Robert 147
Bioenergy 202
Biofuels 38
Biological diversity 138
Bioproducts & Biosystems Engineering, Department of (U of MN) 133, 155, 157, 159, 163
*Bioscience* 204
biotechnology 214
Bodegas Salentein (Argentina) 63
Bologna, University of (Italy) 50
Boody, George 124, 204
Borchert, John 50
Borlaug, Norman 205
Bormida & Yanzow 63
Brooklyn Park Historic Farm (Minnesota) 196
Brown, Frank E. 13
Brown, Tim 192, 235
Buffalo Ridge (Minnesota) 40, 86
building codes 119, 125, 130
building metrics 117
Burr & MacCallum 74

Burt, Nathan 180

California 59
Camden (Maine) **20**
carbon sequestration 8
Carlson, Bill 169
Carmody, John 118
Cartlidge, Thora 145, 151, 155, 159
Casa Di Diana (Ostia, Italy) **225**
Center for International Food and
    Agricultural Policy (Minnesota) 102
Center for Regional Competitiveness
    (Missouri) 85
Center for Rural Policy and Development
    (Minnesota) 120, 125
Center for Small Towns (U of MN, Morris)
    175
Center for Sustainable Building Research
    (U of MN) 117, 133
Center on Institutional Cooperation 85
*Change by Design* 192
Chicago Council on Global Affairs 85
China Agricultural University (Beijing) 91
Chisago City (Minnesota) 144
Chisago County (Minnesota) 135; County
    Commissioner 143
Church in Polk County (Minnesota) **34**
Citizen Action Team 175
Citizen's Advisory Committee 136
City Twins Association (CTA) (North
    Europe) 94
Clearwater County (Minnesota) 47
cliff dwellings 40, **41**
climate change 56, 116
College of Continuing Education (U of
    MN) 215
College of Design (U of MN) 8
College of Food, Agricultural and Natural
    Resource Sciences (U of MN) 8, 102
*commodity resources* 138
community-based research tools and
    technologies 129
community-based rural design 2
Community Development Society (Ohio)
    208
community paramedics 124
confinement type housing for animals 59
Connecticut 74
Connecting the dots 211
contemporary working buildings in rural
    landscape 63
corn crib **36**

cost of food 60
Costello, Joe 206
Covenhaven Farm (Canada) 230
Coxwell Tithe Barn (England) **16**
creative zoning strategies 60
Crocker, Joe 169
Cross-border collaboration in Northern
    Europe 94–7
Cultural forces 44
Currier and Ives 57
Cusco (Peru) 233
Cuyo Region (Argentina) 63

Dahlberg, Peter 188
dairy barn **38**
Dakota County (Minnesota) 183
Dakota County Parks and Open Space
    Department (Minnesota) 184
Davidson-Hunt, Iain 5
Defining local rural character 172, **173**
Definitions 114
Design: economy 206; *for climate change*
    192; *for community vitality* 193; *for
    ecosystem health* 192; *for rural
    character* 193; is a powerful tool for
    integrating knowledge 1; principles of
    farmsteads 27; thinking 3, 11, 191,
    208; *with rural indigenous people* 194
'design charrette' 147
Designing for food supply, food security,
    and health 205
Designing for wellness: Isanti County Parks
    and Recreation Plan 163–9
Detailed Area Plan (DAP) (Scott County,
    Minnesota) 170
Detroit Lakes (Minnesota) 106
Dieter, Sue 180
Digital Town 214
*Dimensions of place and space influencing
    the health of rural people: A view from
    Canada* 97–101
Dominium Land Survey 44
Donne, John 1
Door County (Wisconsin) **31**
'dotmocracy' 140
Drabenstott, Mark 82, 90
drainage basins 43
Drawing and rural design 229
*Driving Change Through Diversity and
    Globalization* 204

Eaton, Leonard 79

ecology 120
Economic and social issues 123
*Ecosystem health* 114
ecosystem provinces 43
eco-tourism 153
Educating policymakers 195
Emerson, Ralph Waldo 24
Empire Township (Minnesota) 183
Empowering rural communities: Digital
    Town – helping rural communities get
    on the map 181–2
Energy markets 191
*Energy systems* 118
English landscape **19**, 20
Environmental enhancement 204
Environmental Partnerships in
    Communities (EPIC) 210
Environmental Quality Assurance 58
Epilogue (case studies) 144, 150, 155,
    159, 175, 180
Espiritu, Ailene 96
ethanol plant **38**
Europe 203
*Evidence-Based Design for Multiple Building
    Types* 122
Evidence-based rural design 2, 122
Extension Educators 181

Fabric covered dairy barn **201**
factory farming 36, 200
Farm policies 124
Farmsteads 26
feasibility study for graduate program in
    rural design 215
Federal Reserve Bank of Minneapolis
    (Minnesota) 85
Fergus Falls (Minnesota) 24, 30; State
    hospital horse barn 30
fertilizer tanks **34**
First District Association Milk Processing
    Plant (Minnesota) 153
First International Symposium on Rural
    Design 22, 111
Florida, Richard 207
Fluegel, David 180
focus of book 8
focus on areas of public concern 134
Foley, John 11
folk architecture 35
Food and fiber 114, 199, 204
Food supply and food security 125
Forces changing rural landscapes 56

Form follows function, climate, and place
    80
Fosston Map of 1896 (Minnesota) 45, **46**
Fraser Hart, John 89
Free State, University of (South Africa)
    102

Gabler, William A. 58, 90
Gaylord Feed Mill (Minnesota) 32, **33**
General Land Office 45
GeoDesign 159
Geographic Information Systems (GIS) 52,
    98, 153, 158; mapping 149, 171
Geological forces 43
geo-spatial analysis 214
Geo-spatial scenarios 82
geo-spatial technology 58
Germania 226
Gillaspy, Tom 106
Gjerde, Jon 30
Global challenges 220
global climate change 8
global impacts 10
Global Initiative for Food Systems
    Leadership (U of MN) 125
Global issues 56
Google Earth 181, 214
Google Sketch-Up 181, **182**, 214
Graham Foundation for Advanced Studies
    in the Fine Arts 7
Graham, Stephan 199
grain elevators **32, 33**
Great Plains Region 44
Great Wall in China 232
greenhouse gases 12

Hallock elevators (Minnesota) **32**
Hamin, Jan 82
Hangard Township (Minnesota) 47
Hanson, Chris 163
Haparanda (Sweden) 95
Hellevik, Wesley 145, 151, 155, 163
Hershey (Pennsylvania) 72
Hispanics 190
Homestead Act of 1862 21, 45
Hoskins, W.G. 18
Huayna Picchu (Peru) 232
human, animal and environmental health
    (One Health) 9
Human health 124

Illinois barn **26**

image-preference survey 173
immigrants dream 21
Immigration to America 45
indigenous peoples 40, 44
Institute on the Environment (IonE)
    (U of MN) 11, 12, 81
Integrated performance metrics 200
Integrating buildings and landscapes
    227
Integrating human, animal, and
    environmental wellness 124
interdisciplinary design thinking 190
International Building Code (IBC) 132
International Organization for Rural
    Design 219
intrinsic scenic value 138
Iowa church **35**
Iowa stone barn **25**
Isanti County (Minnesota) 163, 168;
    Active Living by Design 164;
    Community Steering Committee 164,
    166; Parks and Bike Path Master Plan
    168, **169**; Parks and Recreation Plan
    167
Isle of Skye (Scotland) 68
Italian landscape 203, 230
Italy 203

Jacobs, Jane 123
Jacobson, Larry 125, 157, 159, 200
Jefferson, Thomas 23, 51
Jennissen farm 153, **154**
Joennimi and Sergunin 95
Johnson, Maureen 169
Jorgenson, Zach 188
*Journal of Rural Studies* 82

Kilka Museum (Argentina) 65
Kinney, Tracy 159, 169, 175, 180, 182, 188
Knowledge-based design 111
Kotkin, Joel 9, 81

Lake Agassiz (Minnesota) 70, 145
Lake Elmo (Minnesota) 24
land-cover complexity 138
landform complexity 138
land-grant universities 128
Landscape Architecture, Department of (U
    of MN) 160
landscape character 60
landscape development suitability 139
landscape patterns 49

Land Resources and Management Sciences
    Department 91; see *also* China
    Agricultural University
Land Use and Administrative Research
    Center 91; see *also* China Agricultural
    University
Land use and the urban/rural edge 198
LaVander, Harold 105
Leadership in Energy and Environmental
    Design (LEED) 117
Lessons learned (case studies) 143, 148,
    154, 158, 163, 168, 174, 178, 182,
    188
Liberri Villa (Tunisia) **14**
Linscheid, Neil 182
*Lippincott's Magazine* 79
Litchfield (Minnesota) 153
Litton, R. Burton 52
livestock farming 60
Lofoten Islands (Norway) 230
Longworth, Richard 85
Loom Architects 71
Lowell Center for Sustainable Production
    120

MacDonald, William E. 224
Machu Picchu (Peru) 232
Managing forces of change through rural
    design 57
Mashalaba, Yandissa B. 102
McKnight Foundation 83, 170
McNeeley, J. 42
Mendoza (Argentina) 65
Metropolitan Council (Minnesota) 105,
    166, 170
Midwest region 90, 191
Midwest rural landscape 21
Millett, Larry 4
Milton Hershey School (Pennsylvania) 72;
    see *also* Animal Center
Minister's Island, Saint Andrews (Canada)
    230
Minneapolis and Saint Paul 44, 49
Minnesota 44; Design Team (MDT) 147,
    151, 175; Environmental Quality
    Assurance Program 159, 202;
    Legislature 182; Map from 1895 **48**;
    Milk Producers Association 58, 159,
    160; Pollution Control Agency 56;
    Rural Partnership 107
Minnesota farmstead **27**
*Minnesota History* 22

*Minnesota 2058: Thriving by Design* 107

Minnesota Zoo 7, **228, 229**

Mississippi River 224

Mitchell-David House (Massachusetts) 74

Moberg, Vilhelm 22

Monticello (Virginia) 23

Moore, Jonathan 83

Morris Elementary School (Minnesota) 175, **177**

multi-disciplinary design process 122, 190

Multifunctional agriculture and land use 202

*Multifunctional landscapes* 112, 120


Nanothechnology 214

Napa Valley vineyard 6, 29

Nashville horse barn (Tennessee) **29**

Nassauer, Joan 24

Native Americans 40

National Energy Policy and Midwest Regional Competitiveness 191

National Register of Historic Places 62, 175

National Science Foundation of China 92

natural and human landscapes 50

Natural Resources, Department of (Minnesota) 149, 167, 183

Netherlands 18

Netherlands dairy farm **18**

New England 18, 74, 120

New design technologies 214

New Rural Economy Project (Concordia University, Montreal) 99

Nimmer, Ken 145

*Northern Experiments: The Barents Urban Survey* 96

Northfield (Minnesota) 71

Northwest Minnesota Initiative Foundation 147

Norway 21, 45, 96, 203, 230

Norwegian immigrants 224


Odor impact **156, 157**

Odor offset model 157

O'Fournier Winery 65

One Health 114, 124, 193

organic farms 59, 205

Ostia (Italy) 224

Orvieto (Italy) 229

*Overall systems* 118

overlay districts 60, **61**

Owatonna Bank (Minnesota) 4

Padua (Italy) 226

Parliament, Claudia 102

Partnership for Regional Competiveness 84

*Past Silos and Smokestacks* 82

Pennsylvania barn **28**

Performance metrics and design guidelines 133

Peterson, Andrew 22

Peterson, Todd 1, 150

Phoenix (Arizona) 40

Pitt, David 42, 52, 136, 143, 163

Planning process 210

Planning Process Ground Rules **137**

Prairie School 23

pre-engineered building systems 59

Polaris Industries 145

pole barn 35, 61, **197**

Polk County church (Minnesota) **34**

population increase 81

post-frame dairy barn **36**

post-frame swine barns **37**

Principles of Rural Design 171, **172**

Problems with animal agriculture 198, 199

process of discovery 224

*Provincia Bothniensis* 96

Public Land Survey System (PLSS) 44, 49

Purina Farms (Missouri) 66


Quailey, Carleton 22

quality of rural life 198, 209, 220


Ralston Purina Company 66

Read Guernsey, Judith 97

*Redefining the Beijing region* 91–4

Red Lake Indian Reservation (Minnesota) 47

Red Lake River (Minnesota) 47

Reimer, Bill 99

regional: landscapes 89; planning 86, 105; vision 86

*Regional definitions* 194

*Regionalism* 113

Regional thinking in Minnesota 105

Renewable energy 125

Research opportunities 123, 126, 213

resiliency 193

Richardson, Jean 51, 210, 219

Riverview Dairy **131, 132**

Robert Woods Johnson Foundation 164

Roe, Keith E. 35

Roman: ritual 14; villa 226
Romans 226
Rome Prize Fellowship 224
Roos, Stephan 52, 136, 145, 151, 155,
    157, 159, 163, 169, 175, 180, 182,
    188, 202, 215
Roseau (Minnesota) 1, 145; Civic Center
    151, **152**; Community Vision for the
    Future Committee 148
*Roseau: A Vision for the Future* 148
Roseau River: flood **46**; Watershed District
    147
Rostovtzeff, M. 15
Round barn (Minnesota) **31**
Rudofsky, Bernard 79
rural: architecture 7, 50, 62, 79; change 7;
    character 5, 172; character defined 50;
    definitions 142; design as a new way of
    design thinking 3, 191; design ethic 6;
    design principles 6, 134; design process
    6, 101; design strategies 130;
    landscape 9, 42, 213; policy 54; quality
    of life 9, 42; science and rural society
    10, 213; towns 49, 62
Rural: character: Scott County – defining
    the rural character of the Detailed Area
    Plan 169–75; character units map 171;
    community scale: City of Roseau,
    Minnesota – aftermath of the 2002
    flood 145–51; conflict: Visualizing
    Offset – identifying and analyzing the
    spatial relationships between feedlot
    odor and residential dwellings 155–9;
    design certificate program 216–18;
    design education 215; design principles
    221; development (external) 209;
    development (internal) 209;
    environmental protection:
    Environmental practices on dairy farms
    – protecting the environment while
    protecting the dairy industry 159–63;
    heritage 42; outreach 134; planning
    211; sustainability 218
Rural Centre at Dalhousie University
    (Canada) 97
rural design is a process 116, 128, 212,
    222
rural design methodology 82
rural economic development 209
Rural farmstead scale: Community Dairy
    Partnership – protecting farming and
    the environment 153–5

Rural health in Canada 97
rural landscape character 52
Rural Policy Research Institute 84, 85
Rural town scale: Community of the City of
    Morris – creating a vision and reuse
    plan for the elementary school site
    175–80
Rural township scale: Wyoming Township
    – conflict at the urban/rural fringe
    135–45

Sacsahuaman (Peru) 233
Saint John's Abbey and University
    (Minnesota) 38
Salado indigenous people (Arizona) 40
San Juan Island (Washington) 76
Schalkwyk, Herman van 102
Schilling, Andy 180
Schiltgen farmstead (Minnesota) **25**
Schiltgen, Peter 24
Schmidt, David 159
School of Architecture (U of MN) 180, 224
School of Architecture and Landscape
    Architecture (U of MN) 7
Schultz, H. 226
Scott County (Minnesota) 87, 169
Scully Jr., Vincent 23
Semmingsen, Ingrid 35
Senge, Peter 116
sense of place 134
Shaping rural futures 8, 235
Sheep farm (Minnesota) 71
Sherping farmstead (Minnesota) **24**
site metrics 118
Social capital 126, 207
solar collectors **39**
Somis hay barn (California) 77
Southern Minnesota Initiative Foundation
    83
Southwest Initiative Foundation 84
spatial science 214
Stearns County (Minnesota) 153, 178
Stinson, Tom 106
Straitsview barn (Washington) 76
Strategies learned (case studies) 129–30,
    144, 149, 155, 159, 169
Streng, Stephen 11, 145, 188, 220
StudioKap (Scotland) 68
Studio Palia Fetice Architects (California)
    77
subsidies for agriculture 54–5
Sullivan, Louis 4, 23, 79

sustainable agriculture 115
Sustainable Design Guidelines 178
Sustainable rural community development
    210
Sustainability 125
Sustainability challenge 117
Sustainability today 57
Swedish farmstead **17**
Swine barn (Minnesota) **38**
systemic planning 213, 236
Systems thinking and entrepreneurship
    124

Taj Mahal (India) 232
Task Force on National Energy Policy and
    Midwestern Regional Competitiveness
    191
*The Architecture of the Roman Empire* 224
The arts of a region 126
*The Fifth Discipline: The Art and Practice of
    the Learning Organization* 116
The kinds of agriculture 124
*The Making of the English Landscape* 18
The relationship between rural planning
    and rural design 123
Thief River Falls (Minnesota) 47
Thompson & Rose 76
Thompson, Maryann 76
Thorbeck Architects 66, 70
Thorbeck, Dewey 11, 130, 145, 147, 151,
    155, 175, 180, 182, 188, 216
Tigh na Dobhran (House of the Otter)
    (Scotland) 68
Todeschini, E. 104
Tonn, Bruce 206
Tonto National Memorial (Arizona) 40
Torino (Finland) 95
Tourism Center (U of MN) 121, 147
*Transferring design skills to rural
    communities* 194
transformational change 11
Travel sketches 234
Tromso, University of (Norway) 94
Tunisia 15
Twin Cities Metropolitan Area (Minnesota)
    135, 169

Uco Valley (Argentina) 63
UMore Park (U of MN) 182
United Nations Population Fund 205
United States Green Building Council 117
University of Minnesota, Crookston 70

Upper Midwest 21, 51–2
*Urban and rural connections with South
    Africa* 102
'Urban Master Plan of Beijing (Years
    2004–2020)' (China) 91
urban planning 3
urban/rural edge 11. 60
Urban/rural edge: Concept Master Plan for
    Vermillion Highlands 182–9
urban/rural synergy 196
urban/suburban and rural issues 114, 120,
    123
Urubama Valley (Peru) 232
U.S. Army Corps of Engineers 147
U.S. Department of Agriculture (USDA)
    114, 180, 219
U.S. Department of Housing and Urban
    Development (HUD) 175
U.S. Federal Farm Bill 113
U.S. Fish and Wildlife Service 167
USLegal, Inc 114

*Values of the Agrarian Landscapes Across
    Europe and North America* 204
Vermillion Highlands (Minnesota) 182
Vermillion Highlands Concept Master Plan
    **185, 186, 187, 188**
Vermillion Highlands Regional
    Connections **184**
Vermont 51
vernacular architecture 79
Veterinary Medicine, College of (U of MN)
    133
vision (Center for Rural Design, U of MN)
    129
Vision and Reuse Plan for the Elementary
    School Site 178, **179**

Washington County (Minnesota) 24
Water resources and water quality 126
*Water systems* 118
Weatherhogg, J. 3
White House 214
Wightman, E. 226
Wildlife Management Area (Modified) 188
wind turbines **39, 87**
Wright County (Minnesota) 160
Wright, Frank Lloyd 23
Wood, Susan 159
World Commission on the Environment
    and Development (Brundtland
    Commission) 219

World Future Society 206
World Health Organization (WHO) 99
world population 205, 223
Wyoming, City of (Minnesota) 145
Wyoming Township (Minnesota) 106,
    135

*Yale Environment* 11
Yale University (Connecticut) 23, 224

Zalamans, Dennis 96
Zhang, Fengrong 91–4
Zuccardi winery (Argentina) 65